The Ressurrection of Jesus the Jew

Midrash and the First Easter

PETER KEENAN

columba
BOOKS

columbaBOOKS

Block 3b, Bracken Business Park,
Bracken Road, Sandyford,Dublin 18, D18 K277
www.columbabooks.com

ISBN: 978-1-78218-406-5

Set in Freight Text Pro and Freight Sans Pro 11.5/15.5
Cover and book design by Barra Carlin

Frontcover image:
Watercolour illustration © 'Come and have breakfast'
by Thomas Plunkett PPRWS.

Printed by SprintPrint, Ireland.

ABOUT THE AUTHOR

PETER KEENAN, author of *The Birth of Jesus the Jew: Midrash and Infancy Gospels* and of *The Death of Jesus the Jew: Midrash in the Shadow of the Holocaust*, was born in Dublin. He was a friar but left before ordination.

Peter has studied at Rome's Angelicum University, and his B.A. (Mod.) degree in theology was obtained from TCD, where he also studied for the H.Dip.Ed. (history and religious studies). His degree thesis was on Vatican II, and for the diploma qualification he submitted a dissertation on the educational philosophy of P.H. Pearse (which provided a few ideas, long ago, for some of the material now "resurrected" in Chapter 4 of this book).

For many years, in North West London, Peter taught 'A' Level courses, specialising in religious studies (moral philosophy in particular) and history (Nazi Germany), in addition to having spent sixteen years as adviser to the Catholic Bishops' Conference of England and Wales, in which capacity he served as secretary to its Committee for Catholic-Jewish Relations.

He has worked at an ecumenical centre in the Rhineland, which also involved numerous visits to what was then East Berlin. Peter has lectured extensively at gatherings for students, teachers and clergy. He has led visits/pilgrimages to the Holy Land, in addition to having visited Auschwitz-Birkenau.

Peter describes himself as a post-Holocaust Christian.

Contents

Dedication

This book is dedicated with gratitude and fond memories to the approximately 1,200 students of 'A' Level Religious Studies [represented by Nancy Conoby (née Parsons) and Sonya Remmen], whom I taught for many years at St. Dominic's Sixth Form College, in North West London.

They, our hope for the future, will appreciate the irony that the syllabus focused chiefly on moral philosophy and the philosophy of religion, seldom venturing into the even more contentious field of New Testament Studies.

It is also dedicated with much affection to Shay Mc. Gurrell, my oldest friend, who has been 'a sturdy shelter in whom I have found a great treasure' (Ecclesiasticus 6:14).

As with the two other books constituting this trilogy, the children of the Holocaust and their children's children are always in mind:

Do not forget the things your eyes have seen,
Nor let them slip from your memory...,
Making them known to your children's children.

Deuteronomy 4:9, adapted

A note on nomenclature and some resources

In *The Misunderstood Jew: The Church and the Scandal of the Jewish Jesus* (p. 193-196), Amy Jill Levine addresses this complex and sensitive issue, observing that, as with many well-intended efforts to re-label the Bible (Hebrew Scriptures replacing Old Testament and Christian Scriptures instead of New Testament, for example), it is fraught with difficulties.

Following her wise advice, *The Resurrection of Jesus the Jew* (RJJ), for the most part, uses traditional designations and vocabulary, mindful of the remark that the problem is not so much with "labels" as it has to do with 'a combination of cultural attitudes and Christian education' (p. 196).

Readers are encouraged to read Levine's fascinating book, and not least because - to paraphrase Kant - it has contributed to awakening me from my religious slumbers. *The Misunderstood Jew*, together with Sr Mary C Boys' *Has God Only One Blessing? – Judaism as a Source of Christian Self-Understanding*, the Holy See's *Notes on the Correct Way to Present Jews and Judaism in Preaching and Catechesis in the Roman Catholic Church*, *Denying the Holocaust: The Assault on Truth* (abridged), by Deborah Lipstadt, *The Anguish of the Jews*, by Fr Edward Flannery, *The Christian Problem*, by Stuart E. Rosenberg, Sr Ena Gray's *The Healing of the Past: Catholic Anti-Semitism, Roots and Redemption* and Edward Kessler's *An Introduction to Jewish-Christian Relations*, are excellent resources for the promotion of dialogue between Jews and Christians. In addition, many online resources are available, at www.jcrrelations.net, www.icjs.org/ and het.org.uk, for example.

Similarly, following the suggestion of Bart D. Ehrman in The Triumph of Christianity: How A Forbidden Religion Swept the World, regarding the use of "Christianity"/"Christians, RJJ adopts this advice (p. 301):

My view is that the very basic notions that made the Jewish followers of Jesus distinct among other Jews were already in place by the time Paul converted. These were the beliefs that Jesus' death had somehow brought about salvation with God and that God had then raised Jesus from the dead and taken him up to heaven, "to sit at his right hand". Such views were known to Paul even before he himself became a follower of Jesus, and I think there is no harm in calling anyone who subscribed to them a Christian (without denying, of course, that the person could also be a Jew).

PK, Kinsale, Easter 2025

Acknowledgements

Similar to the previous volumes in this series, once again I make my own the words of Peter de Rosa: 'Knowledge does not bring wisdom; ignorance never does.' For any insights made known to readers in this book, thanks is owed to many people, too numerous to list; but where any ignorance may remain, the fault is mine.

I wish to recognise nonetheless the involvement of Sr Louisa Poole and the assistance provided by the late Ron and Eileen Pluck at the genesis of this project, in London, many years ago.

At that time, Louisa and I had been cooperating on writing a book: *Was Jesus a Pharisee?* A redacted version of our work is now Chapter 3 of this volume. Valentine Irwin, then living in Kinsale (Ireland), also participated in this early endeavour, in addition to Charlie and Maggie Windmill, and I am most grateful for their generous support at that time.

The assistance of Sr Elizabeth Byrne IBVM, who proofread the penultimate manuscript, has been invaluable, and I am also appreciative of the suggestions made by Paul Higginson, Fr Diarmuid O'Murchu MSC, Dr Helena Shaw, Dr Catherine O'Callaghan, Hugh Barriscale, Dr Manfred Weltecke, Sr Anne Walsh OP, and Rev Paul Hewitt, all of whom read some draft chapters.

Thomas Plunkett, a very gifted watercolour artist, is responsible for the book's evocative cover, depicting an interpretation of Jesus' resurrection appearances (see Jn. 21:9-14). Thomas has also produced arresting and original images for the two previous volumes in this series. I owe him an enormous debt of gratitude for these imaginative and thought-provoking creations.

I acknowledge also, and with much affection, the support down the years of Fr Nicholas Madden ODC; his kindness and erudition have motivated me in ways unsuspected by Nicholas, of whom it may be said: *The blessings released through his hands caused windows to open in my young mind.* (John O'Donohoe, adapted)

Above all, however, my heartfelt thanks to the late Rabbi Lionel Blue. It was Lionel who gently awakened me from my *dogmatic credulities*, to paraphrase the great Immanuel Kant. Without Lionel's generous friendship, wisdom and gift for enabling genuine dialogue between Christians and Jews, this trilogy would never have seen the light of day.

By the time of his death, in 2016, Lionel had become something of a national treasure, famous for his Monday morning slot on BBC's *Thought for the Day*, when Lionel ended every broadcast with a gentle and poignant sense of humour, typified by this joke:

Nazi to Jew: 'You Jews are the cause of all the trouble.' Jew to Nazi: 'Yes, Jews and bicycle riders.' Nazi: 'Why bicycle riders?' Jew: 'Why Jews?'

Finally, my thanks to Garry O'Sullivan and his team at Columba Books for their commitment and assistance since 2020; it is much appreciated.

Foreword

In his editor's introduction to the voluminous *Ethics and Theology after the Holocaust*, Didier Pollefeyt – Professor of Theology and Religious Studies at Louvain University – mentions how, during his time as a young student at Louvain in the early 1980s, the Holocaust was not yet a common subject of teaching and research in European faculties of theology. When he spoke with fellow students of his 'work on the Holocaust', they thought he was referring to some new author as yet unknown to them!

Pollefeyt's reading on the Holocaust began with a work entitled *After Auschwitz: Radical Theology and Contemporary Judaism* (1966). This work weighed heavily on him; in fact, he found himself in 'deep shock' because, in his work, Richard L. Rubenstein interrogates some of the most fundamental beliefs of Judaism and Christianity and radically contests traditional understandings of ethics and theology.

What impressed Pollefeyt, however, was that while Rubenstein rejected the traditional God of history, he did not become an atheist, but sought, instead, to reconstruct the Jewish moral and religious identity, by re-reading the Jewish tradition in the light of the Shoah.

For Pollefeyt, reading Rubenstein changed him forever and, since that time, his own scholarship has centred on how

THE RESURRECTION OF JESUS THE JEW

'to re-read and reinterpret the Catholic tradition in such way that it could be an answer "from within" to the tragedy of the Holocaust'.

I have known Peter Keenan since the late 1970s, when we were both undergraduates at Trinity College Dublin, during a time when interdenominational and lay study of scripture and theology was evolving there. He came to college a few years older than the rest of us with the experience of having spent time in Germany, where Peter had been exposed, through various involvements, to the reality of the Holocaust.

Not unlike Pollefeyt, Peter was profoundly shocked by what he discovered and carried in his mind and heart many of the questions raised by writers like Rubenstein. In contrast, we, his university contemporaries, were like Pollefeyt's companions at Louvain, hardly aware of the Holocaust. Yes, we had learned about it in history lessons at school, but the tragedy of it, the unspeakable malevolence of it, had gone largely over our heads. For Peter, however, the tragedy and evil of it was, and has remained, central.

Our own maturing and life experience has, by now, brought us to a deeper engagement with the questions raised by the Shoah, but, back then, they were all there for Peter and became the very springboard for his theological studies, his later work in education, and his many years served as secretary to the Committee for Catholic-Jewish Relations of the Bishops' Conference of England and Wales.

Returning, briefly, to Pollefeyt's *Ethics and Theology after the Holocaust*: In a chapter co-authored with David Bolton – Pauline scholar and theologian – the topic addressed is that of *post-Holocaust Biblical Hermeneutics*. Speaking to what they refer to as 'Texts of Terror' (a term borrowed from Phyllis Trible), Pollefeyt and Bolton argue that because Christian anti-Judaism led to the creation of 'the atmosphere and mentality that made the Holocaust possible', post-Holocaust scholars must rethink biblical texts that appear to legitimize hate towards 'the other'. The New Testament, they assert, contains a number of passages that can be characterised as anti-Jewish or, at least, have been historically interpreted as such.

Rethinking these hermeneutically problematic texts, which are also seen as authoritative for the churches, is, they argue, of critical importance.

Peter Keenan's *The Resurrection of Jesus the Jew* takes up this rethinking – begun in the earlier volumes of the trilogy – as we are led carefully through the Pauline references and gospel accounts of the resurrection of Jesus and shown how the evangelists, by means of the literary technique known as 'midrash', are communicating testimonies of faith in Jesus and his resurrection rather than writing historical accounts of what took place. Indeed, great care is needed when applying the word 'historical' to the resurrection narratives. While their accounts are authentic, the evangelists are describing what is, in essence, indescribable and we are urged not to treat them as literal accounts of what occurred, but rather to understand them as an affirmation that 'Jesus was alive in a new way, beyond the power of death' (Peter Kelly, see endnote 15).

Other volumes of the trilogy have made clear that the political and religious backdrop against which the New Testament writings originated meant that certain seemingly anti-Jewish texts emerged from first century tensions between the early Jewish-Christians and the Pharisees, and between Gentile and Jewish-Christians. Over time, the erroneous interpretation and misuse of such texts contributed to the radical 'othering' of the Jewish people through the ages and the emergence of the distorted, anti-Semitic thinking that brought about the Holocaust. Such distortions are still with us, typified by the absurd and heinous phenomenon of Holocaust Denial.

This volume takes a closer look at the various strands and strains of anti-Semitism prevailing within Christianity and, more specifically, within the Roman Catholic tradition, with its talk of 'good' and 'bad' anti-Semitism appearing with regularity in Church publications up to the early twentieth century.

After the Shoah, Christians can no longer speak that way, and if we are to witness authentically to our own faith tradition, we must appreciate and value the religion of Jesus. Gone must be a literalist understanding of the New Testament writings; and gone, too, the idea that the resurrection of Jesus proves his messianic status, somehow trumping those Jews who look to the messianic age to come. Indeed, it is one of the principal arguments of *The Resurrection of Jesus the Jew* that, after the horror of the Holocaust, Christians must not only develop a new theology of Judaism, but also recast the entire Christian narrative.

On a visit to Auschwitz-Birkenau several years ago, it was the horror that stayed with me the most. The eerie silence of the place, the railway leading to a literal dead end, the vastness of the camp, and the idea that acres and acres of space was dedicated to human destruction is almost beyond belief.

Walking where so, so many people died in the worst of circumstances is chilling, indicative of what we human beings are capable of without grace, without the humility to question our beliefs and where they may lead us.

In a way similar to the other volumes of the trilogy, *The*

Resurrection of Jesus the Jew may unsettle and disturb us on different levels. Nonetheless, this work is an honest attempt to rethink and reframe what many of us have uncritically taken for granted.

Thank you, Peter, for staying with the questions and for writing these important books.

Elizabeth Byrne IBVM
Parish Catechist, Dublin
Easter 2025

Introduction

A man sent by God

The *Resurrection of Jesus the Jew: Midrash and the First Easter* (RJJ) is the sequel to The Death of Jesus the Jew: Midrash in the Shadow of the Holocaust (DJJ), preceded by The Birth of Jesus the Jew: Midrash and the Infancy Gospels (BJJ – a second edition is in preparation, with a new subtitle: Midrash and the First Christmas).

This trilogy has the objective of introducing readers to current reputable theological and historical thinking about Jesus. Some of this book's chapters, '10' and '11' in particular, are designed to assist students of 'A' Level Religious Studies in England and Wales in preparation for their final examinations, and also for candidates in the Irish Republic who are studying for the equivalent qualification. The trilogy is also intended, as appropriate, for undergraduate students of theology.

The successive phases of 'Jesus Research', effectively dating from when Ernest Renan published his sensational Vie de Jésu in 1863 and with particular reference to the so-called third quest, have much influenced the writing of the trilogy. In this regard, Geza Vermes' Jesus the Jew (1973) is seminal, and I endorse Maurice Casey's assessment that everyone 'trying to contribute to our knowledge of the historical Jesus should benefit from Vermes' work' (see endnote 35).

'*Jesus the Jew*' is frequently cited as a marker for the beginning of the third quest' (Hilde Brekke-Moller); and Vermes, for James Dunn, has been its 'John the Baptist'. In the context of these observations, brief comments are pertinent:

- The term 'historical Jesus' should not be equated with the 'real Jesus'. Following Fr John P. Meier (d. 2022), it is a theological construct 'that coincides only partially with the real Jesus of Nazareth', a Palestinian Jew of the first century.

- Meier has noted that the phrase "Jesus the Jew", in the fifty+ years since the publication of Vermes' ground-breaking book, has become something of an academic cliché, echoing William Arnal's remark that 'the simple assertion that Jesus was a Jew is categorically not sufficient to tell us what kind of Jew he was' (see endnote 35). That aim, of throwing greater light on the specific character of the Jewishness of Jesus, is an important task, but one beyond the scope of these books. Readers interested in that objective could do well to read Paula Fredriksen's When Jews Were Christians: The First Generation (Yale University Press), where she writes that 'Jesus' staccato resurrection epiphanies functioned as a kind of charismatic down payment towards his future, definitive return' (p. 118).

- Any tendencies to read Rabbinic Judaism - which did not emerge until after the First Great Jewish Roman War - back into the time of Jesus need to be treated with caution.

- The titles of the trilogy have been suggested by Vermes' famous book and two of the late Raymond Brown's: *The*

Birth of the Messiah and *The Death of the Messiah*.

This volume is an effort to understand the meaning of Jesus' resurrection, rooted in Jewish belief and practice and focused on the conviction that the defeat of crucifixion had been transformed into a Jewish triumph. (James Carroll, in *Christ Actually*. p. 135; see endnote 130).

In the final analysis, however we interpret the scriptural and other relevant data, claims made about the resurrection from the dead of a first century Jew born in Nazareth of Galilee are addressed to *faith*. Such assertions cannot be reduced to categories of empirical verification, whilst acknowledging nonetheless that historical theologians exercise an important role in trying to determine "what really happened".

Honest encounters with that undertaking (Carroll (p. 138), are to be measured by the circumstances prevailing in our time, in addition to taking proper cognizance of the worldview inhabited by first century Jews, especially St Paul.

What was possible for them (perhaps taking Daniel's poetic language, for instance, as 'descriptions of physical and metaphysical events') is likely possible today only for biblical literalists who embrace fundamentalist-type interpretations of religious texts.

This trilogy abjures all such approaches, on the basis that they are inimical to our search for genuine meaning, and, as Tim Crane suggests, leave people prey to 'the emotional appeal of charismatic preachers or demagogues'.

In *The Meaning of Belief*, Crane makes the point that, even if a belief ('Christ is the first fruits of those who have fallen asleep', for instance) may be wrong, this does not mean that it is irrational, a consideration seldom appreciated by proponents of the New Atheism (pp. 155-57).

That understanding has governed the writing of this trilogy, mindful of the reality that the examination of disparate religious views is central to purposeful engagement with issues of existential significance.

DJJ in particular has been written against the background of the long shadows cast by Auschwitz, in the conviction that Christianity after the Holocaust necessitates brave and imaginative revision if it is to be an authentic witness to religious values in this new century.

This *revision* applies not only to Christianity's relationship with Judaism; the imperative is for a transformation of Christian theology altogether, with regard to the reputable findings of the social and physical sciences (see O' Murchu, Chapter 11).

And *RJJ* is cognizant of the necessity to situate all discussions of Jesus' resurrection in the context, to paraphrase Hans Küng, of the reality that *resurrection belief, if it is to have any meaning, must always focus on our daily struggles to make sense of pain and suffering in an often indifferent and cruel world.* "Resurrection" is not about 'cherishing a feeble optimism in the hope of a happy end' (Küng), but about our identification with oppressed, broken, poor and defeated human beings. Our *resurrection faith* must be the proclamation of liberation from death in the here and now, not some academic study of *a past event or sentimental longing* for eternal life.

"Resurrection" is not about "dogma"; it is a call to discipleship, an invitation that, in the twenty-first century, summons the churches to reformulate all theological statements that denigrate Judaism, because the covenant between God and Israel endures forever (see Rom. 9:1-5; cf. 11:1).

The proclamation 'Christ is risen, he is truly risen', at

the Easter Vigil, is an invitation to turn swords into plough-shares, to commit our lives to the building-up of freedoms, in the thought of Dorothee Sölle, in such manner that *the crucified one lives forever with God, as hope and obligation for us*.

In that endeavour, Christianity has often been found wanting, most particularly in the last century, during *Hitler's War Against The Jews*.

When *The Death of Jesus the Jew* was published (2023) and regarding its treatment of Pope Pius XII (d. 1958), it had gone to print by the time David Kertzer's *The Pope at War* was available.[2]

Written after Pope Francis authorised further access to the Vatican archives for the years 1939 to 1945, it is a com-prehensive, if controversial, account of Pius' dealings with Mussolini and Hitler, observing that 'as a moral leader, Pius XII must be judged a failure'.[3]

Kertzer insists rightly, contrary to some popular *myths* about Pius, that he was not "Hitler's Pope" (the tendentious title of a book by John Cornwell), whilst at the same time arguing that Pius was intimidated by Hitler, as he was by Mussolini, concluding with the pronouncement that 'Pius XII clung firmly to his determination to do nothing to antag-onize either man. In fulfilling this aim, the pope was remark-ably successful' (p. 480).

Vladimir d'Ormesson, French ambassador to the Holy See between early June and late October 1940, said of Pius, 'I fear that his personal character is not equal to the dramatic situ-ation found in Europe today.'[4]

An important feature of Kertzer's book is that it provides a detailed account of the extent to which the majority of Italian clergy supported the Axis powers, illustrated by the bizarre example of one Catholic bishop who declared in 1941 that Mussolini was 'a man sent by God, the first one to understand the need for extending a friendly hand to Germany in order to see so many injustices righted'.[5]

This prelate continued by lamenting the fact that so many Christian nations had extended the hand of friendship to 'the descendants of those Jews who had crucified Jesus', concluding with the vow that in the new European order there would be no place for Jews.[6] One hundred years earlier and extending into the early years of the twentieth century, such sentiments were commonplace, propagated by newspapers and periodicals supporting the Vatican's policies (see Chapter 12).

The phrase "injustices righted" would have been understood by the bishop's listeners to echo the rallying cry "peace with justice", code for those who saw in the Versailles Treaty of 1919 a betrayal of Germany at the end of World War I, known colloquially as the "stab in the back". Mussolini and Hitler, during World War II, milked this falsehood for all it was worth, ludicrously claiming they were but seeking "a just peace".

It is unfortunate, to say the least, that at times pronouncements by Pius seemed to endorse, even if obliquely, such misrepresentations of reality, contributing to what one ambassador has described as the influence of a "fascist milieu" at the Vatican.[7]

That same year (April 1941), President Roosevelt's envoy to the Holy See had an informal encounter with Monsignor Bernardini, the papal nuncio to Switzerland, who advanced the view that, even if America joined the war, Germany could not be defeated. Bernardini then advised the envoy, Harold Tittmann, that should this occur, America's best course of action would be to negotiate 'a compromise peace' with the Reich.[8]

Tittmann then enquired of Bernardini how, given his vocation, he could propose an arrangement whereby Hitler would have effective control of Europe, to which the monsignor replied that 'the Vatican had no reason to be alarmed', because within a few years 'Nazi prejudice against Catholics was destined to die out'.

This depressing conversation is indicative of the degree to which fascist ideology had come to influence the thinking of many (but not all) high level Vatican officials; they were incapable of recognising the extent to which it inhibited their ability to counteract the vile anti-Semitic policies implemented by Germany and Italy. It was a failure of moral and political imagination resulting from a collapse of institutional nerve.

What Europe needed in 1940 was not an over-sensitive diplomat running the Holy See, but a prophetic figure such as Pius' successor – John XXIII (d. 1963), who greeted a visiting Jewish delegation with the words, 'I am Joseph, your brother'.

A weakness of Kertzer's book, however, is that it does not acknowledge sufficiently the practical assistance provided by Pius XII to Jews fleeing Nazi persecution (see endnote 9).

Kertzer confirms nonetheless the overall position adopted in *The Death of Jesus the Jew*[9], about which three additional points need to be emphasised, in addition to those outlined above:

- ❖ Church institutions, both Catholic and Protestant, failed to muster the necessary courage and resolve when confronted by the (unique) malfeasance that was Nazism. This failure will forever be a stain on Christianity's record, 'for when the Church was confronted with unmistakable evidence of Nazi evil, it chose, at best, to respond with feeble measures, rather than mass protests.'[10]

- ❖ Europe's legal and religious institutions proved inadequate in the face of the terrors unleashed by totalitarian

Fascism, on a continent that was nominally Christian but most certainly not Christ-like.

❖ It is seldom appreciated that Pius' reactions when confronted with the *Fascist Menace* were influenced by what Frederich Heer terms the Augustinian Principle, by which he means that the world was viewed primarily in dualistic terms. A consequence of this perspective was that the Vatican was 'a prisoner not only of its own history of anti-Semitism, but it was also the product of a historical conditioning as strong as that of any other human institution' (see *good anti-Semitism*, Chapter 12).[11] This mindset was influenced by the neo-Platonic notion that the Church, as distinct from its sinful members, somehow constituted a mystical entity incapable of manifesting serious moral deficiency. Pius laboured under this misapprehension, with disastrous consequences, because it produced a false imperative for him to be 'scrupulously neutral in his appraisal of world-shattering events, believing that National Socialism was a lesser evil than Soviet Communism.'[12] He could not have been more wrong, and this *mystical delusion* continues to haunt Catholicism, and the many abuse scandals are in part a consequence of this dysfunctional theology.

Catholicism, as presently constituted, is on kamikaze autopilot. If it does not soon embrace major changes, it will perish.

There is urgent need to re-anchor Jesus in the flow of history, by encountering – perhaps for the first time – the *Gospel of Jesus* as distinct from the *Jesus of the gospels*.[13]

He lived most of his brief life in Galilee, a loyal son of the covenant, prior to that fateful journey to Jerusalem:

> Jesus, born in Nazareth, was and always re-
> mained a faithful Jew; the religion about him,
> whose foundation he inspired, is Christianity.

Jesus died most probably on 7 April 30, a victim of Roman hegemony, and soon thereafter his followers proclaimed him to be alive: 'God raised His Son from the dead – Jesus, who rescues us from the wrath that is coming' (1 Th. 1:9-10, redacted).

This is the first known written reference to Jesus' resurrection, c. 50, complemented by this more famous one, probably written a year later: 'Christ died for our sins ..., he was buried ..., and he was raised on the third day' (1 Cor. 15:3-4). These verses were written by St. Paul (executed c. 67), our first "Christian writer" (see Chapter 10).

RJJ argues that they provide the basis for the development of later traditions, typified by 'guards at the tomb' (Mt. 27:65), similar to how *DJJ* maintains that the gospels' accounts of Judas' treachery derive from 1 Cor. 11:23-24, with its reference to the betrayal of Jesus, and how *BJJ* argues that Jesus was born in Nazareth, not in Bethlehem.

The above illustrations are midrashim (see Chapters 1 and 12). The gospels were largely written using this methodology – 'guards at the tomb', for instance, comes partly from the story of *Daniel in the Lions' Den* (see Dan. 6:10-28).

These books make no claim to originality.

RJJ maintains that great care needs to be exercised when the adjective 'historical' is applied to the resurrection narratives. The four evangelists have made Herculean attempts to describe the indescribable, and their accounts are honest, but we must not treat them as literal descriptions of what occurred on, and after, the notional date of 9th April 30.

Regarding the accounts of the passion, the Catholic Bishops' Conference of England & Wales states that the passion Narratives do not offer eyewitness accounts or a modern transcript of historical events.[14]

The bishops are right and their advice is even more apposite when it comes to interpreting the resurrection narratives, which encapsulate what Sandra M. Schneiders IHM terms a Saturated Event (see Chapter 11).

These narratives share three unmistakable characteristics:

- No one saw Jesus rise from the dead. [Mt. 28:2ff. comes nearest to a description; cf. the (apocryphal) Gospel of Peter, vv. 34-41, addressed in Chapter 11.]

- There is wide divergence about what occurred on "April 9th" and thereafter.

- Jesus' followers were convinced that he had risen from the dead. In other words, he was now in some way once again alive.

The point is missed if we interpret this third characteristic to mean there are ways for establishing the precise manner and nature of Jesus' resurrection, for the simple reason that these narratives were not written as history (for a contrary view, see 'Wright', Chapter 11). What they affirm is that 'Jesus was alive in a new way, beyond the power of death'.[15] Historical investigation can neither prove nor disprove the resurrection; it is ultimately a matter of faith, not of empirical research.

This observation nonetheless requires a nuanced interpretation. Paula Fredriksen, an expert in *Jesus Studies* who agrees with the above opinion, argues that 'treating supernatural claims as historical data is cheating, unless we are willing to honour all such claims as historical'.[16] David Mishkin, however, rightly adopts a more flexible view, whilst recognising the unique context of assertions made about Jesus' resurrection: 'not only is it not "cheating" for historians to examine the resurrection, but the data seems to require it'.[17]

The Birth of Jesus the Jew (2) examines the argument that Matthew's account of the virginal conception was inspired by the Greek translation of Isaiah 7:14, where it translates the original 'young woman' of the Hebrew as 'virgin'; a mistranslation followed by Matthew: 'Look, the virgin shall conceive and bear a son' (1:23, c. 85 CE). In other words, the Greek text *created* the virgin birth tradition, as "midrash". "Isaiah" was not confirmatory of an "event" that had been prophesised some 735 years earlier about Jesus, who was born in Nazareth, the brother of at least six other siblings (see Mk. 6:3). On balance, however, it is more probable that the anonymous author of this gospel happened upon *Greek Isaiah* and used it to augment a tradition already in existence, since we know that Luke also availed of it independently of Matthew (see Lk. 1:26-38). The important consideration is that this belief is best understood as having originated in a Gentile Jewish-Christian context, in a milieu influenced by 'the dozens of virgin births of classical mythology' (Marina Warner).

In other words, the virginal conception tradition is a function of Diaspora, not Palestinian, Judaism. It arose, at least in part, by way of trying to address a serious problem: the non-return of Jesus after the resurrection-ascension, as indicated by our earliest New Testament document, 1 Thessalonians (50 CE): 'For the Lord himself ..., with the sound of God's trumpet, will descend from heaven, and the dead in Christ will rise first' (4:16). By c. 85, Jesus had still not returned, and there was the need to highlight – for Christians in the Diaspora (Palestinian Christians seem to have rejected the virginal conception belief) – the conviction that 'Jesus had been constituted messiah from his mother's womb' (Thomas Sheehan).

The claim is a Christological one, having nothing to do with biography or biology, contrary to what the late Pope Benedict XVI, in his book on the subject, maintains: 'It seems natural to me that only after Mary's death could the mystery be made public and pass into the shared patrimony of early Christianity.' The virgin birth is really about Jesus' resurrection and its aftermath, not his conception. To paraphrase Hubert Richards, if we don't take the (death and) resurrection of Jesus as our starting point, as Matthew and Luke did, then the infancy stories will read like fairy tales.

It is unfortunate that the historical issues surrounding the resurrection of Jesus are not similarly capable of "easy resolution", but the challenges impacting "resurrection" are far more complex. For one thing, St Paul certainly believed that the Risen Christ appeared in a "spiritual body" (*pneumatikon*), but what does this mean?

Attempts, therefore, to interpret the *First Easter* in simplistic categories are unnecessary and ultimately counterproductive, for the reason that the accounts of Jesus' resurrection, like those about his birth and death, contain legendary and mythological elements (*the third day* tradition, for example, has symbolic precedents in both the Old Testament and extra-biblical literature).

A *Christian tragedy* of our time is that 'myth' is interpreted by many believers to be something that is not true, similar to how we understand the story of Cinderella, when in fact mythological language points to deep truths about what it means to be a human being.

We can read biblical texts in one of two main ways,

fundamentally or *contextually*. The former holds, as a general principle, that anything that can be taken historically and literally should be so taken.

Contextualism, on the other hand, maintains that scripture must be understood with regard to its full contextual (including literary) situation, and this is the position adopted in *RJJ*, with particular regard to how midrash has shaped the resurrection narratives.[18]

Our failure to read these narratives ignoring 'context' is bad history and even worse theology, rather like driving a car with negligent attention to the speeding limits.

Since c. 1975, thousands of scholarly books have been written about Jesus' resurrection, not to mention the vast quantity of catechetical and devotional ones. As a rule of thumb, these academic works fall into two broad categories, at the risk of simplification:

- ✢ *Naturalist interpretations* argue that resurrection belief(s) can be explained in various ways as subjective phenomena arising from the disciples' responses to Jesus' death. Dom Crossan's position, for example, is that Jesus was crucified and remained dead (see Chapter 11 and end of Chapter 10).

- ✢ *Supernatural theories* maintain that Jesus was raised from the dead; that something happened to him rather than merely to his followers. *Supernaturalism* accommodates different ways of understanding the appearance stories. Tom Wright's argument, for instance, is that Jesus rose bodily from the tomb (see Chapter 11 and end of Chapter 10).

It's a *sine qua non* of this book that contemporary theological statements are coherent   only if they honour the famous caution of Johann-Baptist Metz (d. 2019), that the entire Christian narrative, and not merely its theology of Judaism, necessitates emendation after the Holocaust (see Chapter 12).

Metz said this in 1984. Four decades later, Christianity still has a long road to travel, and the vast majority of believers remain unaware of the problem, an ignorance that is contributing to, but by no means the sole cause of, Christianity's arguably terminal decline in the West.

Related to this consideration is a seldom acknowledged Christian anxiety, though fringe movements like *Jews for Jews* are manifestations of its lurking presence in the *Christian psyche*: why did nearly all Jews 2,000 years ago reject Christianity? The Jews, after all, produced the scriptures that Christians claim to provide the evidence for their beliefs about Jesus (Isaiah 53, for example).

As David Klinghoffer has remarked, Jews knew these writings better than anyone, yet the vast majority of them persisted in their refusal to acknowledge Jesus as the Christ, seeing in him – at best – yet another instance of a failed messiah, one whose followers, Paul in particular, were in the process of undermining the ancestral faith, 'prophesying out of their own imagination' (Ezek. 13:3).

Additional considerations addressed by Klinghoffer in *Why The Jews Rejected Jesus*, in a section dealing with how Medieval Judaism answered the charge that Jews wilfully denied Jesus' messianic status, are that

a) Jews 1,200 years earlier knew both Jesus and Paul, b) the rabbis knew the prophets and the post-70 traditions, leading them to the conclusion that it would be the height of arrogance on their part to contradict such esteemed authorities (p. 171; see endnote 203).

Repressed anxiety, for much of Western history, has constituted a threat to Christian self-identity, producing a psychic dissonance camouflaged by increasingly pretentious assertions, often dressed up in a language of faith that would have been wholly alien to the *Rabbi of Nazareth*. That language, by the end of the nineteenth century, even promoted the absurd terms good *anti-Semitism* and bad *anti-Semitism* (see Chapter 12).

This explains, in part, the process, accelerated after the conversion of Constantine, whereby this new religion set about the persecution of *the people of the book*, in a world where fixed doctrinal understandings sought conformity of faith across the Roman Empire, by suppressing other expressions of the religious impulse, to paraphrase Diarmuid O'Murchu.

Another presupposition of *RJJ*, alluded to earlier, is that Christian fundamentalism, be it 'doctrinal' or 'scriptural' (or a combination of both) has no place in responsible and mature religious discourse. Fundamentalists are incapable of dealing with complex realities, preferring simplistic (often dishonest) answers to questions of meaning.

One instance of their inability to engage with reality is how many fundamentalists have embraced the pseudo-science of Creationism. It was Karl Popper (d. 1994) who said that ignorance is not so much the absence of knowledge but the refusal to acquire it.

The vast majority of creationists, under the guise of championing "true Christianity", choose to ignore Popper's maxim, advocating the ludicrous notion, for example, that the Earth is less than 10,000 years old. They often adopt the biblical chronology of Archbishop James Ussher (d. 1656), derived primarily from the genealogies in the Book of Genesis and St. Luke's Gospel, dating the creation of the Earth to (October) 4004 BCE.

Creationism, a pseudo-science, is a deceitful and sometimes dangerous movement. If mainline Christianity is to survive, it must face down the challenges posed by the *Evangelical Right*, in addition both to embracing the vision of Metz and the need for the adoption of a new theological paradigm, characterised by *Evolutionary Theology*.

It advocates the position that Christianity should move beyond a *disaster and rescue* theology to one celebratory of the *Christ Event* in an evolutionary context.

This reflects Laurel Schneider's observation that it is sheer hubris for the churches to insist, against the background of modern scientific and theological findings, that their doctines are definitive arbiters of how the significance of *Jesus as the Christ* is to be understood.

For centuries, Catholicism had promulgated variants on the doctrine *Extra Ecclesiam Nulla Salus – Outside the Church there is no Salvation*. Since Vatican II, the more politically correct term describes the Church as *the universal sacrament of salvation*, but in essentials the message remains the same:

With the coming of Jesus Christ, the Saviour, God has willed that the Church founded by him be the instrument for the salvation of all humanity.[19]

In the same document, *Dominus Iesus*, Cardinal Ratzinger (as he was then) acknowledges that other religions possess salvific value, 'but they acquire meaning only from Christ's own mediation', by which is meant that their worth 'cannot be understood as parallel or complementary to his' (n. 14, quoting John Paul II in *Redemptoris Missio*).

It is difficult to see how it is possible to reconcile Schneider's position with Ratzinger's. Suffice to say that people might ponder the tragic repercussions of the fact that, unlike Judaism, Christianity is a missionary religion, often unwilling to recognise that its past (often aggressive) proselytising is deeply offensive to Jews and others.

Judaism makes no claim that salvation is to be found only within its own tradition, a belief that would have been foreign to the historical Jesus, notwithstanding these words attributed to him: 'Go, therefore, and make disciples of all nations, baptizing them in the name of the Father, the Son and the Holy Spirit' (Mt. 28:19; cf. 15:24).[20]

This verse, with its reference to 'all nations', is indicative of the consideration that, by c. 100, the Jesus movement was already on its way to becoming a new Gentile religion. Soon thereafter, having lost contact with its Jewish origins, early Christianity pursued a course that provided the seedbed for what almost two millennia later contributed to the Holocaust.

The Shoah has been a major focus of this trilogy and its poisonous legacy continues to cast long shadows across our political and religious horizons.

One manifestation of that legacy is the vile phenomenon of *Holocaust Denial* and the threat it poses to the memory of the six million, and to the still living survivors of the Shoah and their children's children.

The concluding chapter of *RJJ* will examine this issue, *The Greatest Lie Ever Told*, because 'the living have no right to forget' (Chaim Herzog).

It was a consideration happily far removed from the thoughts of an old lady in the United States about half a century ago (who appreciated a wise observation of C.S. Lewis, that 'much depends on the seeing eye'). Her interest lay elsewhere, with *The Greatest Story Ever Told*, immortalised in the famous movie of that name.

CHAPTER 1

Zoroastrianism: The Origin of Resurrection Belief?

'I just glories to hear it again.'

North Carolina in the early 1970s had a religious information centre. Its window displayed an image of the dead Christ in the arms of his mother. One day, an old black lady opened the door and pushed her head round the corner:

> 'That Jesus dead in your window?'
> 'Yes.'
> 'He done been killed by the bad mans?'
> 'Yes.'
> 'Done dead and gone forever, that poor Jesus, done gone and dead forever, huh?'
> 'No, he rose again on Easter morning.'
> 'Rose again? You mean he live again? He really truly rise from the dead?'
> 'Yes – you must have heard the story of the Resurrection?'
> And with a broad smile, her face bubbling with joy, the old lady said,

'Oh, I done heard it before. I guess I done hear
it a million times before.
But I just glories to hear it again.'[21]

This story is a master class in pathos. It would need a
heart made of granite not to be moved by it.

The old lady rightly 'gloried' in a narrative that is 2,000
years old. Like all transforming religious stories, it has a long
prehistory, one that oddly has survived in India to this day.[22]

Richard Holloway relates that south of the city of Mumbai
tourists occasionally catch a glimpse of 'a mysterious stone
tower rising above the trees with a flat roof comprising three
concentric circles'.

Carrion-eating birds can be observed on it, 'devouring the
dead bodies that are arranged there, men on the first circle,
women on the second circle and the tiny bodies of children
on the third circle'.[23]

At first sight, this might seem to be an act of outrageous
disrespect but in reality it is a work of profound reverence,
the ancient funeral rite of the Parsees, India's smallest religious community. They believe that dead bodies are unclean.

Burial pollutes the earth, 'and if they burned them they
would pollute the fire that consumed them'. The Parsees are
also kind to scavenger birds because they believe the birds
help to keep the environment clean, 'so they build these
Towers of Silence on which they expose their dead to the
withering heat of the Sun and the sharp beaks of crows and
vultures', as Richard Holloway explains (see endnote 23).

When the skeletons disintegrate into dust, their remains
eventually reach the sea, thereby ensuring that everything is
returned to nature.

The Parsees' beliefs originated in (Persian) Zoroastrianism, a religion that emerged about the time of the Babylonian Exile, when thousands of elite Jews in two batches had been taken captive to Babylon. In 597 BCE, Nebuchadnezzar, the Babylonian king, laid siege to Jerusalem and ten years later he captured it, destroying Solomon's Temple.

Zoroaster (assassinated c. 551) 'founded' this religion and, writes Holloway, he is one of history's most influential figures, because:

- Zoroaster believed that the struggle between good and evil had its origins in the nature of the Godhead, known as the 'Wise Lord' who had fathered non-identical twins. One chose goodness, the other chose evil, and they fought a battle to win human beings to their side, and – like the twin sons of the Wise Lord – 'we too have to decide whose side we are on'.

- He also maintained that good and evil would not forever be 'caught in a standoff'. After death, people would have to face the consequences of their actions: When crossing the 'Bridge of Reckoning' each soul would encounter the destiny that it had prepared for itself – eternal life, be it in Paradise or in Hell.

- Zoroaster, like Jesus centuries later, was an apocalyptic visionary who anticipated that 'God would bring the world story to a conclusion'.

- He believed that goodness and justice would ultimately prevail, facilitated by the emergence of a saviour figure.

- In Zoroastrianism, 'we first find the idea of individual resurrection' (Holloway).[24]

When St. John's Gospel has Jesus say, 'I am the resurrection, ... and whoever lives and believes in me will never die'

(11:25-26) a case can be made for its being a very remote *midrash* on Zoroastrian beliefs.

Midrash ('to search out/interpret') is a literary-theological genre whereby stories related in the New Testament have been largely sourced from the Hebrew Bible. They are ways of expressing the conviction that everything to be honoured in the present must somehow be related to sacred themes from the past. A good example is Herod's *Massacre of the Innocents* (Mt. 2:16-18), derived from the account in Exodus about Pharaoh's attempt to kill the baby Moses (1:15-22).

Stories of this kind serve an important religious (often polemical) function, but they usually provide us with no verifiable historical or biographical information.

The evangelists' intentions are distorted if we force their narratives to conform to some idealised ('infallible') notions about doctrinal and historical orthodoxy, not to mention the fallacious claim that the Bible is 'inerrant'.

Midrash originated during the Babylonian Exile, when the Jews searched their sacred writings to make sense of the disaster that had befallen them, and in this way 'a whole new tradition not only of re-reading but of retelling the Bible grew up', in which old texts were reinterpreted to make them relevant to new circumstances.[25]

One way of understanding how midrash works is by way of analogy. Materials from an old house are sometimes used in the building of a new home, a practice very common until a few generations ago, and 'fire' was frequently part of that process.

It is noteworthy that Zoroastrians honoured the Wise Lord using the symbol of fire.

Their temples maintained a small and perpetual fire, which is why 'they have been wrongly described as fire-worshippers'.

It was very important to them, but only as 'a symbol for the eternal life of the Wise Lord'.[26]

We find a similar emphasis in other belief systems – Judaism, for example, when commemorating the Exodus Event, it describes God as one who leads the people in a pillar of cloud by day and in a pillar of fire by night (Ex. 13:21). In the *Acts of the Apostles*, at Pentecost, we are told that the Holy Spirit came upon the apostles in 'tongues as of fire' (2:3).

The phenomenon is not confined to monotheistic religions. The ancient Greeks had a specific word for the family which translates as *near the hearth*, beside the floor of a fireplace, from which light and heat emanate. It symbolised the family's unity and it was the father's sacred duty, passed in time to the eldest son, to ensure the fire was never extinguished, because its *eternal life* embodied the security provided by the household's gods.

It was not possible for gods to be shared by families, with the exception of a bride's initiation as a member of her new family, when she was quite literally carried across the threshold. There followed a short ceremony before the *eternal flame* to confirm her new status.[27]

When the Romans and Greeks built cities they incorporated these customs into remote prototypes of what nowadays we call urban planning. At Rome, the law fixed two and one half feet as the width of free space between two houses, and that space was consecrated to 'the god of the enclosure'. Such practices very loosely laid the foundations for what today we recognise as 'detached housing' and 'rights of way'.[28]

For obvious reasons, no estate agent is going to make a connection between ancient Rome and the selling of a detached house, but the illustration nonetheless indicates how midrash works, albeit in a manner far removed from its original context (and see 'Peter Enns', Chapter 12).

Central to our understanding of midrash is the God-given human impulse to adapt former situations to new circumstances, and to make them 'holy', illustrated in *The Death of Jesus the Jew* by the account of Paddy Leneghan – the father of Mary Mc. Aleese, Ireland's former president – having been given the task of carrying in a tin can the smouldering embers of the grate from the old house to light the fire in the new family home.

Some biblical scholars – the former Dominican priest Thomas Brodie, for example – argue that midrash is far more radical than a simple reapplication of one story to another context.

They understand it not so much as the *reassembling of bricks* but rather as the *pulverising of a house to mortar and ashe*s used as the foundations of an entirely new structure, which is what metaphorically Paddy Leneghan was doing.

McAleese observes that her dad was 'following an old tradition', and she is absolutely right, one that can be traced back more than 2,500 years, and to long before that, when about 70,000 years ago biological consciousness gave rise to biographical awareness.

The period from about 70,000 to 30,000 years ago witnessed 'the invention of boats, bows and arrows and oil lamps', during the *Cognitive Revolution*.[29]

At that time, *Homo Religiosus* was born, when story-telling around glowing night-fires provided the occasion and opportunity for human beings' early experiences of religion and God, questions about which we cannot be neutral, for the simple reason that we are not neutral about the answers, as John Shea has remarked.[30]

Paddy Leneghan's can of embers, however strange the

idea, has much in common with the perpetually lit sanctuary lamps in Catholic churches – old traditions reach back a long way (to Zoroastrianism and beyond it), similar to how mirdash works.

Fire and light are ancient divine symbols. St Matthew has John the Baptist say, 'I baptise you in water ..., the one who comes after me ... will baptise you with the Holy Spirit and fire' (3:11).

In addition to symbolising the divine presence, the eternal flame represents the belief that, in some manner, human beings are immortal, which is typically understood in two ways:

- ✜ Reincarnation is the idea that we have lived many times before and there are more lives to come, in this world.

- ✜ Zoroastrianism seems to have originated the notion of personal resurrection from the dead, which by the first century of our era had developed to mean that it is a sovereign divine act: 'God raised Jesus from the dead' (1 Th. 1:10, redacted).[31]

When Cyrus, the King of Persia who had defeated the Babylonians, permitted the Jews to return home from their exile in Babylon (538 BCE), they set about building a second, more modest, Temple (520-515), which in turn was destroyed by the Romans in 70 CE.

Herod the Great (d. 4BCE) had carried out extensive renovations on it, to the extent that, by the time of its destruction, work was still underway days before Rome breached its defences. It constituted thirty-five acres, roughly equivalent to the combined square area of twelve football stadia today, with a capacity to accommodate 400,000 pilgrims, one of the wonders of the ancient world (see Mk. 13:1, with its reference to 'large stones').

Historians speculate about whether the Temple was destroyed by accident or design (probably the former), but they all concur that its loss was a trauma which far surpassed the one subsequent to the destruction of the first Temple.

When the Jews returned from their *Babylonian Captivity* in Persia, they brought with them two key concepts: midrash and the idea of personal resurrection.

And by the end of the third century BCE, there is clear evidence that some Jews believed in survival of the soul after death, as the way to reward the righteous and punish the wicked, probably influenced by their interaction with Greek culture and the philosophy of Plato (d. 348).

Others were again hinting at belief in bodily resurrection, and whilst not encapsulated in this earlier verse from the Book of Ezekiel (it is a metaphor for Judah's rebirth after the Exile), v. 12 nonetheless came by the early second century BCE to *represent midrashically* the individual's yearning for post-mortem existence:

> Thus says the Lord God: 'I am going to open
> your graves, and bring you up from your graves,
> O my people, and I will bring you back to the
> land of Israel.' (37: 12, part of the famous *Valley
> of Dry Bones* unit, vv. 1-14).

The originating idea, however, seems to have emerged during the Exile: 'Belief in the resurrection of the body probably came from Persia', maintains Keith Ward, formerly professor of theology in the University of Oxford.[32]

This chapter has a '?' in its title because scholars are divided regarding the extent to which Zoroastrianism has influenced Jewish resurrection belief, though this book favours Ward's hypothesis.

One argument against its assumed influence is that we have 'no Zoroastrian texts that support the idea of resurrection prior to its appearance in early Jewish writing', writes Bart D. Ehrman.[33]

It may be that the concept arose in response to difficult political and social circumstances (see Chapter 3), and also not least because a problem for monotheists is how to reconcile their belief in one God, who is said to be sovereign in all things, with the reality of moral and natural evil.[34]

This dilemma is not much of a problem for polytheists. Their belief in many gods allows them to assign responsibility for such evils to lesser, or malevolent, deities. In the course of its long history, Judaism also embraced polytheistic ideas, but by 538 BCE monotheism had become a defining feature of the religion, a conviction that it bequeathed to Christianity but with a convoluted twist – its doctrine of the Trinity (three persons in one divine nature).

In the 608 years between 538 BCE and 70 CE, Judaism underwent many changes, and from the ashes of the Jerusalem Temple two "new" religions would in time emerge: Rabbinic Judaism and Christianity.

The latter – like the old lady from North Carolina – 'gloried' in Jesus' resurrection.

There is no way of knowing how she might have responded to an image of Zoroaster alongside that of Jesus in the window of the North Carolina religious information centre, or indeed what she would have thought about Geza Vermes' claim that, 'In the mind of Jesus, the distinction between resurrection and mere spiritual survival was minimal'.

It seems that the subject did not play a major role in his

teaching (see Chapter 11), as reflected in the synoptic gospels, where Jesus emphasises that what matters is the realisation of the Kingdom of God, albeit with reference to the need to be saved (see Mk. 10:17-25 and parallels).[35]

Before turning to the resurrection accounts, we need to survey the four groups that characterised Late Second Temple Judaism, particularly the Sadducees and Pharisees.

—

CHAPTER 2

A Tale of Three Philosophies

*'Blessed are you, Lord, you give life
in the face of death.'*

At the heart of Jewish life for 600 years was the Second Temple, the centre of Israel's economic, religious and political life. Its main purpose, as God's dwelling place, was to meditate forgiveness through the sacrificial system.

It is no exaggeration to say that Judaea was, 'for all intents and purposes, a temple-state, and the word "theocracy" was coined specifically to describe Jerusalem'.[36]

The significance of the Temple's and of Jerusalem's destruction cannot be overstated, notwithstanding the ambivalence towards it entertained by most Jews, who - according to Josephus - resented the Temple's priestly nobility as 'lovers of luxury'.

More Jews, proportionate to population, are estimated by historians to have died during the Great Jewish-Roman War of 66 to 73 than perished in the Holocaust.

Josephus (d. 100), a first century Jewish aristocratic historian with the dubious distinction of having supported both sides during the War, described the Zealots, Rome's antagonists during the War, as the "Fourth Philosophy", to distinguish them from the Essenes, Pharisees and Sadducees

(Chapter 3 will focus exclusively on the Pharisees).

He blamed the Zealots for the disastrous outcome of the Great Jewish-Roman War.

[The Scribes, who are not a focus of this book, were experts in the interpretation of Torah, and their origin can be traced back to Ezra, who is considered to be the 'founder' of post-Exilic Judaism (see Ezra 7:10)].

The Hebrew Bible conceives almost exclusively of salvation (meaning 'health', from the Latin) in this-worldly categories: punishment and reward are a function of life in the here and now. It is little exaggeration to say that, in the entire Old Testament (with the exception of the Book of Daniel, see Chapter 4), there is barely a mention of the idea that God will raise the dead.

However, as we have seen, many Jews during and after the Babylonian Exile, influenced by Persian and Greek ideas, inclined to the belief in a world-to-come where the righteous would inherit eternal life, albeit in a rather vague manner and without regard to any belief in original sin, a concept integral to Christian theology, but alien to Judaism. It understands sin as transgression against God, rejecting the obscure Christian doctrine that original sin is 'contracted' and not 'committed'.[37]

Belief in "eternal life" before the Exile had centred on Sheol ('Hades'), a place of shadows and the abode of the dead, situated at the Earth's centre. 'Its primary purpose was to give some personification to death itself', rather like a bottomless pit that devoured life after the analogy of a monster: 'Sheol has enlarged its appetite and opened its mouth beyond measure' (Is. 5:14). This focus was exclusively on Israel.[38]

After and during the Exile, the concept of eternal life was expanded beyond tribal boundaries to embrace a universal perspective, but its orbit still focused on the tribe as the basic unit of society. In other words, punishment and reward were experienced by 'the collective'.

At this time, there was no understanding of the integrity of the individual as we interpret the concept, which is the significance of 'carrying the bride over the threshold', related in the previous chapter.[39]

Great ideas never develop in a straight line (we need but think of how Evolution is now established as a demonstrable scientific fact) and it is naïve to imagine that the Jewish concept of eternal life followed a uniform progression.

It did not, but no later than c. 160 BCE there had emerged the belief, associated particularly with the Pharisees, that 'the King of the Universe will raise us to everlasting life, because we have died for his laws' (2 Macc. 7:9, and see Chapter 4).

The Sadducees rejected utterly this notion, disagreeing with the Book of Job: 'I know that my Redeemer lives, ... and after my skin has been destroyed, in my flesh I shall see God' (19:25-26).

We are familiar with these verses courtesy of Handel's masterpiece, 'Messiah', but the Sadducees would have had little sympathy with his theology, because they rejected the idea of eternal life and Handel's belief that the messiah had to die a sacrificial death.

The Sadducees adopted the position of the author of Ecclesiastes: 'The people of long ago are not remembered, nor will there be any remembrance of people yet to come, by those who come after them' (1:11).

About 300 years after this verse was written, Mt. 22:23 corroborated their standpoint: 'Sadducees came to Jesus, saying there is no resurrection' (redacted).

The idea is renounced by them because eternal, life, in whatever form, is not taught in the Torah, the first five Books

('Pentateuch') of the Old Testament, and the Pentateuch is Judaism's most sacred text.

The word 'Sadducee' derives from the priestly Zaddokite family and to their number belonged most of the Temple priesthood. Josephus relates that the Sadducees were aristocrats, closely involved with the Temple cult and they cooperated with the Romans for the purpose of ensuring the continuation of the Temple's sacrificial system.

Nowadays, we would probably classify the Sadducees as biblical literalists. There is irony in this description because literalists of our day, insisting upon the historical veracity of the empty tomb tradition, are appealing to scripture to validate an argument that the Sadducees, also citing scripture, objected to vehemently.

There is further irony in that, unlike Christian fundamentalists today, the Sadducees did not subscribe to a post-mortem system of rewards and punishments.

They disappeared from history at the end of the first Great Jewish-Roman War, for an obvious reason: the Temple cult had ceased to exist.

Many practising Jews today subscribe to belief in life after death, notwithstanding the consideration that the notion is indeterminate, to say the least, for most of Jewish history prior to and after c. 200 BCE, and it continues to be a conundrum for contemporary Jews.

It is noteworthy that for these Jews the question of the afterlife is a completely open one. What matters to them is the living of this one in accordance with Torah precepts.

The point is illustrated by the "Eighteen Benedictions", beginning with:

Blessed are you, Lord, you revive the dead.

The prayer book of Progressive (German) Judaism keeps this (Hebrew) version, but alongside it provides a German translation:

> Blessed are you, Lord, you give life in the face
> of death.

The purpose of the second version 'is intended to accommodate all those who pray, even if they do not believe in bodily resurrection'.

Judaism is primarily a religion of orthopraxis ('right conduct') and, unlike Christianity, it does not obsess about orthodoxy ('right belief').

As many Jews understand the matter, the Christian emphasis on a messianic (divine) redeemer, allied to the (largely) Protestant mantra of 'salvation by faith alone', has tended to deflect the interests of Christians 'away from the ethical demands God makes upon the human community'. Judaism emphasises humankind's 'spiritual potential, not its spiritual failure'.

Indeed, many contemporary Jews much prefer to speak of a "Messianic Age" rather than subscribe to the idea of a personal messiah. For this reason, to paraphrase Stuart E. Rosenberg, it is naïve of Christians to expect them to embrace the notion of *Jesus the Messiah*. Their focus is on the "Days of the Messiah" (see endnotes 41 and 203).

Judaism shares with Christianity and Islam a commitment to monotheism: 'Hear, O Israel, the Lord our God is one' (Dt. 6:4, abridged).

The Zealots were the *über monotheists* of the first century and, as we shall see in Chapter 4, when on 24th April 1916

Patrick Pearse declared the *Irish Republic*, he was tapping into a long historical and religious vein, one that preceded the Zealots' insurrection against Rome.

Their origin can be traced loosely to 6 CE, when Judas the Galilean led a revolt against Roman taxation, but they only became a major influence immediately prior to the War of 66 to 73.

Josephus, who despised them, maintained that the Zealots held beliefs similar to those of the Pharisees, but would accept only 'the King of the Universe' as their ruler. This explains in part why they (foolishly) took on the might of the Roman Empire - it tolerated many gods, to the extent - as the previous chapter has shown - of respecting their presence when building houses.

Most ordinary Jews saw the Zealots as freedom fighters (but we should not romanticise them), seeking to rid Israel of Roman domination, and they prosecuted the War that led to their (almost complete) defeat at Masada, in 73, following the destruction of the Temple three years earlier.

Their remnant lived to fight another day, but the Zealots were finally defeated at the end of the second Great Jewish-Roman War, 132 to 135, when the Jewish state ceased to exist. It was 'resurrected' almost 2,000 years later by UN charter (1947).

A few years before the Temple's destruction, the Essene sect known to history as the Qumran Community was obliterated by the Romans as they proceeded south from Damascus, to challenge the Zealots' control of Judaea and of Jerusalem in particular.

In a little known book, written somewhat tongue-in-cheek, Jeffrey Archer and Fr Francis Moloney speculate that Judas Iscariot died at Qumran, crucified by the Romans.[42] They are mistaken.

Judas most likely died in his bed, innocent of the betrayal charge levelled against him, with calamitous repercussions for the descendants of Jesus the Jew. *Rolling Stone Magazine*, many years ago, advocated Judas' innocence. It had a point.

The New Testament's two (mutually exclusive) accounts of Judas' death are combined exercises in midrashim, virulent polemic and religious theatre, as are Jesus' putative trials before the Sanhedrin and Pilate.

Judas no more betrayed Jesus for thirty pieces of silver (Archer and Moloney agree) than did Captain Alfred Dreyfus in 1894, another Jew, betray French military secrets to the Germans. Dreyfus, after an appalling ordeal in exile, was eventually exonerated (see Chapter 12).

The Essenes (their name probably means 'healers') disapproved of the Temple's priestly leadership and moved to the Judaean wilderness, at Qumran (c. 130 BCE), where in 1947 their library, known as the Dead Sea Scrolls, was discovered.

It was the group, next to Jewish-Christians, most interested in employing a type of biblical interpretation known as Pesher, one form of midrash. The focus of *Pesher* ('explanation') is on the 'end time', meaning that such groups expected the imminent end of the world.[43] They were mistaken, which in large measure explains why there is a New Testament.

Pesher is typically understood as a kind of fulfilment citation whereby the significance of a text, usually 'prophetic', is identified with people 'roughly contemporaneous with the commentator as individuals in whom the ancient prediction is thought to have been realized'.[44]

The most famous example of this phenomenon, for Christians, is how the author of St Matthew's Gospel applied a mistranslation of Isaiah 7:14 – 'Look, the young woman is with child and shall bear a son, and shall name him

Emmanuel' - to Jesus' birth: 'Look, the virgin shall conceive and bear a son, and they shall name him Emmanuel, which means God is with us'.

When Matthew wrote this verse, c. 85, the Qumran Essenes had been dead for probably fifteen years, having earlier applied a similar methodology to other verses in the Old Testament, referenced to their founder, 'the Teacher of Righteousness', and by extension to the belief that late Second Temple Judaism would produce not one, but two, messianic figures: 'king' and 'priest'.

These observations demonstrate both the vagueness and diversity of beliefs about *messiahship* at the time, and the primitive Jesus movement - contrary to the assertions of later Christian orthodoxy - had no unique or privileged information regarding the concept. Scholars are divided concerning how Jesus would have understood the matter.

In addition to providing a focus for vague predictions, Pesher also 'simultaneously declared the person or the event of the fulfilled prophecy ordained by God', leading to the view that 'the chosen individuals and members of the group associated with them were both divinely predestined and approved'.[45]

Such ideas clearly influenced the Jesus movement as it sought to make sense of Jesus' death and its subsequent belief in his resurrection (there is no need for Christians to literalise the *third day tradition* - see Chapter 5).

The Essenes, according to Josephus, believed in the survival of the disembodied soul, resembling Plato's thinking.

The Pharisees, to whom we now turn, advocated bodily resurrection of the dead, a belief that matured during the Maccabaean Rising, perhaps having its remote origins in Zoroastrianism.

'Pharisees' means 'separated ones', a derogatory term probably coined by the Sadducees, and we misunderstand the movement by thinking they wished to impose legalistic restrictions upon people. At the same time, they had their faults, as Etiennnne Trocmé, in *The Childhood of Christianity*, has pointed out:

> City people like the seventeenth-century Puritans, the Pharisees scorned the peasants, whom they thought to be sunk in superstition and moral laxity (p. 5).

They have much influenced Western society, and we are best introduced to this consideration by telling a story about how two sons smuggled their live Pharisee father out of Jerusalem in a coffin. It contained 'some persuasively reeking object', writes Simon Schama. Their purpose, as we shall see, was educational.

Was Jesus a Pharisee?

*'Jesus was perhaps closer to the
Pharisees in his religious vision
than to any other group of his
time.' Catholic Bishops' Conference
of England and Wales*

About eighteen months before the Temple's destruction, there is a tradition (probably apocryphal) that Rabbi Johanan ben Zakkai, leader of the Pharisees, was smuggled out of the city disguised as a corpse. The story goes that ben Zakkai met with Vespasian, the Roman commander, and predicted that he would soon be emperor.

Impressed by his courage and 'prophetic abilities', Vespasian agrees to ben Zakkai's "harmless petition" that he should be permitted to establish a school, at Jamnia south of Jerusalem, for the study of Torah.

(Vespasian became emperor in 69. His son, Titus, led the final assault on Jerusalem in 70 and he became emperor in 79, reigning until 81).

Simon Schama notes that, regardless of the story's provenance, its meaning is that Judaism would thrive regardless of the Temple's destruction and, from that time on, teachers

- not priests - would be 'the source of Judaic authority'.[46] As a result, Judaism, the religion of Jesus, flourishes to this day, long after the fall of the Roman Empire.

Another tradition has ben Zakkai walking through Jerusalem's ruins when a disciple asks how Israel, without its Temple, can now atone for sin. The answer is that 'We have a means of atonement as effective as the Temple – acts of loving kindness'.[47]

The reply is astonishing from someone who, eighteen months before the city's virtual destruction, had 'devoted his time not to alleviating the suffering of those in Jerusalem but to establishing the school at Jamnia'.[48]

The point, however, is that 'acts of loving kindness' made possible the survival of Judaism after 70/73 and, applying this principle - strange though it may seem - the Pharisees laid the foundations for what today we recognise as access to elementary education, universities and the welfare state.[49]

In the first century, *parental Judaism birthed the emergence of two daughter religions*: Rabbinic Judaism and Christianity, both of which owe much to the Pharisees. At that time and ever since, the vast majority of Jews have thought of Christianity as the "errant daughter", having far more to do with Paul than with Jesus.

These two religions are of equal validity, having arisen from the common matrix of Second Temple Judaism. The mainstream Christian denominations – Anglicanism and Roman Catholicism, for example – quite properly renounce efforts to convert Jews, whilst at the same time continuing to proclaim their belief in Christ as *Redemptor Hominis – Universal Redeemer. The Death of Jesus the Jew* has examined this claim, and it will be returned to later in this book.

Contrary to popular opinion, the followers of Jesus in the

few generations immediately after his death and resurrection had no particular interest in separating themselves from the parent religion, an observation applicable also to St Paul, whose role in the emergence of nascent Christianity was crucial, but also frequently misunderstood.[50]

What we now recognise as Christianity only became gradually aware of itself as an entity distinct from Judaism, though it is also the case that, from virtually the beginning, each addressed its own agenda, soon coming to perceive the other party through a veil of incomprehension and mutual antipathy.

One indication of this fact is how, at Jamnia c. 90, the decision was taken by the majority of synagogues to ostracise from their congregations those Jews, particularly Jewish Christians, who refused to subscribe to the Pharisees' blueprint for preserving Judaism in the wake of the catastrophic Great Jewish-Roman War.[51]

This *exclusion process* was notionally complete by c. 125, when 2 Peter, the New Testament's last document (in date sequence) was probably written, but as late as the 390s - and perhaps for longer - many Christians attended synagogue, especially on the great feasts of Passover and Yom Kippur.

It is against this background that we should interpret St. John Chrysostom's infamous words in a sermon delivered at Antioch, the "birthplace of Christianity" (see Acts 11:26):

> If the Jews are ignorant of the Father, if they
> crucified the Son, and spurned the aid of the
> Spirit, cannot one declare with confidence that
> the synagogue is a dwelling place of demons?
> God is not worshipped there. ... Indeed, not
> only the synagogue, but the souls of Jews are
> also the dwelling places of demons.

Chrysostom (d. 407) was not inciting Christians to acts of violence against Jews. Such rhetorical hyperbole, tragically, was a subtlety not appreciated by later generations and exploited in the twentieth century by the Nazis.

His listeners would have been aware of this consideration. In the ancient world, invective of this nature was frequently understood as a mode of entertainment, not to be taken literally.

The point is that Chrysostom's words were those of 'a leader troubled that his people were attracted by the aura of a religion more ancient and in some ways more venerable than his own'.[53]

One way of interpreting the Bible is the allegorical method, a figurative reading of texts. Isaiah's famous *Suffering Servant passages*, for example, were interpreted by Jewish Christians to mean Jesus when their original context referred to Israel. In other words, the literal text stands for something else, illustrated by Handel's Messiah, mentioned previously.

Chrysostom, however, was opposed to this type of interpretation, insisting that Scripture must be interpreted literally.

Notwithstanding the theatrical nature of his rhetorical hyperbole, the invective was almost certainly influenced by a literal reading of Mt. 23 (and other texts, notably 1 Th. 1:13-16 and Jn. 8:44-45), where Jesus supposedly castigates the Pharisees as 'hypocrites ..., like whitewashed tombs, which on the outside look beautiful, but inside they are full of the bones of the dead and of all kinds of filth', v. 27).

There is about as much chance of Jesus having spoken these words as there is of finding Elvis on the Moon, but the tragedy is that the Pharisees are remembered by history as hypocrites, 'snakes, a brood of vipers' (v. 33), when in reality they have laid the foundations for a yet-to-be realised civilisation of love.

This verse is typical of the opprobrium heaped upon them by some of the New Testament's authors and, sadly, these and similar libels/slanders continue to be disseminated by Christian homilists and teachers in the twenty-first century.

They should know better. It makes as much sense to argue that Jesus could not have been a Pharisee, because of his supposed polemics against them, as it is to say that the late Hans Küng was not a Catholic because he championed radical Church reforms.

[I recently attended a Sunday Mass where the celebrant, blithely and without intention to cause offence, remarked that 'the decision to kill Jesus is the only democratic one in the entire Bible'. This kind of homiletic faux pas should not be occurring sixty years after the close of Vatican II.]

The point is that these polemical verses were not influenced by the facts. They served the purpose of enabling the embryonic Jesus movement to establish its identity over against "the other".

They are instances of polemical anti-Judaism (but not of racial anti-Semitism, a chiefly nineteenth century development), and they need to be read in the context of the febrile situation pertaining after the Great Jewish-Roman War.

The irony is that Jesus was almost certainly closest to the Pharisees in his thinking than to 'any other group of the time': *love your neighbour as yourself* '(Mk. 12:33). This verse is a quintessential expression of the Pharisees' commitment to 'acts of loving kindness'.

At the heart of this undertaking was the Pharisees' promotion of the practice of table fellowship ('commensality', the sharing of meals without regard to social and economic status).

It was a revolutionary development in Late Second Temple Judaism, and one practised by Jesus (see Lk. 7:36-50).

Thus, even long before the destruction of Jerusalem, the Pharisees had implemented strategies for developing Judaism's power structure away from the Temple priesthood, with its emphasis on sacrifice, to embrace a vision of the Jewish home as one where its 'table' was understood as 'being like the table of the Lord in the Jerusalem Temple (see 'Rosenberg', below)'.

Fr John T. Pawlikowski remarks that the injunction, 'You shall be a kingdom of priests and a holy people', was interpreted quite literally by the Pharisees.[54]

In other words, everyone is a priest, meaning that there is no requirement for intermediaries, 'sacrificial' or otherwise, between God and human beings. Because of his or her inherent dignity, everyone has the right to address God as 'Father', who is no longer simply perceived to be 'Father of the Patriarchs'.

Jesus subscribed to this position, which associates him with the teaching of the Pharisees; 'association', however, does not mean 'identification'.[55]

They inaugurated a new understanding of the relationship between God and humanity, to the extent of having developed new names for Him, and one of these was Abinu She-Bashamayim: 'Our Father, who art in Heaven'.[56]

When, in the Sermon on the Mount, Jesus invokes The Lord's Prayer (Mt. 6:7-15), he is appealing to that sense of special intimacy between God and human beings, a manifestation of Oral Torah.

Mk. 14:36 reports Jesus saying 'Abba, Father!', in the Garden of Gethsemane, and it is not uncommon for homilists and teachers to comment that it is an affectionate

Aramaic word used by children, but they are wrong. It is certainly Aramaic, but 'Abba isn't Daddy!', contrary to popular (and some academic) opinion. It simply means 'father'.[57]

The concept was clearly prominent towards the end of the Second Temple period, made popular by the Pharisees (who appear in history c. 160 BCE and disappear from it c. 230 CE) and embraced by Jesus, who seems also to have endorsed their belief in (a general) resurrection from the dead (see Mk. 12:18-27).

Belief in resurrection needs to be understood in the context of the Pharisees' invocation of the 'Our Father'. It is entirely natural to believe that the sense of intimacy evoked by this beautiful prayer should endure beyond the grave.

This conviction is an instance of *Oral Torah* (rather loosely 'Tradition' in later Catholic theology).

In *Why the Jews Rejected Jesus* (see Introduction), David Klinghoffer maintains that, contrary to the position advanced by most Catholic and Protestant historical theologians today, Jesus rejected the *Oral Torah*: 'For Jesus, *Oral Torah* was a man-made accretion without transcendent authority' (p. 58).

Klinghoffer observes that he might more accurately, if less succinctly, have entitled his book *Why the Jews Who Rejected Jesus Did So* (p. 90), by which he means that it was really Paul, not Jesus, who most Jews repudiated:

> What outraged so many of the Jews who heard
> Paul is that he presented himself as an expo-
> nent of, and an expert in, their faith, but what
> he really sought to do was undermine it from
> within. While maintaining, in broad outline,
> some of the major assumptions of Judaism, he
> otherwise wished to hollow out the accepted

meaning of the Hebrew Scriptures, replacing it
with a new religion, albeit fitted out in biblical
trappings (p. 106; see endnote 203).

This observation has the merit of identifying how difficult it is to ascertain Paul's convoluted thinking, since *RJJ*
adopts the counter position that the Apostle to the Gentiles
was not, as such, abrogating Judaism (see endnote 50, also
Chapters 10 and 12).

RJJ agrees with Klinghoffer, however, that St Paul did not
believe Jesus to be God, notwithstanding texts such as Phil.
2:6-11 and 1 Cor. 8:6, often quoted in support of this premise.
Son of God, an appellation Paul applies to Jesus (*as the Christ*)
'in itself did not attribute divine personhood to Jesus' (p. 103).

Attempts to establish certainty in this area are, to say the
least, difficult, but it is probable that Paul thought of Jesus
in a manner similar to the view held by Arius (d. 336), who
maintained that Jesus was the highest of creatures but less
than God, to encapsulate in a sound bite his complex theology of the Father-Son relationship.

Klinghoffer would applaud these moving lines of Goethe
(d. 1832), echoing Jesus, Judaism and primitive Christianity,
to paraphrase Geza Vermes in his *Christian Beginnings: From
Nazareth to Nicaea* (CB, p. 243 and see endnote 169):

> Jesus felt purely and thought
> only of the One God in silence;
> Whoever makes him into God
> does outrage to his holy will.

At Nicaea (325), *the Christ* was declared *homoousion* ('of
one substance') with God the Father, and ever since 'Jesus

is God' has been avowed by orthodox Christian believers. In the words of Jacues Dupuis SJ, 'Jesus Christ is God humanized, not man divinized'.

Pawlikowski articulates this insight by saying that 'faith in Jesus depends not primarily on the miracle of the resurrection, but on the sense of the intimacy between humanity and divinity revealed through his ministry and person, and he had to rise because of who he was'.

He thus rejects criticisms levelled at *resurrection belief*, after the Holocaust, that it has been responsible for harmful expressions of *Christian triumphalism*, maintaining that 'resurrection can be retained in a Christology that wishes to be sensitive to Judaism's continuing role'. For Pawlokowski, therefore, "resurrection" is a function of "incarnation", but this interpretation can give rise to circular reasoning: he begins from a premise that "fulfils" the conclusion.

This hermeneutic is a perennial dilemma for Christian theology, typified by St Paul's all-encompassing argument that Jews and Gentiles alike stand in need of a *dying, obedient saviour*, on the basis of the flawed premise that God's justice requires satisfaction: 'Just as by one man's disobedience, many were made sinners, so by one man's obedience, many will be made righteous' (Rom. 5:19, and see Chapter 10).

On this interpretation of Pawlikowski's standpoint (which works only if Paul's atonement theology works), it is difficult to see how 'Judaism's continuing role' can be preserved on its own terms, as the following anecdote illustrates.

A legend in the Talmud tells of Moses, in Heaven, listening to a learned sermon by (the future) Rabbi Akiba, but he has no idea what the rabbi is talking about. Only when Akiba was pressed by an earnest pupil, did it become clear to Moses that the rabbi's talk was about 'doctrine given by God at Sinai to Moses', relates

Vermes, who then poses this rhetorical question (*CB*, p. 243):

Would Jesus, hearing about his consubstantiality with the Father, be as perplexed as Moses of the legend was when confronted with the rabbinic interpretation of his Law?

However one responds to Vermes' question (the logic of Pawlikowski's argument suggests 'no'), it could never have been asked in the first place 1) had not the Pharisees invoked the 'Our Father' of *Oral Torah*, and 2) had Paul adopted the anti-Judaism of which he is accused by Klinghoffer.

His important book fails to be convincing in these two respects and, to paraphrase Pawlikowski, we should therefore best understand Jesus as loosely part of the Pharisaic movement, recognising that he held some distinctive viewpoints where both *Oral Torah* and the Pentateuch were concerned.

Oral Torah extended the teachings of the Pentateuch to take realistic account of contemporary situations, a move fiercely resisted by the Sadducees, with lessons for the Church of our time: the Sadducees disappear from history; the Pharisees, in the traditions of modern Judaism(s), *survive* to this day, celebrating belief in a resurrected afterlife.

It is possible, however, that the historical Jesus preferred to understand claims about life after death in terms of 'eternal life', without necessarily committing himself to "resurrection" (see Mk. 10:29-30)".

Jesus, as Pawlikowski suggests, was most likely not a Pharisee in any formal sense, but scholars dispute the issue.

Hyam Maccoby, in *The Mythmaker: Paul and the Invention of Christianity* (*MPC*), answers the question in the affirmative, arguing that the gospels are complex, edited versions of oral and written sources, from which he deduces that 'it is possible to identify many details from the earlier accounts which show that Jesus was not in conflict with the Pharisees', and that he was one of their number.[58]

One main illustration will suffice by way of summarising Maccoby's lengthy analysis of the material: the well-known story of *Healing on the Sabbath* (Mk. 2:23-28). It is often used by Christian homilists to point to Jesus' *opposition to legalism*, ignorant of the consideration that the Pharisees used the same argument to show the permissibility of healing on that day.

The famous words, 'the Sabbath was made for man, not man for the Sabbath' (Mk. 27), is a saying of the Pharisees, emphasising their commitment to the principle that the saving of life must always take precedence over religious observance.

Its original pre-gospel context was probably a criticism of the Sadducees, later directed at the Pharisees as an instance of the polemics that prevailed subsequent to 70/73, for the simple reason that it is illogical to argue that Jesus was criticising the Pharisees by invoking against them a central tenet of their own teaching.[59]

A similar interpretation applies to Mt. 12:14, where some Pharisees are said to have plotted Jesus' death (cf. Lk. 13:31 - other ones warn him against a plot by Herod Antipas), which makes no sense: why should the Pharisees seek to kill some one who largely agrees with them?[60]

It is also significant that, at the *Sanhedrin Trial* (Mk. 14:53-65 and parallels), no charge about defiling the Sabbath is made by the Pharisees or anyone else. It makes as much sense to excoriate the Pharisees for Jesus' death as it does to blame Texans for President Kennedy's assassination (and see endnote 208).

The trial accounts are largely polemical fictions, religious theatre masquerading as history, and we need to approach them with a sensitive and critical eye.

A corresponding observation applies to the Good Friday liturgies and the *Oberammergau Passion Play* – these are *dramas derived from text*, reminding us that serious questions lie behind the anomaly that Palm Sunday's acclamations led without adequate explanation to the condemnations of Good Friday.[61]

They serve a theological purpose, one that originated in the oral traditions that began to emerge not only after Jesus' crucifixion but also in the context of his failure to return after the resurrection. 1 Thessalonians, our earliest New Testament document (c. 50), is much exercised by this concern (see Chapter 12).

Notwithstanding the fact that the Pharisees were not complicit in Jesus' death, this does not mean he was one of their number.

Pawlikowski concedes that Jesus' teaching closely resembles theirs, but he provides good reasons for pointing also to differences between them.[62]

A major consideration is that the Pharisees concentrated most of their activities in urban centres, but Jesus' ministry was in a rural setting – the Galilee, with a few likely minor exceptions.

In addition, it is difficult to imagine how, given the short duration of Jesus' ministry (perhaps no longer than nine months), there could have been the amount of interaction between him and the Pharisees postulated by Maccoby.[63]

We cannot determine the whole truth of the matter, but it is credible to argue for some kind of positive relationship between the Pharisees and the Jesus movement, extending from c. 29 to about 130, and central to that relationship was their shared belief in the resurrection of the dead. There can be little doubt that the latter inherited this conviction from the former, and even less doubt that the gospels' portrait of the Pharisees is an exercise in propaganda, bearing little resemblance to fact.

Of related interest is St Paul's claim that, 'circumcised on the eighth day', he was 'blameless under the law' and 'a Pharisee' (Phil. 3:5-6, abridged), but Maccoby and other Jewish scholars, whilst acknowledging Paul's commitment to resurrection belief, are very suspicious of the avowal that he was formally a Pharisee.

Chapter 10 will address the Apostle's understanding of the resurrection, but the point here is that if his "Pharisee credentials" are suspect, then what by implication is to be made of Paul's vehement insistence in 1 Corinthians 15:8 that 'Last of all, as to someone untimely born, he appeared also to me'?

These scholars remark, amongst other considerations, that few enough Pharisees as there were in the Galilee (as opposed to urban Jerusalem), it is very hard indeed to imagine that Tarsus, far to the north, had them in abundance, if at all.

The most telling objection, however, is that whenever Paul quotes from the Old Testament, he uses the Septuagint translation (in places erroneous, of which Paul is unaware), leading David Klinghoffer to say that 'Paul could not read Hebrew', which in turn calls into serious question the claim that he was a pupil of the famous Gamaliel, one of the leading Pharisees of the era (see Acts 22:1-5; cf. 5:35-39).[64]

Of Gamaliel, the Talmud declares that, at his death, 'the glory of the Law has ceased'. The irony is that Paul, (a Roman citizen) by turning to the Gentiles, caused the eclipse of Judaism's 'glory', though it must be emphasised that the religious genius of the Pharisees ensured Judaism's survival following the *Great Catastrophe* of 70/3.

Simultaneous with the Pharisees appearance, the institution of the synagogue also made its advent, about 170 years before the birth of Jesus. The interesting and controversial account in Lk. 4:16-30, of his visit to the Nazareth synagogue, most likely preserves a historical memory, with a caveat.

Verse 29's reference to the attempt to hurl Jesus from a cliff suggests a fair bit of literary creation on Luke's part, or that of his source(s): Nazareth is not built on a cliff. I know this, having visited it a few times.

After 70, the synagogue effectively replaced the Temple's religious functions, in   addition to having served as 'the mother of the Christian Church and also of the Muslim mosque' (Albert Reville).

But the widespread presence of synagogues in Palestine and cities of the Diaspora most definitely did not serve as votive shrines, chapels or sacred places, in our manner of understanding such institutions, observes Pawlikowski.

And, transcending the Temple in the lives of ordinary Jews, it was not so much "the House of God", but rather 'the House of the people of God' (Stuart Rosenberg).

Ellis Rivkin and others have noted that *Pharisaic Judaism* did not consciously create the synagogue, but the movement nonetheless 'enacted a profound structural change in Judaism by gradually replacing the Temple with the synagogue'.

Contemporaneous with the emergence of the Pharisees in the middle of the second century BCE was the Maccabaean Uprising (166), led by Judas Maccabaeus and his brothers. 'Maccabaeus' is derived from the Aramaic word meaning "hammer".

The Maccabees' victory over their enemies was to play

an important part in the popularisation of resurrection belief among a large number of Jews, and it is also noteworthy that their military success contributed to the re-Judaizing of Galilee, to the extent of pursuing a policy of forcible conversions, notes Geza Vermes.

When Jesus was alive, the region was surrounded by non-Jews and it is possible that he would have worked in Sepphoris, an important (largely) Hellenistic city located about six kilometres from Jesus' birthplace in Nazareth.

—

CHAPTER 4

Insurrections, Resurrection and a Surgical Procedure

*'The old heart of the earth needed
to be warmed with the red wine of
the battlefields.'*
Patrick H. Pearse

The Maccabees liberated the Jews from the rule of Antiochus IV, a Seleucid king. His dynasty was centred in Syria, with Antioch as its capital, and it arose following the premature death of Alexander the Great in 323 BCE, whose tutor was Aristotle.

Alexander's conquests resulted in the Hellenization of much of the Ancient Near East, where Greek language and culture became a dominant influence, one that aristocratic Jews welcomed even prior to Antiochus' attempts to impose it on Judaea by force.[65]

An extraordinary illustration of the extent to which upper class male Jews – including the Temple's younger priests – embraced Hellenization was their adoption of a medical procedure: 'epispasm'.

These Jews were granted Antiochene citizenship status, which effectively made Jerusalem an extension of the Syrian capital, resulting in considerable economic and political benefits.[66] Jerusalem's new status required a novel institution: the gymnasium, an important cultural, sporting and educational focus, but it came with a price.

Greeks exercised in the nude (discus throwing their sport of choice), but for Jews to do so would expose their circumcision, a practice 'Graeco-Roman society regarded with both disdain and horror'.[67]

This left young Jewish men who were committed to Helenization with no option other than to "reverse" their circumcision, using 'the cosmetic surgical procedure of epispasm'.[68] It involved a partial restoration of the foreskin.

The author of 1 Maccabees, writing c. 80 BCE and extolling the merits of the Maccabaean Uprising, considered these Jews to be apostates: 'They built a gymnasium ... removed the marks of circumcision and abandoned the covenant' (1: 14-15, abridged).

What had begun as an initiative by upper class Jews 'soon deteriorated into a violent clash of cultures between Syrian Greeks and Jerusalem'.[69]

Antiochus (d. 163 BCE) posed the greatest threat to Judaism's survival until the rise of Hitler. Had Antiochus succeeded, it is highly unlikely that nascent Christianity would have emerged as an entity in its own right in the latter half of the first century of our era.

He ignored opposition to his policies and, in 167 (on 25th December in our calendar), Antiochus made the disastrous mistake of dedicating an altar to Zeus in the Temple, having first breached the city's defences and murdering thousands of Jerusalem's citizens.

The Book of Daniel recounts this act of sacrilege as the 'abomination of desolation' (11:31; cf. Mk. 13:14, where its author has Jesus refer to it by way of predicting the Temple's ultimate destruction).

Rebellion broke out a year later, led by Mattathais Maccabaeus and his five sons who led a guerrilla campaign against the Syrians, culminating against all expectation in Judas Maccabaeus, following his father's death, recapturing the Temple, three years to the day after Antiochus had set up the 'abomination of desolation'.

The symbolism was powerful. His victory has been commemorated ever since on the Feast of Hanukkah (*Festival of Lights*), one that is even more poignant in the shadow of the Holocaust.

The Maccabees and their allies succeeded in defeating the might of the Seleucid armies, providing the small Jewish state with relative stability and independence, chiefly under the Hasmonean Dynasty, until the Roman occupation from 63 BCE to c. 395 CE.

It is difficult to overstate the magnititude of the Maccabees' success (nowadays, they would probably be thought of as religious fundamentalists). One commentator has compared it to the Easter Rising of 1916, led in the opinion of some people by political fundamentalists. If that Irish rebellion against the British had succeeded, it would have been analogous to the Maccabees' victory over the Syrians.

Patrick Pearse, the Rising's "commander-in-chief" - who exhibited a messianic consciousness based on a version of Christian atonement theory - understood, like Judas Maccabaeus, the value of religious symbolism, and for this reason he insisted that '1916' had to be at Easter.

Pearse would have identified with the example of the 'seven brothers', martyrs in the revolt against Antiochus, one of whom says that dying unjustly by the hand of others gives the hope of being raised again to life by God (see 2 Macc. 7:14).

The background to his optimism that God will raise the martyrs 'again to life' is a theme articulated by the late second century author of the Book of Daniel: 'Many of those who sleep in the dust of the earth shall awake, some to everlasting life, and some to shame and everlasting contempt' (12:2).

Its claim is that, in the end, goodness will ultimately triumph over evil, an optimism shared by Pearse, who would have interpreted that hope both metaphorically (Ezekiel's *Vision of the Dry Bones*, see 37:12) and literally (Daniel's conviction that *people will arise for their reward at the end of time*, see 12:13).

He 'knew' that the Rising was doomed to defeat, but the triumph of that failure, to paraphrase one of Pearse's biographers, ensured *Ireland's ultimate resurrection to new life*.

Pearse had envisioned Jesus' death as a martyr's sacrifice, reflected in his controversial poem of 1915 with its reference to the 'red wine' of Europe's battlefields, an obvious allusion to Jesus' attributed words at the Last Supper: 'This is my blood of the covenant which is poured out for many' (Mk. 14:24; cf. 1 Cor. 11:23-24.[70]).

By identifying with a tradition that had associated sacrificial death with renewal and the triumph of good over evil, Pearse was reflecting St Paul's distinctive (and problematical) atonement theology. It was focused on belief in the resurrection:

> Christ died for our sins in accordance with the
> scriptures, he was buried, and he was raised on
> the third day (1 Cor. 15:3-4, abridged).

When St Paul wrote these words (c. 51), the majority of Jews had come to accept belief in an afterlife of reward and punishment. He understood the concept in exclusively

Jewish terms, for the simple reason that Christianity did not exist then, but within a century – influenced by Hellenism – it began 'to synthesise the resurrection of the body with the immortality of the soul in ways that made sense to its growing Graeco-Roman audience'.[71]

It is easy to forget that Paul's (seven) genuine writings antedate the rest of the New Testament. In addition, he seems to have known very little about the historical Jesus, apart from the fact of the crucifixion, to which he makes ten references, but without the detail provided by the four evangelists and later apocryphal writings, which is significant.

Paul's emphasis is important, because it seems that, for him, it was not death by stoning or some other means that had significance, but the act of crucifixion, a clear allusion to Dt. 21:23, where anyone hung on a tree is said to be under God's curse.[72]

According to Bart D. Ernham, Paul had postulated that because Jesus was nailed to a "tree" – that is, 'crucified on a stake of wood – he bore God's curse'. This 'curse' was underserved and owed to others.[73]

Ernham writes that what mattered to Paul was not just that Jesus died, but that he died a victim of crucifixion. The implication, which Ernham does not develop, is that atonement theology as espoused by the Apostle to the Gentiles may have been unique to him, having nothing to do with the historical Jesus, contrary to the above quotation from St Mark's Gospel. On balance, Paul probably did inherit some version of it from the Jesus movement, even if it may not go back to Jesus himself.

The phrase 'for many' is traditionally understood to mean that Jesus intended his death to have an atoning significance, but this interpretation stands only if he had foreknowledge of it.

The Death of Jesus the Jew argues that we best understand 'for many' in the context of Jesus having looked forward to the imminent arrival of God's reign on Earth.[74] This aspiration almost certainly preserves a memory of the historical Jesus, but it is now transposed into an atonement framework many years after his death.

Atonement belief (as we now have it), meaning that Jesus has reconciled sinful humankind to God, seems to have originated with St Paul: 'Christ died for our sins' (1 Cor. 15:3), an idea expressed in a slightly different way in Romans, arguably the most influential book of the New Testament's twenty-seven: 'By the blood of Christ, we were saved from God's wrath' (5:9), and there is much truth in the claim that Martin Luther (d. 1546), pondering 'God's wrath', launched the Protestant Reformation on the basis of his interpretation of Paul's Letter to the Romans.

Many books have been written about atonement theory. When St. Paul introduced it, against the background of Yom Kippur (the Day of Atonement), he unwittingly began a process whereby the concept assumed the character of a disastrous 'honour- and shame-based way of thinking among Christians', in the words of Richard Rohr OFM.[75]

In recent decades, some women theologians have criticised the idea that Jesus' torture and execution 'saved the world', arguing that 'atonement theology is the deepest betrayal of Christianity ever perpetrated'. Rita N. Brock, for example, characterises it as 'not just one way of understanding salvation, but a betrayal of salvation, a doctrine that has abandoned the life and ministry of Jesus for loyalty to Caesar and his legions'.

Nonetheless, Paul – a religious genius – has, through his

use of the Old Testament, provided us with a kind of *mid-rashic template* for how later New Testament writers developed their own interpretations of the *Christ event*.

That 'template' encompasses references to Jesus' post-resurrection appearances, most famously in 1 Cor. 15:3-7, where St. Paul includes himself in the list of those to whom the risen Lord appeared (see Chapters 10 and 11).

The significance of these verses, taken in conjunction with Gal. 1:2, where the Apostle says that his credentials to preach the gospel 'came through a revelation of Jesus Christ', is that they are some of the most important verses in the New Testament, from the standpoint of establishing "what really happened" pertaining to Jesus' resurrection.[77]

A discussion about "what really happened" is a focus of later chapters, but suffice to say for now that *RJJ* endorses the historical inference that stories about the tomb are late in the tradition.

There is no convincing evidence for them prior to when St. Mark wrote his Gospel, immediately subsequent to the Temple's destruction in 70 (see Mk. 13:1-8; verses attributed to Jesus).

St Paul knew nothing about a tomb, contrary to how many scholars have interpreted his reference to Jesus' burial (1 Cor. 15:4).[78] Or, to express this claim another way: the tradition about a tomb is a midrash on the appearance stories.

We are so accustomed to thinking of burial preceding appearance that we dismiss the likelihood that Jesus was not buried. The probability, however, is that his body was consigned by Roman soldiers to a charnel pit.

As far back as 1973, in a little known book, *The Virginal Conception & Bodily Resurrection of Jesus*, Fr Raymond Brown (the late doyen of Catholic biblical scholarship) remarked that 'Christians believe in Jesus, not in a tomb'.

In his magnum opus, *The Death of the Messiah*, Brown (d. 1998) deduces nonetheless that, 'in all likelihood', Jesus was buried in a tomb provided by Joseph of Armiathaea (see Mk. 15:42-47 and parallels).

DJJ challenges this deduction, arguing that Joseph of Armiathaea is a middrashic construct derived from Is. 53:9a – 'They made his grave with the wicked and his tomb with the rich.' And the reference to 'the wicked' almost certainly generated the moving story of the two thieves crucified either side of Jesus (see Mk. 15:27 and parallels).

Jesus probably died utterly alone, save for the presence of a cohort of Roman soldiers, which is the plain implication of Mk. 14:50: 'All of them deserted him and fled.'

Brown has observed that the story about Pilate's wife suffering a great deal because of her dream about an innocent Jesus is 'a pious legend' (see Mt. 27:19). He is right, and so, too, is 'a pious legend' that women 'looked on from afar' (see Mk. 15:40 and parallels), which is almost certainly a midrash on Ps. 38:11 – 'My friends and companions stand aloof from my affliction, and my neighbours stand far off' (cf. Ps. 88:8).

Another 'pious legend' is that women visited the tomb on 'the first day of the week'. In my opinion, they did not, because there was no tomb to visit. For these and other reasons, we have no actual knowledge of the location of Jesus' body after his death.[79]

When St Paul references "in accordance with the scriptures", he is saying that the way to understand the present is to seek clues for its meaning in the sacred history of the past, and this midrashic procedure was employed by Jesus' disciples and his later followers when they came to interpreting the significance of his life, death and resurrection.

Pearse employed an analogous procedure when, at his court martial, he invoked religion in defence of the decision to proceed with the Rising, thereby contributing to the emergence of the *Sacred Myth of Easter 1916* (and see Schneiders' *Saturation Event*, Chapter 11).

In a similar manner, America's Revolutionary War (1776 to 1783) soon assumed mythological proportions, for the reason that people were willing to give their lives in service of a noble ideal, one that eventually gave rise to a common tradition of American identity, with its now iconic symbol of the 'stars and stripes'. In some parts of the south, a counter myth still prevails, with its romanticising of the 'Spirit of the South', famously portrayed in the movie *Gone With The Wind*.[80]

Or, to express these observations another way: "1776" and "1916" are the *foundation myths* for how most Americans and the majority of people living on the island of Ireland now relate to their understanding of nationhood, which originated in violent insurrections.

As the stories of "1776" and "1916" came to be told and retold, the boundaries between factual history and mythological accretions became blurred, and the matter is no different with regard to how the gospels' narratives about Jesus' ministry, death and resurrection came to be written.

One key to unlocking a deeper appreciation of the meaning of Jesus' resurrection is to explore the significance of the mythology of *The Holy Mountain*.

Thomas Fawcett, in *Hebrew Myth & Christian Gospel*, has written that the evangelists made use of symbolism derived from myths when they portrayed Jesus' resurrection as they understood it.[81]

It is in this context that 'on the third day' needs to be understood as it relates to the myth of the sacred mountain, which makes its first known written appearance c. 2,800 years ago, as recorded by the Book of Genesis (see 22:1-19, especially v.4).

There is little doubt that it had a long oral history before achieving written form and, together with theological developments in the wake of the Maccabees' Uprising, 'on the third day' provided a springboard, so to speak, for a now full-bodied form of resurrection belief that had begun life c. 530 years earlier, in Persia, during the Babylonian Exile.

The 'third day tradition' appears about eighteen times in the Hebrew Bible and its most famous representation is the story of *Jonah and the Whale*, most likely dated to c. 300 BCE. "Jonah" is the focus of the next chapter.

—

CHAPTER 5

Jonah's Whale (on the third day) and the Holy Mountain

*'Christians of the earliest period
showed no interest in the tomb.'*
Thomas Fawcett

On 12 May 1865, the Jerusalem Chamber of Westminster Abbey, where seventeen years later the body of Charles Darwin was interred close by, hosted a meeting of what later became known as *The Palestine Exploration Fund*, 'blessed' by Queen Victoria and funded mainly by Angela Burdett-Coutts (England's second richest woman at the time, after Victoria). She, in addition to having been a social reformer and close friend of Dickens, was also patroness of the British Goat Society, relates Simon Schama.[82]

The *Fund* set itself the task of vindicating the Hebrew Bible's narratives as the 'true history of Israel', precursor to the coming of Christ. These Victorian worthies never doubted their mission, but many of them had the good sense in 1865, six years after the publication of *On the Origin of Species*, to qualify them by recognising that 'Jonah and the Whale' and other miracle stories recounted in the Old Testament were 'most improbable'.[83]

Jerusalem was a particular focus of their interest and military engineers were dispatched there, with a view to surveying it pursuant to the belief that the engineers' findings would further illuminate the 'true history of Israel', including verification of the location of Jesus' burial and resurrection, assumed to be the site of the Holy Sepulchre.

The *Fund's* ambitions were laudable but misguided. It failed to take into account the myth of the holy mountain – Moriah, and its *truths* are not accessible to engineers' surveys.

'Myth' functions at many levels (the fairy stories of Hans Christian Andersen, for example) and one of the Bible's most perplexing myths is the account in Genesis 22 of Abraham being told to bind and sacrifice his son Isaac, which according to some Jewish traditions occurred at Passover.

Christians subsequently came to interpret Isaac as a prefigurement of Jesus, both in light of 'on the third day' (Gen.22:4) and Abraham's words addressed to Isaac that 'God himself will provide the lamb for a burnt-offering, my son' (Gen. 22:8).

Abraham had another son, Ishmael, by Hagar (his wife Sarah's "surrogate"), but he is told to sacrifice his "only son", thereby emphasising Isaac's role as the inheritor of Abraham's covenant with God.

At the last moment, as Abraham is about to kill Isaac, a voice from Heaven is heard: 'Do not lay a hand on the boy', in response to which Abraham instead sacrifices a ram (an uncastrated adult male sheep).

Historians and theologians debate the original context of *The Binding of Isaac*, but for our purposes three considerations are pertinent:

- ❖ Isaac carries the wood that is to provide the means for his sacrifice, 'on the third day' after he and Abraham had set out from Beersheba. This is the probable *midrashic origin* of the account of Simon of Cyrene helping to carry Jesus' cross-beam to Calvary (see Mk. 15:21 and parallels[84]).

- ❖ Jews of the first century were familiar with the later association of Isaac with Passover, and this provided the basis for St Paul's proclamation that Jesus' death, freely suffered, was 'the perfect fulfilment of the redeeming, self-offering of Isaac', which in the Apostle's estimation was of universal significance: 'For this end, Christ died and lived again, that he might be Lord of both the dead and the living' (Rom. 14:9).[85]

- ❖ Jesus' resurrection 'on the third day, in accordance with the scriptures' (1 Cor. 15:4), clearly echoes Abraham's intention to sacrifice Isaac.

In the context of these observations, it is no exaggeration to suggest that 1 Cor. 5:7b – 'Christ, our paschal lamb, has been sacrificed' – is arguably the most important statement in the New Testament.

Not only is it the matrix for atonement theology, but it also implicitly situates Jesus' death and resurrection in the context of *The Binding of Isaac Myth*, which Jewish tradition identifies as the site of Solomon's Temple (see 2 Chr. 3:1).

The moving story of Simon of Cyrene, a midrash (as suggested above), reinforces that symbolic identification and Mark almost certainly intended this association when he shaped a written narrative of the passion from oral and other sources against the background of the Jewish liturgical calendar.

Psalm 22, with its famous opening -'My God, my God, why have you forsaken me?' - influenced that narrative development, and it is also likely to have contributed to the account of the women's visit to Jesus' tomb 'on the third day'.

The Holy Sepulchre is the place tradition assigns to Jesus' burial and resurrection. A church was first built there c. 335, supporting Fawcett's observation that interest about the location of Jesus' burial is a late development. In other words, the lateness of this tradition complements the position taken in *DJJ* that his body was not placed in a tomb.

Kathleen Corley has pointed to a multitude of evidence showing that, for a long time preceding Constantine's conversion in 312, Christians participated in a tradition of the cult of the dead unrelated to a particular location for Jesus' tomb. It is 'the earliest evidence for Christian worship in antiquity'.[86]

Her findings confirm both Raymond Brown's insistence that 'Christians believe in Jesus, not in a tomb' and this book's premise that the resurrection narratives' tomb accounts are best understood as having their origin in appearance stories related to 'on the third day'.

Much scholarly ink has been spilt studying variations of "on the third day". Matthew, for example, uses the formulation 'for three days and nights' when he has Jesus say that the Son of Man will be in the earth for that length of time, after which people will recognise that 'something greater than Jonah is here' (12:40-41).

If taken literally, this would mean that the resurrection occurred not on Easter morning but on the evening of the following day, Monday. He inherited "after three days" from his main source, Mark, but it is noteworthy that Matthew also uses 'on the third day'.[87]

Biblical scholars are able to show that "on the third day" is a later attempt to reconcile "after three days" (a phrase used by Jewish Christians) with a later Gentile Christian tradition, which we now find preserved and redacted at Mark 16:2: 'Early on the first day of the week, when the sun had risen, they went to the tomb.'[88]

The use of "on the third day" confirms two virtual historical certainties:

- ❖ The story of the empty tomb is not part of the earliest resurrection tradition(s). The answer to the question *Who Moved the Stone?*, the title of Frank Morrison's famous book (first published in 1930), is that no one moved the stone because there was no tomb in the first place, despite Morrison's engaging arguments to the contrary.

- ❖ St Paul referenced the 'first day of the week' as the day on which the Corinthian brethren put their offerings aside to be kept until his next visit to them (see 2 Cor. 9, *The Collection for Jerusalem*). The implication is that it was the day when they gathered to worship Jesus as Lord, so "on the third day" is 'a mechanism for reconciling an ancient tradition with a secondary one'.[89] Of course, it is 'secondary' in the sense of its employment in the context of the resurrection narratives. The phrase itself is present many times in the Hebrew Bible (see Ex. 19:10-11, 16-17, for example: "Sinai", and Chapter 12 of this book: "paucity of witnesses").[90]

The denotion "three days", in whatever form, is not a reference to calendar time. It is a Jewish eschatological symbol referencing the end of the world (at dawn, "on the third day" after its end) and Jewish Christians would have interpreted it to mean that Jesus' death and resurrection had brought about the dawning of the Kingdom of God.[91]

Over time, the sacred number 3 came to be identified with "the day of the Lord", which enabled Christians to relate their story of Jesus' resurrection in terms of "on the first day of the week", with the proviso that he would come a second time, to establish "the final day of the Lord" (see Mt. 25:31-46).[92]

That 'final day' has not yet materialised and the New Testament is largely the result of Jesus' non-return. We should interpret in that context the gospels' two infancy narratives, which represent a phase of the developing understanding of Christ unknown to earlier (Palestinian) Jewish-Christians.

It is noteworthy that in Jewish tradition people were considered not to be truly dead until after the third day, during which time the individual's life force (*nephesh*) was said to hover over the grave, when it then 'departed for the regions of Sheol'. It is against this background that we should understand the raising of Lazarus: 'When Jesus arrived, he found that Lazarus had already been four days in the tomb' (Jn. 11:17).[93]

Sheol, the mythological abode of the dead located at the Earth's centre, is to where Jesus would have been consigned after his death, known also as Hades, a belief curiously affirmed in the Apostles' Creed: 'He descended to Hell' (see 1 Pet. 3:18-22).

The belief, known also as *The Harrowing of Hell*, is curious because the New Testament barely mentions it. The significance is that it probably contributed to the development of traditions about Jesus' burial, involving the *midrashic* figure of Joseph of Arimathea (see Mk. 15:42-47 and parallels).[94]

When St Paul, for example, refers to Jesus' death and burial, it would have been understood to mean a descent into Sheol, an idea that certainly resonates, but should not be identified, with Pagan beliefs about gods rising from the dead.

In this context, it is best interpreted as what the Pharisees hoped for at the end of time, when 'the righteous' would be constituted a 'new creation'. They, no more than Jesus' disciples, had a belief in Jesus' divinity, a concept unknown during his lifetime.

Reputable scholars are 'certain' that the evangelists, despite the clearly legendary character of the empty tomb tradition, did not create it 'in order to provide a mythological basis for a subsequent cultic veneration of the site'.[95]

They had another reason, because nowhere in the New Testament (with the unlikely exception of Acts 2: 29-35) do its authors use the empty tomb as an argument for the resurrection, making it clear that 'the empty tomb merely puzzled the disciples or drove them deeper into despair' (see Mk. 16:8 and Lk. 24:22-24).[96] Jesus' appearances made known the resurrection. It was not, contrary to popular opinion, deduced from the empty tomb tradition.

That 'other reason' had to do with the evangelists' emphasis on Jesus' death in Jerusalem, in effect the site of the holy mountain on which Abraham, "on the third day", had decided to sacrifice Isaac, his "only son". And this account reflects the Jonah story.

In addition, close to the city was the Hinnom Valley, where Pagan sacrifices had been practised; in Hebrew, 'Gehenna', that is, 'Hell'.[97]

These considerations are the background for understanding The Harrowing of Hell, interpreted by later Christian tradition to mean that Christ had descended there in order both to chain the Devil and preach to its captives.[98]

The empty tomb story would have been suggestive of these ideas, supported by the extraordinary account in Mt. 27:51-53 of tombs being opened and the dead coming forth at the moment of Jesus' death, the point being that 'the dead are raised from their tombs only by virtue of the fact that Jesus himself enters the domain of death in order to free its prisoners'.[99]

In the first century, the idea of death as a prison was deeply entrenched in Jewish thought and 'the gates of Hades' was a common synonym for mortality, with a huge stone placed in front of its gates, symbolising the 'locked door' at the entrance to Sheol/Hades.[100]

It was Jewish practice, when affordable and practicable, to entomb the dead, representative of the above symbolism, but it is unlikely in the extreme that this was Jesus' fate. The location of his grave was almost certainly unknown to family, disciples and friends, though it is a reasonable assumption that burial sites close to places of execution would have been visited by the acquaintances of deceased victims.

We best understand the tomb story as reflecting the evangelists' desire to associate Jesus' death and resurrection with the sacrificial connotations attendant upon the mythological story of Abraham and Isaac.

The "empty tomb" and the "Binding of Isaac" are not historical data, and for this reason Angela Burdett Coutts' engineers were doomed to failure in their quest, despite what Mk. 16:6b says: 'Look, there is the place they laid him.'

That assertion is really an apologetic/missionary strategy employed by the primitive Jesus movement, for the reason that no one had been witness to the resurrection. In other words, *experiences of the risen Jesus* gave rise to the story of an empty tomb, not the other way round, contrary to what Tom

Wright argues (see Chapter 11).

As Norman Perrin expresses it: 'Scholars are coming increasingly to the conclusion that the empty tomb tradition is an interpretation of the event – a way of saying "Jesus is risen!" – rather than a description of the event itself.'[101]

We turn now to the women who witnessed Jesus' postmortem appearances: 'Jesus met them and said, "Greetings!". They came to him, took hold of his feet, and worshipped him (Mt. 28:9).

Before doing so, however, it should be noted that this reference to the holding of feet probably reflects a very early stage in opposition to the belief, later known as Docetism, that Jesus' resurrected appearances were not of a bodily nature.[102]

—

CHAPTER 6

The Empty Tomb: Women and a Greek Conjunction

'It is in the gatherings of ordinary women to mourn and lament the death of Jesus, not in the closed circle of male disciples, that we should seek the origins of the resurrection traditions.'
Kathleen E. Corley

Our earliest gospel is that of Mark (c. 71). Karen F. Mc. Carthy, in her riveting book *The Other Irish*, relates the amazing stories of those Northern Irish who, from the 1700s, largely tamed and shaped what is now known as America's Deep South – its 'Bible Belt'.

Pastor Jimmy Morrow's ancestors arrived in Tennessee from (what is now) Northern Ireland about 300 years ago and for many years he ministered to a small community in the Appalachians (*The Edwina Church of God in Jesus Christ*). [103]

Morrow has a dangerous speciality: snake handling, a practice that was said to have originated in first century Jerusalem. He was inheritor of a tradition that subscribed to the Bible as the literal word of God; 'the result was supernatural encounters and an emotional outpouring from people striving to have complete faith in His will and to be freed from the fear of death'.[104]

For Morrow and for most Evangelical Christians in the "Deep South", the emphasis is on heartfelt conversion to Jesus, combined with a deep suspicion of 'Christian rationalists' who advocate the importance of 'learning', and not only of 'preaching', when it comes to having a contextual understanding of religious narratives, be they scriptural or doctrinal.

This book champions the 'learning' approach, mindful of the late Jonathan Sacks' profound insight that Judaism arose from the need to escape Egyptian oppression and the urgency today is to ensure that we do not succumb to the despotisms (often interrelated) of religious fundamentalism and political totalitarianism.[105]

Christianity, in the wake of Darwin and of the Holocaust, necessitates what has been called a 'hermeneutic of suspicion'. Jimmy Morrow rejects this imperative, as do many others who subscribe to more fundamentalist and even orthodox expressions of belief, but it is a myopic view indicative of the sclerotic condition in which Christianity now finds itself, regardless of the 'promise' of Mt. 28:29b: 'I am with you always, to the end of time'.[106]

Should Pastor Morrow ever decide to leave off "the preaching" for a day or two and instead take up "the learning", he will be surprised to discover that the main scripture text (Mk. 16:18; cf. Acts 28:3-6) supporting his ministry is a later addition to St. Mark's Gospel.

Of itself, this is no great matter, but literalists have difficulty acknowledging the complexities behind the composition of the New Testament, preferring to ignore the findings of reputable scholarship.

St. Mark's Gospel originally ended at 16:8, with the phrase 'for they were afraid' (in Greek, *ephobounto gar*) and '*gar*' is a conjunction.

Scholars have long debated the significance of this grammatical barbarism, but there can be little doubt that vv. 9 to 20, inclusive of a reference to snake handling, are a summary pastiche drawn from other sources, chiefly the endings of Matthew's and Luke's Gospels, and this composition encompasses reference to an empty tomb appearance story: 'After he rose early on the first day of the week, he appeared first to Mary Magdalene' (16:9a; cf. Mt. 28:1-10 and Lk. 24:1-12).

The author of this gospel was making a point. The women who visited the tomb and fled it in fear were acting in keeping with an important theme in the Gospel of Mark, where the disciples sooner or later fail Jesus: 'All of them deserted him and fled' (15:50), and it is noteworthy that the women 'said nothing to anyone' (16:8b).

We should understand this motif both in terms of what probably happened at the time of Jesus' crucifixion and with regard to the difficulties experienced by followers of the Jesus movement a generation later, at the time of – and subsequent to - the Temple's destruction. The account in Mk. 14:66-72 of Peter's triple denial of Jesus, for example, most likely reflects such 'difficulties'.[107]

St. Mark's account of women at the tomb reinforces the hypothesis that the original version of this gospel had no resurrection appearance stories associated with the sepulchre, and if this premise is correct it means also that the reference to Mt. 28:9, at the conclusion to the previous chapter, supports this deduction, because the Gospel of Mark was the primary source for the two other synoptic gospels – Luke and Matthew.

How, then, are we to understand the origins of the moving accounts of the women at the tomb?

Before outlining Kathleen Corley's hypothesis concerning these reports, a misunderstanding often voiced by Christian homilists and scholars, including some Jewish ones, requires attention.

It is not true that the disciples refused to believe in Jesus' resurrection because the testimony of women at the time was inadmissible. It was not believed for the simple reason that his disciples were unwilling to acknowledge the claim (see Lk. 24:11; cf. Jn. 20:24-26).

Geza Vermes (d. 2013), the doyen of Jesus scholarship, thinks otherwise: 'In the patriarchal society of inter-testamental Judaism, a woman's testimony could not be trusted'. This judgement needs to be tempered by the consideration that 'we are not talking about a Jewish court of law in which witnesses are being called to testify'.[109]

This observation of Bart Ehrman is supported by his noting that oral traditions, not formal testimonies, lie at the back of these stories, commenting further that women could have invented them since we know that 'they were particularly well represented in early Christian communities'.[110]

St Paul, for example, writes about Junia 'as foremost among the apostles' (Rom. 16:7[111]) and it is obvious that women played a key role in the life of the historical Jesus.[112]

These considerations augment Corley's position that funerary cults involving meal rituals were a significant factor influencing Christian origins, giving participants 'a sense of *the presence* of the dead person, of communion with the dead person, and of *memorialisation of* the dead person'.[113]

Contrary to the earlier writings of many academics, there is now extensive archaeological evidence that Jews of the late

Second Temple period practised 'cults of the dead', despite numerous attempts to suppress them, where 'funerary feasting' was a common practice, patterned to some extent on Hellenistic customs.

Participants in these "funeral clubs" consumed much bread and wine at the burial site(s), in addition to other foods.[114] Strange though it may seem, these 'clubs' are the forerunners to the Medieval guilds of 'butcher, baker and candle-stick maker'.

Corley argues with considerable erudition that we should understand these original practices against the background in antiquity of lamenting women visiting graves on the third day after death, a perspective that has influenced the composition of our first passion story in St Mark's Gospel.

Its reference to 'women looking on from a distance' (15:40), is also indicative of 'noble death scenes' from the period – Plato's dramatised *Death of Socrates*, for example.[115]

If Corley is right, it means that we need to evaluate anew the origins of the passion and resurrection narratives against the background of the famous kerygmatic formulation of 1 Cor. 15:3-4: 'I handed on to you as of first importance what I had received – that Christ died for our sins in accordance with the scriptures, and that he was buried, and that he was raised on the third day' (abridged).

The involvement of women in cults of the dead 'on the third day', though certainly orderly, 'was treated with considerable suspicion because of its necromantic associations'. Necromania is the evocation of spirits of the deceased for the purposes of fortune-telling.

For this reason, it is probable that the reference at 1 Cor. 15:4b ('he was raised on the third day') had to be subsequently modified c. 71 (when Mark's gospel was written), and the consequence was the empty tomb tradition.

Corley's point is that it marginalised Jesus' female disciples, 'thus weakening their claim to having seen the risen Christ', because at that time in popular Greek, Roman and Jewish religion the presence of women at graves (and tombs) 'on the third day' had magical associations, their lamentations allegedly having the power 'to stir up the dead, especially to exact vengeance'.[118]

The gospels' midrashic device of an empty tomb is 'a modification of a literary and cultural connection between women, magic and tomb cults' and also present in Hellenistic romances - when Chareas, for example, goes to mourn the death of Callirhoe his wife, he discovers an empty tomb (and see Chapter 11, *Greater than Moses*).[119]

Corley's thesis is that the empty tomb narrative(s) served the purpose of emphasising women's inferiority to men when it came to proclaiming the risen Christ.

This hypothesis is supported by St Paul's failure to include women as recipients of Jesus' resurrection appearances, when he identifies 'Cephas and the Twelve' (1 Cor. 15:3-8), notwithstanding the fact that this letter (c. 51) antedates St. Mark's Gospel by about twenty years.

Significant also is the reference to 'the Twelve'. St. Paul clearly had no knowledge of Judas' putative betrayal of Jesus. It is an exercise in political and religious propaganda, derived probably from what he says in 1 Cor. 11:23, about the night of Jesus' arrest. It has had disastrous consequences for the Jewish people. Judas (if he existed at all) most probably died of old age.

The resurrection narratives are inextricably linked to the passion narratives, and an unusual but compelling feature of Corley's hypothesis is that rather than being exclusively the product of a document written by well-educated men, 'as virtually all scholars suppose', she argues that the latter have their origins 'in a grassroots liturgical context dominated by women', influenced also by ordinary people from what nowadays would be called the 'working classes'.[120]

In addition, she postulates that back of the (first) appearance stories recorded in 1 Cor. 15:3-8 were spiritual (ecstatic) visions of Jesus, 'not experiences of a bodily risen Lord'.[121]

Corley is probably right, supporting the complementary deduction that St Paul had no knowledge of Jesus' burial in a tomb, for the simple reason there was no such interment: 'With regard to the body of Jesus, by Easter Sunday Morning, those who cared did not know where it was, and those who knew did not care.'[122]

It has been suggested by Richard Swinburne that Paul failed to mention the tomb because he didn't need to[123], but this claim hardly fits with the fact that the apostle seems to have known virtually nothing about the life of the historical Jesus, so why should knowledge of a burial site be an exception to this pattern? It makes little sense.

Furthermore, Palestine in the first century was known for the popularity of its tomb sites associated with well-known figures and a literal empty tomb would have 'increased the likelihood of a physical site commemorating Jesus' resurrection, not decreased it'.[124]

The absence of such a tomb, in addition to veneration at a site not occurring until the fourth century supports Corley's argument that the gospels' tomb traditions are late additions to the embryonic Christian story.

Her impressive and extensive analysis of the data, having researched comprehensively Jewish and Graeco-Roman material, leads to the further conclusion that the visions of the women at some point became associated with a third day funerary ritual, and in turn this gave rise to the empty tomb stories as we now have them.

An inference of Corley's proposal is that we should understand the resurrection traditions as liturgical representations, similar to how *The Death of Jesus the Jew* maintains that the passion narratives are religious dramatisations set in part against the background of the synagogue's liturgical calendar. Matthew, for example, patterned his account of Jesus' last day on a twenty-four hour synagogue service divided into eight segments.[125]

Her extensive research is also relevant to contemporary situations. The ancient grieving rituals that she examined have parallels today. In 2012, for example, Diarmuid O'Murchu, the Irish priest and social scientist, was facilitating a series of conferences in the Philippines on the theme of Christian spirituality when another of the facilitators, Sr Elsa, invited him to dine out one evening (31st October), at *The Graveyard*, which he took to be the nickname of a local restaurant.[126]

Soon after setting off, O'Murchu realised that he had been very naïve when they found themselves merging into a large crowd walking in the same direction, similar to what he had experienced in the UK before important football matches (and see Chapter 11, *O'Murchu on the Resurrection*).

Their destination was indeed a literal graveyard, where relatives and friends of the deceased gathered at graves to mourn and celebrate their memory (in story-telling, music, song and prayer), between 30th October and 2nd November (All Souls Day), frequently remaining overnight.

In the course of the vigil, at least one special meal was eaten at the graveside and it had to include a complete stranger, which was the role of Sr. Elsa's guest.

O'Murchu explains that what to contemporary people may look like a primitive and morbid custom has not only been a feature of ancient societies but it is also practised today throughout the Philippines and in some Central and South American countries.

The implication of this observation is that just as the original passion-resurrection narrative had its origins in a liturgical context centred on women and ordinary people, women's laments in our time continue to have the potential to transform experiences of grief into ones of hope.

Many people will disagree with Corley's interpretation of the material, but it has the merit (amongst others) of reminding us that the voices of women, and not only those of men, lie behind the stories of Jesus' death and resurrection.

This is a great irony given how Christian theology continues to be influenced by patriarchal stereotypes and prejudices, a consideration even more ironic when scholars are now examining the likelihood that funerary meals facilitated by women may constitute some of the backstory to the Last Supper narrative(s), with particular regard to the Eucharist's sense of "memorial" and "presence" in the context of folk laments.[127]

—

CHAPTER 7

No Guard at the Tomb:
Joseph Fiennes in Risen

*'No one knows what happened
to the body of Jesus. Stolen?
Buried elsewhere? Miraculously
resurrected? It does not matter and
Christians should not care.'*
Thomas Sheehan
(slightly redacted)

Sheehan, in *The First Coming – How the Kingdom of God Became Christianity*, argues that 'the proper response to the 'empty tomb' is silence, even silence about that silence. The women who came to the tomb had the correct reaction. ... They did not say anything to anyone.'[128]

'Hollywood' has not read, let alone taken to heart, Sheehan's book. Its job is to sell movies and, in 2016, it released Risen, starring Joseph Fiennes as the Roman officer (tribune) charged by Pilate to find Jesus' corpse, because - according to St. Matthew's Gospel - the chief priests and Pharisees, the day following Jesus' death, petitioned the procurator to secure the tomb, 'otherwise his disciples may steal him away and tell the people Jesus has been raised from the dead' (27:62-64).

Pilate declines the request, and we are then informed that it was secured 'by sealing the stone' (27:65-66). In *Risen*, the 'sealing' was achieved by the placing of big red seals on it, which were not to be removed before sunset 'on the third day' (see 'Daniel', Chapter 8).

These verses are unique to this gospel. There is little doubt they are not historical and it is of interest that, in *Risen*, the soldiers placed at the tomb were Romans, when St. Matthew implies they were a Jewish guard (27:65b[129]). He, like the director of *Risen*, was not unduly concerned with historical facts, and for good reason. In their own ways, they have provided us with powerful dramatisations of a famous story, not with an historical account of it.

Or, to express this observation another way: When the fictional tribune tells Pilate that he personally placed the stone at the tomb's entrance, Fiennes is portraying a *fictive midrash* on Mt. 27:62-66, a redaction of Mk. 15:42-47, and the latter is a midrash derived from the Hebrew Bible (see below).

When the author of Mt. 27:62-66 wrote this passage, he was not writing history as we interpret it in a post-Enlightenment world that no longer appreciates *the wonder of the religious imagination*. To paraphrase Aristotle's famous statement, *it requires moral imagination to live an authentically virtuous life*.

To read such passages literally, many Christians believe to be virtuous but, by so doing, they embrace a delusion encapsulated by John Dominic Crossan in his oft-quoted aphorism:

My point is not that those ancient people told
literal stories and we are now smart enough to
take them symbolically, but that they told them
symbolically and we are now dumb enough to
take them literally.

In *When The Disciple Comes of Age: Christian Identity in the
21ˢᵗ Century*, Diarmuid O'Murchu demonstrates powerful-
ly how literalism has done incalculable harm to Christians'
faith development.

This book endorses his analysis, arriving at similar conclusions but from a different perspective, influenced chiefly
by the imperative to re-evaluate Christian beliefs in the light
of the Holocaust.

Matthew wrote 27: 62-66 about twenty years after
the Temple's destruction in 70, by which time Jewish-
Christians were promoting the belief that its razing
was a consequence of God's will because of mainstream
Judaism's refusal to acknowledge the messianic claims
made on behalf of Jesus.

It is against this background that we should interpret the
supposed appeal of the chief priests and Pharisees before
Pilate: 'Sir, we remember that the impostor said when still
alive, "After three days, I will rise again"' (27:63).

Jesus did not speak these words and they clearly refer back
to Mt. 26:61: 'This fellow said I am able to destroy the Temple
of God and to rebuild it in three days' (cf. Mk. 14:58), reflecting the mythological 'third day' motif examined previously.

Unless one adopts literalist perspective, that somehow
Jesus really said these things reported verbatim c. sixty years
after his death, the only sensible and responsible conclusion is that we are dealing here with utterances serving a

polemical function.

That purpose was rooted in the need to appease the Romans, subsequent to the circumstances prevailing after the *Great Jewish-Roman War*, when Jewish-Christians and other Jews (the Pharisees, in effect) were vying for dominance subsequent to the Jews' catastrophic defeat.

(James Carroll, in *Christ Actually*, has described it as the 'First Holocaust', observing that the War had an immense influence upon the composition of the synoptic gospels.[130])

The Romans, after the year 73, made no distinction between 'ordinary Jews' and 'Jewish-Christians'. It is a differentiation that we impose retrospectively upon the New Testament and it has led to grave consequences, not least with regard to how Mt. 27:25, 'His blood be on us and on our children', has provided a launching pad for anti-Semitism.

The verse derives from a number of sources in the Old Testament, particularly Jer. 26:15: 'If you put me to death, you will be bringing innocent blood upon yourselves and upon the inhabitants of this city' (cf. Acts 5:28).[131]

By c. 85, when St Matthew's Gospel was completed, that city had become identified with the horrors prior and subsequent to Jerusalem's surrender in 70. On that day (probably 9th August), when the Romans gained final control of Jerusalem, thousands of Jews were slaughtered, many of whom burned to death on the roof of the Temple's Court of the Gentiles, and for a time thereafter countless numbers were crucified on Jerusalem's streets, to the extent that wood and nails became scarce commodities.

Similar to how 'the people' never voiced the notorious Blood Cry, there was no guard at the tomb, for the simple reason that Jesus' body was most likely placed in a communal pit and thus, on Easter Day, when we are told that an angel 'rolled back the stone and sat on it' (dressed in clothing white as snow[132]), the guards could not have 'shook and became like dead men', following an earthquake (28:2-4; cf. 27:50-55).

(Benedict Viviano OP makes the interesting observation that, in antiquity, stones blocking tombs symbolised the victory of death over life. In the above situation, it symbolised life's triumph over death, but there is no requirement for Christians to literalise that symbolism.[133])

It is then narrated, after the angel tells the women to inform the disciples of Jesus' resurrection and they have an encounter with him (vv. 7 to 11), that the chief priests and elders formed a conspiracy to give a large sum of money to the soldiers, with the instruction, 'You must say, "His disciples came by night and stole him away while we were asleep. If this comes to the Governor's ears, we will satisfy him and keep you out of trouble' (28:12-14).

The soldiers take the money, following the above instruction, 'And this story is told among the Jews to this day' (v. 15). In *Risen*, Joseph Fiennes is told that eight or ten of Jesus' disciples stole the body.

What are we to make of this story? Its chief purpose is to distance Rome from involvement in the death of Jesus. The soldiers "witness" the resurrection, similar to how, at Jesus' crucifixion, the centurion says, 'Truly, this man was God's Son' (27:54; cf. Mk. 15:39).

It is no accident that his "confession of faith" is subsequent to another legendary earthquake, which accompanied the rending of the curtain of the Temple's inner sanctum and the extraordinary account of the raising of many bodies from their tombs (Mt. 27:51-53).

None of this is history in the sense that we have come to

understand it. We are dealing here with a combination of midrashic and legendary materials. (See Is. 29:6, for example: 'In an instant, suddenly, you will be visited by the Lord of Hosts, with thunder and earthquake and a great noise'.)

'Witness', referred to above, is in inverted commas because in the canonical gospels nobody actually sees the resurrection; Jesus appears only to his disciples. The apocryphal Gospel of Peter, however, is the exception to this rule; there, Jesus' enemies are "witnesses" to the resurrection. Scholars debate how *appearances* are to be understood and approaches to the phenomenon will be examined in Chapter 11.

Raymond Brown identifies a further literary-theological basis for the story of Guards at the Tomb. Similar to St Matthew's birth story (written after the passion-resurrection accounts), 'it resembles the co-operation of Herod, the chief priests and the scribes, in sending to kill the baby Jesus' (2:16-18), which itself is a midrash on Ex. 1:15-22, pharaoh's (supposed) attempt to murder the baby Moses.[134]

Brown, however, whilst recognising the polemical character of the story, implies that its argumentative nature derives in part from Jewish denials that Jesus was raised bodily from the dead. I think he is mistaken, for three reasons:

✣ Many Jews at the time had no problem with bodily resurrection. Their concern was that the concept had been "hijacked" by the primitive Jesus movement. Underlying this Christian anxiety was the knowledge that mainstream Judaism of the late Second Temple period did not subscribe to the notion of a dead, resurrected messiah. Thus, when Pilate, in Risen, says, 'Without a corpse, we have a potential messiah', he is voicing a popular Christian misconception, all the more ironic given the

New Testament's propensity to use fulfilment citations: 'Christ died for our sins in accordance with the scriptures' (1 Cor. 15:3b), which is one of many examples. In fairness, the phrase 'in accordance with the scriptures' can be interpreted more loosely, in the sense that it is a generic formula arguing for continuation between traditional Judaism and 'Christian messianic Judaism' (alluded to earlier), but that is not how most Christians have come to understand these citations. In summary, the problem is not so much with the claim that someone was raised from the dead, but that Jesus' resurrection (however we are to understand it) is endowed with universal, redemptive significance. Judaism, for 2,000 years, has repudiated this belief.

❖ Brown, in his extraordinarily impressive magnum opus, *The Death of the Messiah* (DoM, 1994), is fond of the noun 'verisimilitude', meaning that something could have happened, as in: 'Pilate asks Jesus if he is King of the Jews. There is nothing implausible about this question' (p.719). Apart from the consideration that the encounter is highly improbable, another difficulty is that Brown applies a similar methodology to the Guards at the Tomb (despite advocating in different contexts that 'Christians believe in Jesus, not in a tomb'), one that is selective rather than contextual. It does not recognise adequately the midrashic character of the tomb tradition(s), with regard to the day of Jesus' death and the subsequent accounts of his resurrection, which almost certainly emerged over a period of many years; they were not determined by a notional time span of three days. Brown, however, implies some historical reality for Guards at the Tomb, where the truth is that we are dealing exclusively with polemical theology.

✢ A third difficulty is that DoM, despite its protestations to the contrary ('this commentary will not ignore the way in which guilt and punishment for the crucifixion of Jesus have been inflicted upon Jews'), fails to live up to its promise to castigate anti-Judaism. His treatment of Guards at the Tomb illustrates this failure, and the book (in two stout volumes), for all its many virtues, never really addresses a problem at the core of how we are to understand the passion and resurrection narratives: the simple fact that it is not merely a question of how these narratives have been misinterpreted, but of the nefarious purposes, however unintended, they have served for 2,000 years.

Related to these problems is the consideration that Brown's methodology is influenced excessively by the requirement to remain within the parameters of orthodox teaching about Jesus, a criticism voiced by Geza Vermes in his assessment of Brown's other masterpiece, *The Birth of the Messiah* (1993): 'Frank Kermode has attributed Brown's refusal to acknowledge the made-up character of Matthew's birth story to his eagerness to secure the Catholic Church's imprimatur for his book.'

'Imprimatur' is a fancy Latin term for 'seal of approval'. The next chapter will examine a seal of a different kind, one that supports Sheehan's conviction that we do not knows what happened to the body of Jesus.

CHAPTER 8

—

The Lions' Den is sealed with a Stone: Midrash at Work

*'Jesus saw himself as the divine
Son of Man.'*
Daniel Boyarin

The drama of *Daniel in the Lions' Den* is one of the Bible's most well known stories and it – like *Jonah and the Whale* – has become part of popular culture.

It can be reliably dated to c. 165 BCE, immediately prior to the death of Antiochus IV. 'Daniel', however, is presented as living at the time of the Babylonian Exile (597 to 538 BCE), but the real focus of the *book* is the Macabean Revolt against Antiochus, a conflict examined in Chapter 4.

'Daniel' is an apocalyptic work, meaning that it promoted the view, dated to at least the second century BCE, that God's intervention in history was imminent. In other words, He would soon reward the righteous and punish evildoers.

Jesus almost certainly subscribed to this outlook, on the assumption that Mk. 1:15 represents his teaching: 'The time is fulfilled, the Kingdom of God is close to hand; repent, believe this good news'.

Litres of scholarly ink have been used elucidating this verse. 'Kingdom of God' is typically interpreted nowadays in three main ways:

- ✣ Jesus proclaimed and inaugurated it, meaning that, in Diarmuid O'Murchu's words, it was 'the ministerial strategy used by Jesus for his mission'. The main emphasis here is on the (later) claim that Jesus is divine (at the Council of Chalcedon in 451, Jesus was proclaimed 'true God and true man').

- ✣ Jesus is 'lesser' than 'the Kingdom', where the latter is understood as God's dream for the whole of creation, perhaps reflected in a Jewish understanding of covenant ('I have set my bow in the clouds, and it shall be a sign of the covenant between me and the Earth', Gen. 8:13). The crucial point here is that 'divinity' is not the central issue. We are dealing with a human being who identifies himself so radically with God that Jesus serves as an ideal exemplar for those of us who choose to identify with that vision. In this context, 'divinity' is best interpreted as the radical living of human life, echoing St. Irenaeus' famous statement: 'The glory of God is man fully alive.'

- ✣ The Church equates with 'the Kingdom', which is effectively (if not officially) the position of the Catholic Church, notwithstanding the reforms initiated by Vatican II (1962-65). This interpretation maintains that, without fidelity to Church teaching, the vision of 'the Kingdom' cannot be realised in the world. In other words, the Kingdom is the Church and an important dimension of the Church's mission is to balance the claim that, in Jesus' person, there are two natures (see

'Chalcedon', above). In reality, however, Christianity for most of its history has adopted 'functional docetism', meaning that Jesus' humanity is always trumped by his divinity. (The exaggerated devotions frequently evident in Adoration of the Blessed Sacrament, for example, are illustrative of this disconnect.)

O'Murchu argues that the second position is the more authentic one, because it reflects both the historical context as we now best understand it and his proper insistence that, in the light of the advances consequent upon the findings disclosed by Evolution and Quantum Physics, it is no longer tenable to postulate unqualified belief in a God who creates *ex-nihilio*.

One implication of the position that God has not created *ex-nihilio* is that the account of *The Fall of Adam and Eve* (Gen. 3), which gave rise to the later Christian myth of *Original Sin*, is that 'there has never been a perfect idyllic time, nor is there likely to be some grand finale at the end of the world' (O'Murchu; see endnote 337).

In his book *How to Read the Bible and Still be A Christian*, Dom Crossan explains how "sin" is an occurrence derived not from Gen. 2-3 but from Gen. 4 (Cain's murder of Abel), where it is not a flaw in human beings but in civilization, that is, 'not in nature but in culture'. In other words, 'original sin is not about individuals and sex but about communities and violence'.[140]

Crossan is not denying the obvious fact that human beings commit evil actions. The force of his observation is that, contrary to St. Augustine's later (and unfortunate) interpretation of the same chapters in Genesis, these actions result not from some 'genetic flaw' passed from generation to generation, but from the reality that 'escalatory human violence has never invented a weapon we did not use, never invented one less powerful than what it replaced, and never ceased to confuse lull with peace'.[141]

The Catechism of the Catholic Church (CCC) disagrees with Crossan's thesis, by maintaining that the Church, 'which has the mind of Christ, knows very well that we cannot tamper with the revelation of original sin without undermining the mystery of Christ', and it goes on to say that whilst the account of the Fall in Gen. 3 uses 'figurative language', it nonetheless 'affirms a primeval event, a deed that took place *at the beginning of the history of man*, and that 'revelation gives us the certainty of faith that the whole of human history is marked by that original fault, committed by our first parents' (nn. 389 and 390, quoting the Council of Trent).

These anthropocentric assertions lack credibility. Or, to express this consideration another way: there was no 'primeval event', because there was no *Paradise* in the first place.

Christianity, if it is to be an authentic and prophetic voice in the twenty-first century, must engage courageously and urgently with these issues, renouncing the siren (often dangerous) voices of Christian Fundamentalism(s). The time is long overdue for (more than) a little tampering with a paradigm necessitating radical adaptation.

These observations suggest that Christians should re-examine titles like 'Son of God' and 'Son of Man' and the claim, traditionally understood, that *Jesus is our Divine Rescuer*.

Leaving aside one atonement context for this belief in St. Paul's genuine writings (he did not believe Jesus is God[142]), Daniel Boyarin, a leading Jewish scholar, writes: 'I want to show that Jesus saw himself as the Divine Son of Man', in his book The Jewish Gospels.[143]

This book cannot address Boyarin's contested thesis in detail, but he does highlight three considerations that can be easily overlooked by historical theologians and New Testament scholars:

- ❖ 'Jews at the time of Jesus had been waiting for a messiah who was both human and divine', that is, *The Son of Man*, an idea they derived from Dan. 7, with particular regard to vv. 13 to 14: 'I saw one like a human being coming with the clouds of Heaven ..., his dominion is everlasting, and his kingship is one that shall never be destroyed' (abridged).[144]

- ❖ 'Jesus entered into a role that existed before his birth, and this is why many Jews were prepared to accept him as the messiah', expressed pithily in the claim that 'The job description was not a put-up job tailored to fit Jesus!'.[145]

- ❖ Boyarin argues in consequence that the contemporary *Messianic Jews Movement* is a genuine concern 'to demonstrate that their belief in Jesus does not make them un-Jewish', with particular regard to their interpretation of the famous *Suffering Servant* material in Isaiah 53.[146]

Bart Ehrman confirms Boyarin's thesis to the extent that he makes a convincing argument for the claim that some Palestinian Jewish-Christians did indeed speak about Jesus as a divine figure.[147]

Ehrman elucidates how Judaism incorporated notions of divinities becoming human beings and vice versa, and how in the first century the Book of Daniel provided a particular, but not unique, context for the belief that Jesus was in some manner divine.

Boyarin's desire is to encourage greater understanding between Judaism and Christianity, but notwithstanding Ehrman's indirect endorsement of his position, there remain some difficulties with it.

For one thing, St Paul seems to have been unaware of any alleged connections between 'Jesus', 'Son of Man' and 'divinity', which is odd, given the consideration - and acknowledged by Boyarian - that the Apostle was steeped in his Jewish heritage (albeit from a background in the Diaspora, the significance of which is usually lost on Christians, and see Chapter 10).

Furthermore, Boyarin has in effect cherry-picked verses to support his thesis. The most obvious instance of this practice is his quoting of Jesus' alleged response to the high priest at *his night trial*: 'Are you the Messiah ..., Jesus said, "I am"; and you will see the Son of Man ..., coming with the clouds of Heaven' (Mk. 14:61b-62 and parallels).

No such encounter took place. It, like the supposed *Trial before Pilate*, is a theological fiction and it is extraordinary – given his deserved academic reputation – that Boyarian seems to have ignored this fact and the virtually unanimous scholarly consensus regarding the Son of Man tradition.

Jewish belief certainly applied the epithet 'coming with the clouds of Heaven' to the messiah and it also taught that, like Abraham, he would 'sit at the right hand of God', but the messiah and Abraham were never thought to be in any sense divine, notes Maccoby.[148]

His observation does not invalidate Boyarin's thesis because Maccoby is writing about 'divinity' in the sense of a thorough monotheistic understanding of the concept.

'Son of Man' means a figure resembling a human being. In the Hebrew Bible, it is identical to 'man': 'What are human beings that you are mindful of them; mortals that you care for them?' (Ps. 8:4)

Daniel 7's treatment of the theme is against the background of his famous dream, where he provides an extraordinary apocalyptic vision of 'four great beasts' (vv. 2-14). They represent the four Pagan empires of the Babylonians, Medes, Persians and Greeks, and the tenth horn of the fourth beast, for example, stands for Antiochus IV, after whose defeat victory will come to the 'saints of the Most High', meaning that the Jews will experience an everlasting triumph over their adversaries.[149]

The Book of Ezekiel also avails of the Son of Man theme, as do the apocryphal works of 4 Ezra and 1 Enoch. In the latter, he is identified as the anointed messiah of the Lord who seems to have some kind of pre-existence, 'a light to the nations', which may point to an angel as 'the embodiment of God's wisdom'.[150]

Daniel believed that at the end of time Israel's anguish would be vindicated: 'Many of those who sleep in the dust of the earth shall awake, some to everlasting life, and some to shame and everlasting contempt' (12:2).

In conjunction with the conviction of the Maccabees addressed in Chapter 4, it reflected the belief of many (by no means all) Jews that there would be a general resurrection of the dead, when God would bring the world to its conclusion and judge it. By this time, c. 165 BCE, Judaism had gradually come to embrace what many scholars consider to be a novel conceptual development: "resurrection".

In reality, however, the notion of the resurrection of the

dead can be traced back to the time of the Exile (see Chapter 1).

Daniel, it should be emphasised, did not advocate belief in individual resurrection *per se*, an idea which, by the first century of our era, had nonetheless become established and famously encapsulated by St Paul: 'Christ has been raised from the dead, the first fruits of those who have died' (1 Cor. 15:20; cf. Rom. 8:29 and Acts 26:23).

All of these ideas influenced how the evangelists crafted their accounts of Jesus' resurrection and, strange though it may seem, when St Matthew came to write his account of the resurrection he drew on Daniel's notion that one like a *Son of Man* 'is given sovereignty over the earth and accorded power and authority to rule over all peoples, *as king*'.[151]

The phrase as *king* is revealing because the story of *Daniel in the Lions' Den* has King Darius command that Daniel should be thrown into the pit, and Darius 'sealed it with his own signet' (6: 16-17).

On the assumption, argued in *DJJ*, that Jesus never had a formal burial, Matthew has taken the *Darius-Daniel Story* and reformulated it as a midrash, whereby a guard of soldiers made the putative tomb secure, 'by sealing the stone' (27:66), oddly mirroring what Darius' minions, following his example, do at the lions' den (Dan. 6:17b, and see Chapter 11).

Matthew was not writing history and he knew it. As with the notorious *Blood Cry* (27:25), his intention is an exercise in religious polemics, demonstrated by the sentiment attributed to the centurion at the foot of the cross, referenced earlier: 'Truly, this man was God's Son' (27:54b), reflecting the words said to have been placed on the horizontal beam of the cross: 'Jesus, King of the Jews' (27:37b).

The intention, derived in part from Daniel, is clearly to assert that Jesus, and not four Pagan dynasties, now has *sovereignty over all the Earth*, inclusive of authority over a *fifth evil empire* - 'Rome', to borrow in a very different context the words of the late President Ronald Reagan, applied to the former Soviet Union.

St Matthew had an additional source to draw on for his account of the story, taken from the Book of Joshua (10:1-27), where its protagonist has a guard of soldiers roll stones against the mouth of a cave within which are incarcerated five of Joshua's enemies (v. 18; cf. v. 27).[152]

He also drew on the Hebrew Bible for other material, giving us what we now term 'Lent', a penitential and liturgical tradition rooted in how the people of Israel are said to have spent forty years in the wilderness (Ex. 16:35).

This story finds its way into the New Testament with the account of *Jesus' Temptations* endured against Satan (Mt. 4:1-11; cf. Mk.1:12-13), a midrash derived from the tradition that Moses spent 'forty days and nights' on Sinai (Ex. 24:18b).

Jewish practice was that on the third Sabbath of Nisan (late April in our calendar) the story was narrated in synagogues.[153]   Jewish-Christians would have been present at these services and it is virtually certain that their familiarity with Jewish liturgical practices also lie at the back of the tomb and *rolling stone tradition*(s), when taken in association with 'Daniel'.

The evangelists were not being duplicitous by *translating one to the other*. Their purpose (c. 80) was to proclaim, as they understood it, the commission 'to make disciples of all nations', one which Matthew situates on a mountain-top following Jesus' resurrection (28:19a).[154]

It reflects this gospel's depiction of Jesus as the *new Moses*, who - in the Sermon on the Mount - is represented as *one greater than Moses*, since it was Moses who had delivered the

Law from Sinai, 'on the morning of the third day' (Ex. 19:16; cf. 20 to 24). In addition, surely it is no accident, following this *Moses theme*, that the location of his tomb is unknown (Dt. 34:6), but Jesus' burial place is 'known' (Mk. 16:42-47).

When, therefore, Joseph Fiennes in *Risen seals the stone*, the movie (for understandable reasons) is buying into a narrative that has everything to do with the *psychology of Christianity* but nothing to do with historical data in our normal way of understanding that term.

Benedict Viviano, OP, reflecting this observation, argues that locating an empty tomb is not essential to Christian faith, noting that St Paul, in 1 Corinthians 15, makes no reference to it, yet he seems to have no problem affirming belief in Jesus' bodily resurrection (see Chapter 10).

Viviano argues that, in strict logic, there is no requirement why an empty tomb and belief in the resurrection should necessarily entail each other: 'Jesus could have risen and the corpse be in the tomb; Jesus could have not risen and the tomb be empty (the body could have been stolen), but the two fit well together.'

"Empty tomb" and "resurrection" certainly 'fit well together', but there can be little doubt that the former is an interpretation of the latter rather than a description of an aspect of the resurrection itself, to paraphrase Norman Perrin. In other words, consequential events give rise to momentous stories by way of proclaiming an experience that cannot be apprehended in ordinary historical categories.

Viviano's assessment is nonetheless apposite because death is a state of utter annihilation, and God's gracious decision to overcome it with regard to Jesus (we should not think of his resurrection as mere post-mortem survival) is not dependent upon "evidence".

At the same time, he would be anxious to emphasise that the resurrection is not some code for saying that, despite his death, Jesus' message continues in the preaching of his followers; that, to paraphrase Gerard Hughes SJ, the resurrection is about Jesus independently of his effect on the disciples or believers in later generations, but Hughes' observation certainly does not invalidate Dom Crossan's pronouncement:

> With regard to the body of Jesus, by Easter
> Sunday morning those who cared did not know
> where it was and those who knew did not care.

Sheehan, therefore, is right: 'No one knows what happened to the body of Jesus' (see Chapter 7). This does not mean, however, that the *Easter Proclamation* is devoid of meaning, as illustrated by the exquisite story of *The Road to Emmaus* (Lk. 24:13-35) and the account in St John's Gospel of Jesus, also after the resurrection, sharing a meal of fish and bread with the disciples (21:9-14).

On the book's cover, Thomas Plunkett, a gifted watercolour artist, has provided a striking interpretation of the verses from John, encapsulating both the ethereal nature of the resurrection appearances and how they relate to open commensality, the practice of sharing meals without regard to socio-religious boundaries.

—

CHAPTER 9

Food, Wonderful Fish: They Recognised Him in the Breaking of the Bread

A Celebration of Hospitable Conversation

For centuries, scholars have speculated about the location of Emmaus but this is to miss the point. 'Emmaus' is not about location, location location; it is about hospitality: 'The eyes of the disciples are only fully opened after they have shown *hospitality* to a stranger'.[156]

Having said that, it seems more likely than not that Emmaus was a real village (approximately eleven kilometres north of Jerusalem), if Josephus is to be relied upon. He narrates that Varus, Governor of Syria, subsequent to the revolts after the death of Herod the Great, burned it to the ground, after which - upon reaching Jerusalem - he proceeded to crucify about 2,000 insurgents.[157]

In her charming, yet problematical, book, *The Burning Word: A Christian Encounter With Jewish Midrash*, Judith Kunst (from an Evangelical background) writes that 'revelation cannot be reduced to facts'. It is really about a *celebration of conversation, not about information.*[158]

Addressing some implications of Kunst's insight, allied to the notion of *open commensality* (the sharing of food without regard to social class, which seems to have been a major feature of Jesus' ministry), it is necessary to first clarify something that often comes as a surprise to Christians.

St Luke's beautiful account of *The Road to Emmaus* has two disciples, maybe wife and husband, dejected that Jesus 'had not been the one to redeem Israel' (24:21), when they are joined by a *stranger* who proceeds to explain to Cleopas and his friend that it was necessary that 'the messiah should suffer these things and then enter into his glory' (v. 26), a disclosure that is soon thereafter made clear when, 'in the breaking of the bread', their eyes were opened to the resurrected Jesus (vv. 29 to 31).

The above quotation from Jesus is clearly a midrash on Hos. 6:1-2 (with another "third day" reference), and the prophet there is the people Israel who are offering repentance for their transgressions.

Kunst is right when she observes that *the conversation between Jesus and the disciples* conforms to how midrash works. Jesus, for her, s a true darshan, that is, a midrash-maker, one who turns stories on their head.[159]

Her claim, however, that Jesus fulfils the ancient descriptions of messiah as 'Saviour of the world' could lead the unsuspecting reader to think that all first century Jews sanctioned this interpretation. They did not.

Kunst is employing midrash, as was St. Luke, to advance a religious conviction, but it obscures the fact that Judaism, both preceding and contemporaneous with emerging first century Christianity, knew of no tradition about a dying and resurrected messiah.[160]

In addition, Jesus, as portrayed by the writers of the New Testament and despite their claims to the contrary, simply did not fulfil the messianic expectations of late Second Temple Judaism. No Jew ever has.

The famous passages in Isaiah 53 (typically, 'he bore the sins of many, interceding for transgressors', v. 12b) refer not to an individual but symbolically to Israel and, more to the point, they are most unlikely to have been understood otherwise by Jesus, with the 'Boyarian/Ehrman caveat' outlined in the preceding chapter.

It is entirely legitimate, of course, for Jesus' earliest followers (*Messianic Jews, the Ebionites*[161], for instance) to have interpreted Isaiah differently, but what is not acceptable is Kunst's implication that normative Judaism 2,000 years ago would have recognised Jesus as the messiah, 'Saviour of the world' (*Redemptor Hominis*).

It did not, for the simple reason that, despite there being no uniform agreement at the time about *messianic hope*, Judaism has never embraced the concept of a dying and resurrected messiah, to emphasise yet again a point previously made.

For much of its history, Christianity has de facto assumed a *divine right* to impose upon Judaism what it claims in the name of *Jesus the Jew*, the title of Geza Vermes' famous book of that name (1973). This imperative has had disastrous consequences for Jesus' co-religionists, who do not - and never will - recognise him as the *Christ*.

Sr Mary C. Boys, in H*as God Only One Blessing?*, reminds us that to read Scripture through the exclusive lens of salvation history is bad theology, by which she means that it leads inevitably to poor interpretations of the *First Testament* (Boys' term for the Old Testament).

By placing Christ at "the centre", the impression is given of 'a clear portrait of Jesus as the long-awaited messiah to whom the prophets had pointed, but the Jews failed to recognise'. The historical reality, however, was very different, because there were diverse meanings of "messiah" in the first century, there being 'no universally portrayed messianic figure, and messianic language was but one way of imagining salvation and, she emphasises, it was not the most important one: 'So, to call Jesus "messiah" is a claim of faith, not a self-evident axiom of prophecy to which history has inevitably led' (p. 214).

One contemporary Jewish scholar of the New Testament, Hyam Maccoby, referenced earlier, argues that how St Paul, for example, understood 'the Christ' had no precedent in Judaism, and that it comes from the mystery religions prevalent at the time (see Chapter 10).

The messianic status attributed to Jesus is probably best understood as a function of his teaching about the imminence of the Kingdom (see Mk. 1:15; cf. 11:10).

In the first century, one strand of Jewish thought linked the coming of the Kingdom (the anticipated inauguration of a universal reign of peace and justice) with the coming of the messiah, and this is the general context against which we should understand the proclamation of the primitive Jesus movement, argues Paula Fredriksen, noting further that 'Jesus himself was not the source of this messianic identification, though his message was its cause'.[163] These observations necessitate contextualisation against the background of the *Boyarin-Ehrman thesis* discussed in the previous chapter.

Characteristic of this message was Jesus' participation in *fellowship meals*, that is *open commensality*, defined at the close of the last chapter and illustrated by the *Parable of the Wedding Feast* (Mt. 22:1-14): 'Go into the streets and invite everyone you find to the wedding banquet ..., both good and bad, and the wedding hall was filled with guests' (vv. 9-10, redacted).

Commensality (derived from *Mensa*, the Latin for 'table') is best understood as an invitation to participate in meals that are celebratory of the Kingdom values advocated by Jesus and his earliest followers, including those of the "Jerusalem Church", led by his brother James, in the decades immediately subsequent to Jesus' death and resurrection. (Strangely, that "church" seems to have had no awareness of *Jesus' Institution of the Eucharist.*[164])

The purpose of these meals was to challenge the boundaries that kept people apart, by proclaiming a community of welcome and forgiveness, one not burdened by the memories of past failures, to paraphrase Prof Tom O'Loughlin.[165]

He makes the important point that 'commensality is not an optional aspect of human existence', meaning that the sharing of meals is central to our understanding of human nature.[166]

This insight is at the heart of "Emmaus", a celebration of conversation and of the sharing of *food, wonderful food*, symbolising the fellowship meals that Jesus would have enjoyed with friends.

Dom Crossan interprets the Emmaus story against this background, making the observation, pertinent to Jesus' blessing, breaking and giving of bread (24:30), that Luke (or his editor) omitted 'fish' as part of this *Eucharist-type meal*, thus anticipating what would eventually become the norm: bread and wine Eucharists.[167]

The evangelist nonetheless alludes to the practice of bread and fish Eucharists later in the same chapter, when Jesus appears to 'the eleven and their companions' and eats a piece of broiled fish in their presence (vv. 36-43).

St. John's Gospel, in the context of a resurrection appearance, also has Jesus eating some fish and the framework is clearly Eucharistic (see cover illustration):

> Jesus came and took the bread and gave it to
> them,
> and did the same with the fish. (21:13; cf. 6:11)

Chapter 21 of this gospel, a late addition and set by the Sea of Galilee, devotes its first thirteen verses to an encounter between the risen Jesus and seven disciples, where from the beach he views some of them fishing. (The gospels have twenty-eight allusions to fish.)

Unsuccessful, Jesus commands them to cast their net 'to the right side of the boat', resulting in a catch of 153 fish; the number is symbolic, representing the universality of the Christian proclamation. St Jerome (d. 420) explained it by saying that 'Greek zoologists of the era had recorded 153 types of fish'.[168]

It would be a gross exaggeration to say that, by the second century, there were as many types of Eucharistic celebration, but the hyperbole underlines the point that, whatever their form and extent, by then the Eucharist had become 'the cornerstone of the cultic edifice of Gentile Christianity and it has remained so ever since'.[169]

Such practices, including evidence of (non-deviant) bread and water Eucharists celebrated into the third century[170], indicate that open commensality during Jesus' lifetime was the origin of later ritualization(s) centred on the Eucharist. *DJJ* has argued that the Last Supper narrative is one representation of this development and the words attributed to Jesus at it are not his *ipsissima verba*.[171]

This deduction is supported by Crossan's additional observation that it is highly improbable Jesus himself had instituted a meal 'in which bread and wine were identified with his own body and blood', for two reasons:

✣ Had this been the case, it is very unlikely that Eucharistic practices using water or fish, for example, would have been celebrated in the earliest communities. And the same point applies to bread-and-fish Eucharists: 'For how could those ever have been created if a bread-and-wine symbolization had already officially antedated them?'

✣ There is a complete absence of body and blood symbolism in the Didache, a teaching/liturgical manual now dated to between 50 and 70 . Strangely, it has two Eucharistic prayers without any words of institution, augmenting the virtual certainty that, in the first century, there was no standard rite of institution.

Crossan, therefore, is justified when he avers that one segment of the primitive Jesus movement created the Last Supper narrative, a ritual that combined the fellowship meals of Jesus' lifetime with a commemoration of his death, and 'it spread to other Christian groups only slowly.'[174]

One implication of this position is that the Last Supper can no longer be used in support of this claim made by the CCC: 'On the eve of his Passion, ... Jesus transformed this Last Supper with the apostles into the memorial of his voluntary offering to the Father' (n. 610, abridged).

In other words, we cannot use it 'as a historical event to explain anything about Jesus' own death', no more than, to quote Kieran O'Mahony OSA, was the Last Supper an ordination service, 'simply because the historical Jesus did not reckon with a body separate from his own Jewish faith'.[175]

O'Mahony, at the time co-ordinator of a biblical studies programme for an Irish Catholic diocese, continues by observing that the churches need to listen to what the Spirit is saying to them.

An urgent requirement for those churches identified particularly with liturgical-sacramental traditions is to embrace reforms compatible with the findings promoted by O'Mahony and other like-minded historical theologians.

O'Loughlin, for example, champions *food theology*, a concept that in the Catholic tradition needs to move beyond its preoccupation with redundant notions pertaining to 'valid celebration' and instead to embrace a theology of the Eucharist which recognises what it truly means 'to break bread'.[176]

He is very critical of how the host has come to be understood with regard to the Mass (and in popular Catholic devotions), characterising it as *the world's first industrialised food commodity*, which amounts also to a representation of functional Docetism (an early heresy advancing the view that Christ's humanity was apparent, not real).[177]

Another important observation is O'Loughlin's insistence that theologies of the Eucharist, which *should be focused chiefly on the Father*, must also be located without equivocation in the context of the proper sharing of meals, patterned on the commensality practices of Jesus and not on some idealised notion of *The Last Supper*, which is not a real time account of the night before Jesus' death.[178]

In other words, whoever nowadays understands the Eucharist without 'a consciousness of food, meals and their place in communities' approaches it with an impoverished imagination, failing also to appreciate the radicalism of the Christian imperative to quite literally share food with the hungry, whatever the cost.

Back of O'Loughlin's thinking is the insight that (official) Catholicism makes the error of thinking that the Last Supper is somehow 'immune to all the problems, long recognized, about the historicity of events in the life of the historical Jesus'.[179]

His observations are timely, reflecting O'Mahony's implicit requirement that Christianity needs to re-anchor both Jesus and beliefs about him in the flow of history, to borrow a term from Fr John T. Pawlikowski, which he applies to the Jewish-Christian dialogue.

It is never acceptable to endorse a remark attributed to Cardinal Manning, that 'doctrine trumps history'. Such positions inhibit dynamic faith development, preventing our recognition of the significant consideration that history, in a very practical sense, is something not so much behind us, but instead a reality that follows us, inviting ways to explore the possibilities for a better future.

The meals of commensality Jesus shared with his friends were inclusive gatherings, open to the possibilities of a better future, because their focus was to counter the shame and honour culture prevalent at the time, which reflected table fellowship as one way of asserting social and political superiority.[180]

My inherited religious tradition, Catholicism, has typically understood participation in the Eucharist as a "reward" for avoiding sin, far distanced from what O'Loughlin calls 'ordinary living', by which he means human beings' *hospitable encounters*.[181]

Pope Francis, rightly, has made an effort to correct this psychological and spiritual distortion, by – for example – characterising the Eucharist as 'medicine for the soul', but his good intentions do not go far enough. For one thing, the pope is unwilling to acknowledge that women have an "entitlement" to preside at celebrations of the Eucharist.

O'Louglin's insistence upon refocusing the Eucharist in the context of 'ordinary living' is an important contribution to our discovering anew the significance of Jesus' fellowship meals, because the Eucharist as we now celebrate it originated almost certainly after Jesus' resurrection, when some of his followers created the Last Supper as a ritual combining those meals remembered from Jesus' life with a commemoration of his death.[182]

In other words, we best understand it as midrash and our theologies of the Eucharist need to be adapted in the light of that consideration.[183]

This is one background against which "Emmaus" *should be understood*. It is about the *religious imagination*. Its meaning is abused when many Christians, ignoring the findings of reputable scholarship, choose to interpret 'he vanished from their sight' (Lk. 24:31b) in a literal manner (but see *Lohfink on Emmaus*, Chapter 11).

Cleopas and his companion recognise the risen Jesus because at table with them, he took bread, blessed and broke it and gave it to them (24:30-31).

It was their *eureka moment*, made possible because they had invited 'the stranger' to eat with them. The *recognition scene* ("anagnorisis") was a typical contrivance in Greek and Roman literature of the period.[184]

For understandable reasons, we interpret this *eureka moment* in the context both of the synoptic gospels' accounts of the Last Supper and the disparate Eucharistic practices adopted by Christians for two millennia, but maybe the time has come to view it in a new light.

Jesus, I am now convinced, as *a fact of history*, did not institute the Eucharist, in the sense that most Christians understand that claim. However, we should - and we must - continue to participate in its celebration, but with a transformed perspective, one rooted more in the revelatory language of the resurrection that gave rise to it in the first place.

In a profound insight, Judith Kunst writes that, at "Emmaus", Jesus *breaks* the disciples' words, 'so that they may be put back together as revelation'.

By coincidence, I am writing this chapter whilst at the same time *side-watching* a repeat of *Broken*, the acclaimed and deeply moving television drama (BBC, 2017), centred on a traumatised Catholic priest and played by Sean Bean. Jimmy McGovern, a Liverpudlian *ex-Catholic*, is its screenwriter.

In an interview with Peter Stanford, he says that flawed priests are of much greater interest than flawed plumbers, a remark McGovern develops by explaining that, contrary to what many people think, Broken is not a metaphor for a 'broken Church' or for 'flawed priests', let alone for a 'broken England'. It represents 'the broken bread of the Eucharist'.[185]

When pressed by Stanford for clarification, McGovern responds by saying that the breaking of bread is not for 'ease of consumption'. It is about the *brokenness of heart, spirit and body*.[186]

McGovern, with his gift for pathos, captures the essential meaning of the Eucharist, reflecting Kunst's intuition that Christian revelation is a dynamic, evolving process. It invites believers to experience the *burning words* at the centre of the Easter experience: 'Were not our hearts burning within us while he talked to us on the road, while he opened the scriptures to us?' (Lk. 24:32)

This invitation becomes real when we celebrate the

Eucharist as sacred hospitality, which is at the heart both of Kunst's *midrashic vision* and O'Loughlin's brilliant elucidation of its origins.

His concern is to ensure that the Eucharist should remain central to how Christians practise their faith, but if this expectation is not reconfigured, with particular regard to the important role of women in that necessary transformation, sacramental life as we know it will soon perish.

In Kunst's words, "Emmaus" should be interpreted as 'a celebration of conversation' and its resurrection significance becomes manifest when people share food together: *food, wonderful food* is what it is all about.

The significance of these sacred meals, with the liturgical formula of 'taking', 'giving thanks', 'breaking' and 'giving' (1 Cor. 11:23-24), was not so much a celebration of the resurrection but more a case of 'a signal to understanding the original meaning of the resurrection'.[187]

At "Emmaus", once Jesus had eaten, we are told that 'he vanished from their sight' (Lk. 24:31), but his formulaic actions at the meal, clearly mirroring the two verses referenced in the preceding paragraph, indicate that Jesus' resurrected presence will in some manner always be available to the believer.

And it is significant that 1 Kings 18:7-12 has an account of Elijah's random appearances and vanishings (a probable basis for the midrashic *Road to Emmaus*), prior to his being taken up to heaven in a whirlwind facilitated by 'a chariot of fire and horses' (2 Kings 2:11).

This verse is part of a section where Elijah and Elisha (his disciple) are walking and talking together, after the former has parted the River Jordan, thereby enabling them to cross onto dry ground (2:8). It cannot be a coincidence that Lk. 24 adopts a similar conversational pattern.

St. Luke's Gospel was intended mainly for Gentile-Christian believers. It is against this background also that we should understand *A Vanishing Jesus*, because it would have made sense to them in the context of "anagnorisis" (explained above).

Such phenomena were not unknown in the ancient world. Plutarch, for example, gives an account of how the dead Romulus (one of Rome's mythological co-founders) appeared to a friend outside the city and then disappeared.[188]

It is clear from the New Testament that the first appearance of the risen Jesus was to Peter, as recounted by Paul: '..., he appeared to Cephas, then to the twelve' (1Cor. 15:5).

Our familiarity with the gospels' accounts of Mary Magdalene first seeing the Risen Christ understandably obscures the significance of 'Peter' (in Aramaic, 'Cephas') for our understanding of the origins of the *Easter Event*.

One school of thought, represented by Thomas Sheehan, maintains that back of the appearance(s) to Simon Peter there was a series of psychological experiences, genesis unknown, which resulted in the belief that, somehow, Jesus had survived death, and Sheehan is at pains to emphasise 'we should not conclude too hastily that Simon had proclaimed Jesus to have been raised physically from the dead'.[189]

Sheehan contextualises this claim by saying that, in the apocalyptic circumstances of the first century, a resurrection did not necessarily mean that a dead person came back to life and literally left his grave: 'Resurrection was an imaginative way of saying that God saved the faithful person *as a whole*, however that wholeness be defined', and he references 1 Cor. 15:35-58 in support of this assertion, typically v.44: 'It is sown a physical body, it is raised a spiritual body. If there is a physical body, there is also a spiritual body.' (And see

"Transfiguration", next chapter.)

Sheehan's contention is that 'a spiritual body' is one way of describing the phenomena experienced by Peter and the other disciples, and this fits with a naturalistic interpretation of the data given in the introduction.

For him, this means that Jesus did not survive the grave: 'The last historical event in the life of Jesus of Nazareth was his death on April 7th 30 CE. ... Jesus had not fainted. He was dead. And, in the spirit of the New Testament, we may add: He never came back to life.'[190]

This appeal to the New Testament is an allusion to St Thomas Aquinas' statement that 'Christ did not come back to life in the usual sense of life as we all know it; rather, he entered a life that was somehow immortal and god-like'.[191]

Sheehan's point, rightly, is to eschew all interpretations of the resurrection that promote the idea that it was 'any form of resuscitation or reanimation'.[192] *The Raising of Lazarus* (Jn. 11:38-44), who would have died a second time, should be classified under this category.

Similarly, *The Resurrection of Jesus the Jew* rejects the *swoon theory* (Jesus, in a comatose state, was placed in the tomb alive and later appeared to the disciples, after which he died[193]), the *wrong tomb theory* (the women mistook the site) and the *theft theory* (Jesus' body was stolen by the disciples[194]).

The notion of 'the whole person' advocated by Sheehan is rather vague ("resurrection" could theoretically encompass it), but his argument referencing 'a series of psychological appearances' enjoys a broad scholarly consensus, with particular regard to the theory of cognitive dissonance (see Chapter 11).

It maintains that the disciples' belief in the resurrection arose from the anxiety (probably related to guilt feelings) following both the death of Jesus and the failure of the Kingdom to materialise.

Paula Fredriksen succinctly explains the claim: 'His death – unexpected, traumatic, bewildering – threw the whole journey to Jerusalem into sudden reverse, inflicting on them a grinding cognitive dissonance. If Jesus were dead, how could his prophecy be true? If Jesus' prophecy were true, how could he be dead? Resurrection both resolved this dissonance and reinforced the prophecy. If Jesus were raised, then the Kingdom truly must be at hand.'[195]

Numerous objections have been made to this hypothesis (typically by Tom Wright). The most common one is that the endurance and sophistication of the Jesus movement cannot be accounted for simply by reference to psychological factors and the "visions" they produced. Its most famous "visionary" is St Paul, to whom we now turn by way of introducing a more general survey of these phenomena.

CHAPTER 10

—

The Resurrection of Jesus the Jew (1): Paul and Other Voices

If Christ has not been raised, then
our preaching has been in vain and
your faith has been in vain.
(*1 Cor. 15:14*)

Jesus is the focus of, and the inspiration behind, the religion that bears his 'surname': *Christianity*; but St Paul is its 'true founder', to borrow a thought from Geza Vermes. Without him, it is most unlikely that what was originally a sect within Judaism would have become the world religion it is today, an outcome certainly not anticipated by Paul when he wrote, c 55, to (formerly Pagan) believers in Galatia:

> When God, who had set me apart and called me through his grace, was pleased to reveal his Son to me, so that I might proclaim him among the Gentile, I did not confer with any human being ..., I went at once into Arabia, and afterwards I returned to Damascus. (Gal. 1:15-17, abridged)

131

Jesus and Paul were not Christians; the former was a Palestinian Jew and St Paul was a Jew of the Diaspora, born in Tarsus. They never met. For all his brilliance, Paul was not a systematic thinker and, for this reason, it is naïve to imagine that his interpretation(s) of Jesus' resurrection can be summarised in a simple and consistent manner.

In addition, and many Christians persist in this fallacious practice, we must stop reading back into Paul ideas that were never part of his thinking – the popular myth that he was a misogynist, for example.

Paul can be understood, however imperfectly, only with reference to his Jewish origins, although ideas from the world of Hellenism also had an influence on his views.

Reza Aslan, in *Zealot* (Z), disagreeing in some measure with Alan Segal (see below), points out that, by the time Paul's mission to the Gentiles was underway, 'certain syncretistic elements borrowed from Greek Gnosticism and Roman religions had crept into the Jesus movement'.[196]

Paul (meaning "little") is truly *The Pagans' Apostle*, to borrow the subtitle from one of Paula Fredriksen's many books.[197] In the preface to the same book, she has a quotation from St Augustine (d. 430):

> The past is gone; and the truth of the past is
> what lies in our own judgment, not in the past
> event itself.

Pinchas Lapide (d. 1997), one of the few Jews to have written a book about the resurrection of Jesus, has remarked that, as an event, it was ambiguous, 'but unambiguous in the history of its effects'.

In the same book, *The Resurrection of Jesus: A Jewish*

Perspective (hailed as an 'ecumenical miracle'), he described Easter as 'a Jewish moment of faith that opens a path to God for the Gentile world'.[198]

Paul would have applauded this sentiment. It is to misunderstand his (complex) thinking when we attribute supersessionism to him, the belief that Christianity has replaced Judaism, by reading out of context passages such as 'regarding the gospel, they are enemies of God' (Rom. 11:28, abridged). Aslan disagrees, maintaining that Paul's reference to Judaism as a 'ministry of death chiselled in letters on stone tablets' (2 Cor. 3:7) represents his true position.[199] David Klinghoffer adopts the substance of Aslan's position whilst disagreeing with John Gager (see below and Chapter 3).

When Paul references Judaism as 'a ministry of death', he is being (albeit viciously) polemical, caricaturing his own religious tradition, but in any case Paul is plain wrong: Judaism never was, and never will be, the atrophied, calcified entity suggested by such intemperate language, which nonetheless echoes a rabbinic form of argument.

The same apostle wrote, 'I ask, has God rejected his people? By no means!' (Rom. 11:1), indicating that v. 28 of the same chapter cannot be interpreted without reference to broader circumstances.

Some commentators, for understandable reasons, suggest that the Apostle to the Gentiles was riddled with contradictions; others assign the contradictory passages to Paul's unresolved feelings following his "conversion", and still others give up, concluding that he was simply incapable of consistent thought.[200]

The most common approach, with disastrous historical and theological consequences, has been to subordinate one set of passages ('All Israel will be saved', for instance) to the anti-Jewish ones ('All who rely on the works of the Law are under a curse', for example), thereby frustrating the development of a positive Christian narrative about Judaism.[201]

By the fourth century, Christianity had come to be defined, and indeed defined itself, by its hostility towards Judaism, and St Paul's writings were frequently cited in support of that rationale, a situation which continued virtually up to the 1960s.[202]

John Gager has demonstrated (but not to everyone's satisfaction, see endnote) that, far from being the 'father' of anti-Judaism, Paul 'is entirely innocent of all charges lodged against him', for the main reason that Paul did not expect Jews to find salvation through Christ. In addition, he did not convert *from* Judaism *to* Christianity.[203]

However, whatever else may be said about St Paul, he would not have been impressed by this sentiment on prominent display in one of Ireland's oldest places of post-Reformation worship:

Our mission is conversation, not conversion.[204]

Notwithstanding an objection to Gager's position, that Christ – as Paul understood him – remains 'the sole avenue to redemption for Jews as well as Gentiles'[205], he nonetheless reminds us that everything Paul wrote is predicated upon the conviction that Jesus, crucified, rose from the dead, and he understood this in a "bodily" (albeit transformed) sense, implying an ontological continuity between the pre-mortem and resurrected Jesus.

That belief is behind the most famous *conversion* in the history of religion(s), known as the *Damascene Experience*, where Paul, on the road to Damascus 'breathing threats and murder against the disciples of the Lord', has a blinding vision of the risen Jesus: 'Saul, Saul, why do you persecute me?' (Acts 9:1-19; cf. 22:6-16 and 26:12-23)

After it, Paul is led, blind and helpless, into Damascus. The account(s) of his conversion are consistent with the Jewish mystical tradition of the period (see below) and, as Rabbi Michael Cook has suggested, we are perhaps better using the terms 'reversion' or 'extension' instead of 'conversion', because 'Paul ultimately switched from one form of Judaism to another'.[206]

It is important to recognise that Paul himself does not provide us with this information about his 'extension'. It comes from Luke the evangelist, in the second part of his two volume work: Luke-Acts.

There is good reason for thinking that Acts is really a kind of eulogy to Paul – 'less an account of the apostles than it is a reverential biography of him; the apostles disappear from the book early on, serving as little more than the bridge between Jesus and Paul' (Z, p. 184).

There can be no doubt, however, that the Risen Jesus was the agent of Paul's decision to embrace the Jesus movement, but we do not know the nature of his objections to it; a likely explanation is that it was the identification of the crucified Jesus with the messiah: 'We proclaim Christ crucified, a stumbling block to Jews and foolishness to Gentiles' (1 Cor. 1:23).

Apart from the admission that his zeal for Judaism led to persecution of the movement (1 Cor. 15:9, Gal. 1:13, Phil. 3:6, Acts 8:1[207]), nothing else is known about the events leading up to Paul's conversion, but that has not prevented many scholars from speculating about it. They effectively adopt St Augustine's observation: *the truth of the past is what lies in our own judgment, not in the past event itself.*

Some commentators have judged the Apostle's likely birthplace, Tarsus, to be significant for his belief in the resurrection, since it was a metropolis (founded by the Hittites) where there was worship of 'the mystery god *Baal-Taraz*, the dying and resurrected deity who gave Tarsus its name'.[208]

The mystery religions (cults emphasising secrecy and elaborate initiation rites, most famously Mithraism) were certainly a feature of life in Tarsus, but Alan Segal (d. 2010), an expert on ancient beliefs about the afterlife, maintains that Paul, who doubtless availed of the vocabulary associated with their rites of death and rebirth, had no specific relationship with these religions.

Segal's interpretation of the data is rather equivocal, particularly given his admission towards the end of *Paul the Convert* (*PtC*, 370 pages of dense reading) that, apart from the visionary experience itself, whatever lay behind of Paul's *conversion* is now lost to us, 'since converts often retell their stories in the language of their new beliefs'.[209]

This assessment echoes St Augustine's reminder about the nature of the *past event itself*. Larry Siedentop's *Inventing the Individual: The Origins of Western Literalism* (2014) offers a perceptive interpretation of 'the event', when he suggests that Paul's *Damascene Experience* is best understood not as an instantaneous occurrence but rather in terms of a process: 'It is more likely that he spent some years pondering the significance of Jesus of Nazareth, finding the terms in which to express his new convictions', and Paul's *vision* gradually became 'a remarkable conception of the Christ'.[210]

Siedentop's analysis has merit:

❖ It supports Lapide's insight that the resurrection was

'unambiguous in the history of its effects', endorsed by Siedentop's astute observation that, within a few centuries, belief in Jesus' resurrection – espoused zealously by Paul – 'provided the individual with a foothold in reality', thereby 'replacing the family as the focus of immortality' (p. 58). Richard Rohr OFM captured the magnitude of this achievement when he said that Paul's encounter with the Risen Jesus gave him the motivation to offer human dignity back to a world that had lost its moral compass.

- Psychological explanations of Paul's *conversion* fit well with the notion that the 'reversion' was a gradual, not sudden, phenomenon.[211]

- It accords with Aslan's observation about the characterisation of Paul in Acts.

Few Jewish scholars, from the Enlightenment until virtually our time, have addressed the claim that Jesus rose from the dead. The majority of those *Other Voices* who have examined it favour psychological interpretations of one kind or another.

A consensus holds that Paul's excitable and vehement character produced a mental paroxysm experienced in the form of visions, perhaps triggered by the cognitive dissonance resulting from his passive involvement in Stephen's death (see Acts 7:58, also 'psychogenic', Chapter 11).

This 'paroxysm' was fuelled by internal religious conflicts arising from a morbid and pathological sense of sin: 'I am carnal, sold under slavery into sin. I do not understand my own actions. For I do not do what I want, but I do the very thing I hate' (Rom. 7:14-15).

A variant of the "paroxysm theory" is "Schizotypy", a propensity to develop schizophrenia which in its early phase has been shown to be associated with religious experiences (Claridge, *Origins of Mental Illness*, 1985). These ides are sometimes complemented by the problematical views of Sigmund Freud (d. 1939), who maintained that religious experiences and the institutions to which they give rise are manifestations of *infantile helplessness* rooted in 'a powerful mix of need and guilt that worked its way out as religious piety' (Nicholas Spencer, in *Magisteria: The Entangled Histories of Science and Religion*, p. 360).

Others have focused on Tarsus as a centre for the worship of Pagan deities, questioning Segal's observation (above). They maintain that Gentile-Christians in Damascus and other centres of the Diaspora had fused together Jesus' original apocalyptic-eschatological message[212] with the idea of dying and rising saviours, patterned on figures like Osiris (see endnote 208).

1 Cor. 5:7b – 'Christ, our paschal lamb, has been sacrificed' – has often been quoted in support of this argument. It is one of the most important verses in the New Testament, commonly understood to refer to atonement theory, the belief that Jesus' (*voluntary*) death effected reconciliation between God and humankind.

Whilst it is true that the notion of vicarious atonement is peripheral to Judaism, it is a gross exaggeration to maintain that St Paul reinvented the theory by mining Graeco-Roman mythologies, though he certainly, as with the Eucharist, places it centre-stage in the emerging edifice of Christian beliefs.[213]

For almost 1,000 years, from the time of St Irenaeus (d. 200), the dominant theory was that Jesus had died as a ransom paid to the Devil for the (*original*) sin of Adam. St Anselm (d. 1109) rejected this *ransom theory*, arguing that the Devil has no rights over humankind.[214]

He promoted *satisfaction theory*, meaning that Jesus' passion and death, as the god-man, satisfied God's honour, which had been offended against by Adam's sin.

Peter Abelard (d. 1142) reacted against these views, arguing for *moral atonement theory*, and, in our time, Richard Rohr adopts a similar position. It maintains that Christ's atoning sacrifice is best understood as a pledge of God's love towards us, and it is also the means whereby human beings are moved to love God: 'God so loved the world that he gave his only Son, so that everyone who believes in him ... may have eternal life' (Jn. 3:16; cf. 1 Jn. 4: 9-10).

At the time of the Reformation, the reformers adopted what has come to be known as *penal substitution theory (pst)*, promoting the view that, because people sin, everyone is deserving of eternal punishment. Christ, however, has borne the punishment in place of us; and, once people place their trust in him, the relationship with God will be restored (see Rom. 3: 9-26).

This fourth theory remains a strong feature of Evangelical preaching and teaching, whereas the mainstream churches, one way or another, tend to favour a moral *theory approach*.

In recent decades, the entire theory, in the light of Darwinian biology and the findings of the social sciences, has had rigorous criticism from many biblical scholars and theologians: 'Jesus, as the agent of God's divine rescue operation, is not a Jesus who will appeal to, or communicate with, the citizens of this century.'[215]

And Rene Girard, the renowned French academic, has been vociferous in his criticism of *pst*, arguing that it is inherently dangerous, succeeding only in reinforcing violence, an observation that others have applied to the Christian Right's strong advocacy of capital punishment, especially in the United States. In addition, *pst*, in the opinion of some commentators, has contributed to defences of slavery and colonialism; and feminist theologians have described it as a type of *divine child abuse*, which has victimised women in particular.[216]

At the core of such objections is the claim that the reality of human mortality has been wrongly interpreted to be 'a sign of the universality of human sin', typically represented by Paul when he implies that our sins necessitated the death of Jesus: 'Christ died for our sins in accordance with the scriptures' (1 Cor. 15:3; cf. 2 Cor. 5:21 and Gal. 3:13).[217]

Richard Rohr, in *The Universal Christ*, has tried for a less negative assessment of atonement theory, represented by this famous quotation from Duns Scotus (d. 1308, another Franciscan) on page 139 of the book:

> Our predestination to glory is prior by nature to
> any notion of sin.

(The word 'dunce' was coined in the Middle Ages. It became a pejorative term used by those Christian intellectuals who disagreed with the Franciscan spirituality and theology derived from Duns Scotus' philosophy, with particular regard to its rejection of certain tenets of Aquinas' thought.[218])

Similarly, Diarmuid O'Murchu's *Doing Theology In An Evolutionary Way* argues that Christians need to move on from the orthodox understanding of atonement theory which is mired in anthropocentric and imperialistic categories of religious discourse.

This is a massive undertaking for the churches, one that is

all the more urgent in the wake of the Holocaust, and there is no guarantee of success.

The challenge is even more daunting in the context of Jewish-Christian Relations. In the words of Amy-Jill Levine, Jesus is a redundant figure in terms of atonement language: 'He is not needed to save us from sin or death, since Judaism proclaims a Deity ready to forgive repentant sinners, and since it asserts, following the Mishnah, that 'all Israel has a share in the world to come'.[219]

Paul is both a bridge and a barrier when it comes to furthering Christian-Jewish dialogue. On the negative side, his frequently misunderstood (seven genuine) letters have contributed to what in time became Christian anti-Semitism, and the pseudonymous Letter to the Hebrews is especially problematic, where it promotes the view that Judaism has become obsolete (8:7).

We now know that, for St Paul, nothing could be further from the truth, but the polemical nature of verses such as '8:7' was hopelessly obscured by the time Christianity became the state religion of the Roman Empire (Constantine is its second most famous convert) , cut adrift from the religion of Jesus.

Recognition of this fact has encouraged a more positive reading of the Pauline literature, typified by Rom. 11:1, quoted earlier. An ironic consequence of this shift in perspective is that it provides a more balanced context for some of the above criticisms directed at Paul by many Jewish scholars since c. 1900.

Having said that, we must never forget the admonition of Dan Cohn-Sherbok, in *The Crucified Jew*, that because 'Christianity in its earliest stages constituted a Jewish messianic sect which claimed to be the true Israel over against an apostate nation', tragic consequences flowed from that characterisation (p.14).

Christians of a fundamentalist disposition, both *Catholic and Protestant*, fail to respect Cohn-Sherbok's caution when they insist that "true interpretation" of the Hebrew Bible is a function exclusive to their understanding of the Jewish-Christian relationship, effectively ignoring the enormous theological and related issues thrown into relief by Hitler's attempt to exterminate the Jews of Europe. The problem with fundamentalists, to paraphrase Richard Holloway, is that they have lost living contact with the originating traditions they are so keen to preserve. The peerless confidence exhibited by fundamentalists gives their apprehension of religion its power, 'but at the price of building into it the cause of its own destruction'.

Christianity, once and for all, must abjure the claim to be the heir and arbiter of biblical prophecy/tradition, for *God does not abandon his people* (Rom. 11:1; cf. 9:11). Biblical literalism, masquerading as "inspired revelation", which often endorses anti-Jewish, sexist and other questionable interpretations of sacred texts, must be called out for what it is: a sin against truth and justice.

Despite such concerns, many contemporary Jews, having hesitantly embraced *Jesus the Jew*, are now in the process of acknowledging *Paul the Jew*, whilst aware of serious criticisms attending that rapprochement (see endnote 203).

When Paul tells us in Galatians that, immediately after his conversion, he did not confer with anyone and went instead for three years to Arabia, it is interesting to speculate how different history might have been had the Apostle gone first to Jerusalem and spent his time there more in conversation than in attempting to convert Peter and the others to his version of atonement theory, which Paul claimed was a consequence of having encountered the risen Jesus, the sole agent of his conversion.

For him, there was no way of anticipating how the notion of atonement, inextricably linked to the death and resurrection of Jesus, would later come to dominate the Christian imagination, a development repudiated by Judaism, and not least because Jews reject the idea that the execution of one man can somehow be morally and ontologically superior to the death of millions of others:

> All unjust killing of human beings (Jesus among
> them) may be commensurate one with another;
> these also include the unjust deaths of count-
> less Jews over the centuries, for the sole reason
> that they were vilified as "Christ-killers".[220]

A number of Jewish academics, Pinchas Lapide amongst them, recognising the importance after the Holocaust of reanchoring Jesus in the flow of history, have turned their attention to the debate about Jesus' resurrection, notwithstanding the above quotation.

Whilst acknowledging the New Testament's many discrepancies in general and difficulties with its accounts of the resurrection in particular, he concludes that 'legends can also be bearers of truths, which by no means deprives the kernel of the narrative of its historicity.'[221] This claim is redolent of the famous statement by C.S. Lewis (d. 1963) that, in respect of the Incarnation, "Myth became Fact".[222]

Lapide argues that the gospels should be understood as Jewish literature, having similarities with both the Old Testament and later (midrashic) rabbinic writings. Despite layers of embellishment, the resurrection story reflects 'traces of authentic Jewish experience'.[223]

At its core there is no exaggeration of the story, for the main reason that, unlike the apocryphal gospels, the canonical ones have not 'accentuated the supernatural elements, seeming to go out of their way to make the resurrection a non-spectacular event.'[224]

Ignoring problems inherent in the notion of 'supernatural elements', Lapide insists that a fictitious report would never have included the account of the women attending the tomb, and their going to anoint Jesus' body *proves* that the resurrection was not expected.[225]

Geza Vermes is the other Jewish academic who has paid close attention to the resurrection, emphasising that – unlike the crucifixion – 'it is an unparalleled phenomenon in history'.

For Vermes, the idea of the resurrection is peripheral to Jesus' teaching, but St Paul 'turned it into the centrepiece of his mystical and theological vision', and soon afterwards it became identified in large measure with 'the essence of the Christian message'.[226]

Chapter 5 has examined the significance of the *Binding of Isaac*, 'on the third day'. Vermes suggests that the formula may have 'haunted Paul's creative imagination', providing a subconscious justification for his uncharacteristic failure to provide a biblical citation supporting his claim that the messiah died, was buried and rose, 'on the third day, in accordance with the scriptures' (1 Cor. 15:3-5).[227]

This failure was occasioned by a simple datum: there was 'no established tradition among Jews about a dying and rising messiah' (Christ).[228] In the words of Steven L. Jacobs, a Reform rabbi from Alabama, 'there is only one Jewish theological affirmation that unites *all* streams of Judaism, namely, that Jesus is *not* the messiah, regardless of how he is understood and affirmed by others.'[229]

Martin Goodman, in *A History of Judaism*, makes the thought-provoking observation that Paul seldom refers to biblical texts about the expected messiah and that 'his image of Christ has more in common with the veneration of mediator figures like exalted angels in the mystical texts from Qumran and elsewhere' (p. 193).

When Paul wrote his letters, that developing messianic tradition depended solely on visions of the risen Jesus: 'He appeared to more than five hundred brothers and sisters at one time ..., last of all, he appeared to me' (1 Cor. 15:6-7). The significance of the reference to himself is frequently overlooked.

Raymond Brown notes that 'Paul is the only New Testament writer who claims personally to have witnessed an appearance of the risen Jesus', and he does so without reference to the phenomena described in the later gospels.[230]

There is irony here, since in the teaching of the historical Jesus, "resurrection" is a marginal concern; for Paul, however, it is central to his message:

> This is the gospel concerning his Son who, in
> terms of human nature was born a descendant
> of David and who, in terms of the Spirit of
> holiness, was designated Son of God in power
> by resurrection from the dead: Jesus Christ,
> our Lord, through whom we have received
> grace and our apostolic mission of winning the
> obedience of faith among all the nations for the
> honour of his name. (Rom. 1:3-5)

In passing, it should be noted that few contemporary scholars subscribe to the notion that the historical Jesus would have promoted a mission 'of winning the obedience of faith among all the nations'. Mt. 15:24 – 'I was sent only to the lost sheep of the house of Israel' – is thought to best represent what Jesus would have believed (see endnote 20 and 'Goodman', below).

Following Brown, belief in the resurrection with its messianic implications does not depend upon the gospels' empty tomb traditions. For Paul, his vision alone validated the conviction that Jesus was the messiah, a term used 269 times in the genuine letters, allied to his complementary belief that Jesus would soon return to establish a reign of everlasting justice and peace.

This proclamation is the kernel of Paul's understanding of Jesus' resurrection, and for this reason in 1 Corinthians 15:12-34 he rounds on those who say there is no resurrection of the dead.

This "attack" should be interpreted as a defence of the Apostle's insistence that those who have *died* in *Christ* will be resurrected, like him, to new life: 'Christ has been raised from the dead, the first fruits of those who have died' (v. 20). Hans Küng emphasises that this famous verse should be understood in the context of 'the Risen One now present', that Christians are called to belief not in a 'past fact', but in a present reality.

On the basis of the claimed appearances to 'the five hundred brothers and sisters', Brown and other biblical scholars have argued that a purely internal vision on the part of Paul 'seems to be ruled out', maintaining that Jesus' appearance to him was through the medium of a transformed (real) body.

The implication is that Paul's experience was both veridical (from God) and in some manner verifiable (theoretically, others could have witnessed it). Such claims are also regarded by many theists to be *evidence* for God's existence.

This position is advanced by Richard Swinburne, a philosopher of religion, using his *principle of credulity* (we are justified in accepting the occurrence of an event unless there is good reason not to) and *principle of testimony* (in the absence of evidence to the contrary, it is reasonable to believe the experiences of others as they report them).[231]

The notion of a 'transformed body' is supported by 'the analogy of sowing in the ground and what emerges from it', exemplified by 1 Cor. 15:37-38: 'As for what you sow, you do not sow the body that is to be, but a bare seed ..., (*and*) God gives it a body as he has chosen, and to each kind of seed its own body.'[232]

Before turning to an examination of "visions", one interpretation of the "five hundred" is a hypothesis proposed by Thomas Brodie, the distinguished, if controversial, Irish biblical scholar and former Dominican priest.

He argues that the visions of Jesus recounted in 1 Cor. 15 have no factual basis; they are *midrashic creations* derived from the Old Testament, the book of Numbers (chapters 11 to 17) in particular.

Brodie's contention is that 1 Cor. 15:5-9 (Paul's list of post-resurrection appearances) turns out to be 'largely a synthesis and adaptation of the diverse appearances and descents of the Lord' during the crises detailed in these seven chapters from Numbers, typified by 11:25 and 16:19 (conflated): 'The Lord came down in the cloud ..., and His glory appeared to the whole congregation.'[233] For Brodie, both Jesus and Paul are literary constructs: in his pithy expression,

'Scripture reshapes Scripture.'

If he is right, then passages such as Mt. 28:16-20, known as *The Great Commission* and where the risen Jesus appears (*from a cloud*) to the disciples on a mountain top, support Brodie's hypothesis that the New Testament's accounts of the life of Jesus are essentially a rewriting of the Greek (Septuagint) translation of the Hebrew Bible.[234]

As far back as 1971, Raymond Brown had postulated that accounts of the prophets, particularly Elijah and Elisha, were literary templates for the gospel writers, but Brodie goes much further. The similarity of 1 Kings 17:17-24 to Lk.7:11-17, the *raising of widows' sons*, illustrates Brown's point.

Brodie argues that the New Testament provides no evidence whatsoever for Jesus as a living person, a claim dismissed by A.N. Wilson's observation that because the gospels' authors wrote about Jesus in a mythological way (the story of his virginal conception, for example), it does not mean we are entitled to maintain that this is all they were doing.

In *The Book of the People: How to Read the Bible*, he criticises Brodie's version of *Christian Mythicism*, but he nonetheless recognises his contribution to scholarship: 'There is a great attractiveness about Brodie's book ..., and to say Jesus did not exist as a historical figure does not mean he has been eliminated. 'Copernicus', quoting Brodie, 'did not eliminate the Earth; he simply saw it in a new way.'[235]

Contemporary scholars identify a three stage process behind the canonical gospels: Events in Jesus' life and oral traditions about him, followed by writings, a position rejected by Brodie: 'The prevailing paradigm of New Testament origins is going nowhere'.

Brodie's *literary paradigm* is persuasive but not convincing.

It is true that Luke-Acts, for instance, relies heavily on 1 Kings, but this fact is best explained by a creative use of midrash. The evangelist weaved material from the stories about Elijah and Elisha into his narrative about Jesus, and this is also how we should best understand other New Testament passages, such as Mt.28: 16-20 and the stories about St Paul in Acts.

Nonetheless, Brodie and other critical scholars 'have done much to enable us to read the Bible with new eyes', and Wilson points to how they have rightly alerted us to the poverty of imagination that is fundamentalism, with particular regard to the nature of the Bible:

> Belligerent, intolerant people have seized on
> the words to mean that *We are Right* and *They
> are Wrong*. But the words really mean: banish all
> preconceptions from your mind about God. Get
> rid of them. Banish idols from your mind. If you
> are making the God of the Bible into an idol,
> banish him too. If you are making the Bible an
> idol, banish that.[236]

The world inhabited by Paul had many "idols" (see 1 Cor. 8), but Jesus triumphed over them all, having been designated "Son of God" by virtue of his resurrection from the dead (Rom. 1:4).[237]

Paul's conviction that God had raised Jesus was an experiential reality, one rooted in Jewish mystical tradition, whereby he moved from *believing* to *knowing*, a state analysed by William James (d. 1910), in his famous book *The Varieties of Religious Experience*. For him, religions carry a "cash value", meaning that an idea's usefulness determines its truthfulness.

At Lourdes (1858), for example, the young Bernadette Soubirious (d. 1879) had apparitions of the Virgin Mary and soon thereafter it became a famous pilgrimage site of healing, but the cures there are occurrences regardless of whether or not Bernadette's visions were veridical. The implication of this position is that it matters not at all how we understand *Paul's Christ Vision*; what matters is that Paul's experience(s) proved beneficial to him and, on one interpretation of his actions, the world beyond Judaism.

In *Varieties*, James explains how auditory and visual (illuminatory-type) phenomena are characteristic of mystical experiences, clearly present in the famous episode of *Paul on the Damascus Road*, outlined above.

It is noteworthy that however we are to understand Paul's vision of the risen Jesus, he maintains that it was no different from what others had experienced. The affirmation is a little odd, since it implies that these appearances were of an identical nature, but Paul's "conversion" to the Jesus movement occurred some years after Jesus' death. We should therefore interpret the claim as a self-justifying exercise in light of the opposition to him in some quarters (see Gal. 2, for example).

This observation strengthens the argument that the empty tomb story was part of a developing tradition and that Jesus' appearances were most definitely not of a physical nature, that is, of a resuscitated body come back to life.[238]

Brown and others suggest that Paul's experience was 'not purely internal', meaning that it was in some manner cognitive (statements that are either true or false, in the sense that 'Ireland is part of Germany'), but it would seem that, by definition, mystical visions are non-cognitive (they are not open to verification or falsification), a consideration that applies also to Jesus' resurrection, which had no eyewitnesses to it.

Another way of expressing this non-cognitive interpretation of Paul's experience is to say that his *Jesus vision* was of a subjective character, and it was later assumed by others to have been of an objective (verifiable) nature. Was his experience *sight or insight*? We cannot know the answer to this question, because Paul – despite being our earliest recorded witness to Jesus' resurrection – never explicitly tells us.[239]

Gal. 1:15-16 – 'God was pleased to reveal his Son to me' (abridged) – illustrates the difficulty of determining the status of Paul's revelation. Biblical scholars note that, in this context, it can mean "insight" or the revelation of 'an actual appearance of Christ'; and, observes Bart Ehrman, 'it probably means both' (see 1 Cor. 15:8). However we (2,000 years later) interpret it, there can be no doubt that Paul's *Christ Encounter* has changed the world.

Scholars have long debated the reasons for Christianity's success as *the* world religion. In addition to the political and social consequences of Constantine's conversion, and leaving to an endnote ('240') the summary reasons advanced by Edward Gibbon in his famous book, *The History of the Decline and Fall of the Roman Empire*, Arthur D. Nock, as far back as 1933, has provided the most convincing reason for this success.

Nock proposes "conversion" as the major factor influencing the shift from Paganism to Christianity (by c. 300, the world's Christian population numbered some five million). Paganism promoted "adhesion": people who adopted a new cult did not have to renounce their previous affiliations. The strength of Christianity, according to Nock, is that its commitment to monotheism, necessitating the renunciation of former affiliations, fostered an appealing sense of radical exclusivity, one that was able to benefit from the ancient world's increasing adoption of henotheism. It is the belief that situated above the mass of deities and cults 'there was one ultimate reality', a position adopted by Constantine, notes Bart Ehrman.

Paul, on one interpretation of the data, would have been delighted: 'Such a proselytizing mission was a shocking novelty in the ancient world'; its success was 'unparalleled and unprecedented, particularly in light of the consider-ation that 'ancient Judaism lacked any genuine missionary impulse'.[240]

A short time after his death (c. 67), the Jews were defeat-ed in a war against Rome (66 to 73) and Jerusalem was de-stroyed. This event led to the emergence of Christianity as an entirely Gentile religion and, as Reza Aslan has observed, it soon required its own distinctive theology, which came from Paul's singular interpretation of the significance of Jesus' death and resurrection.[241]

He certainly subscribed to the belief that Jesus truly rose from the dead, but literalists who argue that the Apostle must have interpreted this reality in an exclusively physical manner are mistaken, confusing "physical" for "bodily" (see 'Schneiders', Chapter 11). They commit the error of thinking that Paul's enigmatic accounts of the resurrection can be re-duced to a simplistic characterisation of that *First Easter*.

The Apostle to the Gentiles *genius* was to reimagine Judaism, but at the same time Paul's *Jesus Vision* led to some (unintended) disastrous consequences for the descendants of this 'zealous and blameless Pharisee' (Phil. 3:6).

Whilst history can assist us in exploring the effects of that particular *Jesus Vision*, it is ultimately a matter of faith regarding what transpired that *First Easter*, before Saul's conversion, and not the subject of historical knowledge it-self. And it was Paul, to paraphrase Richard Holloway, who took that *Easter Vision* into world history.

In the opinion of Mark Lilla (see endnote 208), that *Pauline* mission has resulted in attracting a 'certain sort of mind', with deleterious consequences for the West. Quoting Nietzsche (d. 1900), Lilla agrees that 'there was only one Christian, and he died on the cross'. Maccoby voices a similar perspective when he writes that 'the myth launched by Paul ... has brought mankind comfort in its despair, but has also produced plentiful evil' (*MPC*, p. 205).

This Paul, for Maccoby, 'changed the meaning of Jesus' life and death, so that it became the basis of a new religion in whose central myth the Jews were the villains, instead of the heroes of sacred history, and Jesus would not have under-stood the new meaning attached by Paul to the title 'Christ' (*MPC*, p. 50, edited).

For Martin Goodman, St Paul was the innovator par ex-cellence: 'the single apostle who invented the whole idea of the systematic conversion of the world, area by geographical area' (see endnote 203).

It was Michelangelo (d. 1564) who said that the sculptor's task is more "revelation" than "creation". For Paul, it was a good mix of the two, earning him the epithet 'Christianity's true founder', notwithstanding his inability to condense Christological images and metaphors into a consistent theo-logical framework.

(The) *Catechism of the Catholic Church* addresses this 'mat-ter of faith' by maintaining that 'the Resurrection was an his-torical event that could be verified by the sign of the empty tomb and by the reality of the apostles' encounters with the risen Christ, still it remains at the very heart of the mystery of faith as something that transcends and surpasses history' (n. 647).

John Mc Dade SJ interprets this carefully nuanced statement to mean 'that the resurrection was *real*'. Its use of the phrase 'could be verified' fits with Viviano's analysis outlined in Chapter 8, since it does not say 'was verified', but at the same time the paragraph must be understood in light of a preceding one, 643: 'Christ's resurrection cannot be interpreted as something outside of the physical order, and it is impossible not to acknowledge it as an historical fact.'

St Paul would have agreed with the notion that his vision of the risen Jesus was of a factual nature, but the claim that it is impossible to think of it otherwise is a different matter altogether.

Statements of this order fail to convince *Other Voices*; Lapide, for instance, whose emphasis on the event as 'ambiguous' is cognizant of different Jewish views, and it must be remembered that, in the first century, as now, beliefs about what happens after death embrace the likely possibility that there is no post-mortem existence, the position defended by the Sadducees.

As discussed in Chapter 3, the Sadducees argued that the individual did not endure beyond the grave, and that rewards and punishments were for this life only. Against this background, reports of post-mortem visions of Jesus could mean only that the recipients' experiences were of a delusional nature, notwithstanding how "real" they were for them.

(Nowadays, there is a vast literature on near death experiences (*ndes*), which this book does not address, but suffice to say that the clue is in the preposition "near". People who reported these doubtless genuine phenomena, regardless of how close to death they may have been, were still alive.)

Delusional or not, it was in the context of Pharisee belief promising individual life beyond death that ensured
Judaism's survival after 73 and the emergence of Christianity,
and it triumphed eventually on the basis of faith in the veridical status of Jesus' appearances, typified by this famous
exchange:

> Thomas ..., was not with them when Jesus came.
> So the other disciples told him, 'We have seen
> the Lord'. But he said to them, 'Unless I see
> the mark of the nails in his hand, ... and put my
> finger in his side, I will not believe.' A week later
> ..., Jesus came and stood among them ..., and
> he said to Thomas, 'Put your finger here and
> see my hands. Reach out your hand and put it
> in my side. Do not doubt but believe. Thom-
> as answered him, 'My Lord and my God.' (Jn.
> 20:24-28)

Tom Wright is one scholar who accords veracity to the
above exchange, arguing that Jesus was raised bodily from
the dead; that something happened to Jesus and not just to
his followers. For him, despite there being no eyewitnesses
to the resurrection itself, Thomas and others provide us with
(circumstantial) "eyewitness testimony" after the fact, so to
speak; and the empty tomb traditions, for Wright, are reliable
historical data.

John Dominic Crossan disagrees, insisting that Jesus
died and remained dead, and that visions claiming to be evidence of his post-mortem existence, be they from St Paul
(the emphasis on resurrection comes from him) or anyone

else, are ways of saying that Jesus' message and spirit endure. He would agree with Thomas Sheehan that all religious doctrines are mythical, and that Christianity's foundation story is in crisis.

Wright and Crossan, *scholars in dialogue*, are good friends, notwithstanding their very different understandings of the meaning of Jesus' resurrection.

—

CHAPTER 11

The Resurrection of Jesus the Jew (2): Scholars in Dialogue

I have seen the Lord. (Jn. 20:18)

'It was visions, and nothing else, that led the first disciples to believe in the resurrection.'[242] Other scholars disagree with this view of Bart D. Ehrman, notably N.T. (Tom) Wright, the Anglican bishop and renowned biblical scholar:

> I've shown that we can't account for early
> Christian faith by suggesting that stories about
> appearances and stories about an empty tomb
> have nothing whatever to do with one another,
> and the idea of resurrected faith being generat-
> ed by some kind of cognitive dissonance simply
> doesn't work.[243]

Wright, in his *The Resurrection of the Son of God* (RSG), comes down firmly on the side of maintaining that the resurrection can be demonstrated to be a historical event, and that there was an empty tomb.

His other major work, *Paul: A Biography*, declares that the Apostle was talking about history in the sense of what happened in the real world: 'the world of space, time and matter', by which Wright means that Jesus' resurrection and the visionary appearances associated with it are objective, veridical phenomena.[244]

He dismisses as "armchair psychology" some of the theories – "psychic dissonance", for example – examined in the previous chapter, quoting John Betjeman, 'the *whimsical* English poet':

> St. Paul is often criticised
> By modern people who're annoyed
> At his conversion, saying Freud
> Explains it all. But they omit
> The really vital part of it,
> Which isn't how it was achieved
> But what it was that Paul believed.[245]

Geza Vermes has remarked that Wright's methodology is faith masquerading as scholarship. The Judgement is rather harsh, but it reflects scholarly criticism of Wright's contention that 'the *only* possible reason why Christianity began and took the shape it did is that the tomb really was empty and that people truly met Jesus, alive again'.

Robert M. Price, another New Testament scholar and member of the *Jesus Seminar*[246], has been even more scathing in his criticism of Wright's scholarship, writing that RSG is no more a contribution to the study of the New Testament than creationism is to the advancement of biological science.[247]

One reason given by Wright in support of the empty tomb

is that it has no echo in the Hebrew Bible, maintaining that the evangelists (Mark in particular, with whom it seems to have originated) could not have invented the tradition as an apologetic exercise, or whatever.

Chapter 8, however, has given an excellent reason for thinking the evangelists were indeed "echoing scripture": the story of *Daniel in the Lions' Den* may well lie at the back of the "empty tomb".

There are three other difficulties with Wright's presentation:

1. As *DJJ* argues, the passion narratives exhibit much "theological invention" (the *Sanhedrin Trial*, for instance), so why should we not expect the same phenomenon to be a feature of the resurrection narratives?

Indeed, given their content ("visions" etc), is it not more likely that they are even more inventive than the accounts of Jesus' last day(s)?, without having to endorse the scepticism of David Friedrich Strauss (d. 1874), one of the pioneers of critical biblical scholarship:

> Rarely has an incredible fact been worse attested, and never has a badly attested fact been intrinsically less credible.[248]

2. Thomas Fawcett, referenced in Chapters 4 and 5, also provides a sound alternative to Wright's interpretation of the data, by explaining that 'the resurrection was made known by the appearances of the risen Christ and not deduced from the disappearance of the body from the sepulchre'.[249]

The background to the empty tomb story is that Jesus had to die in Jerusalem, the *Rock of Zion*. Jerusalem was the focus of *the myth of the sacred mountain*, the connecting link between heaven and hell.

In Jewish mythology, this symbolised the 'womb of new birth', into which Jesus is placed prior to his rebirth to new life from the rock. Psalm 110: 2-3 reflects this symbolism: 'The Lord sends out from Zion ..., your people will offer themselves willingly; on the day you lead your forces on the holy mountain, from the womb of the morning.'[250]

3. Fawcett also points to the significance of Abraham's burial (aged "175 years") 'in the cave of Machpelah, ... with his wife Sarah' (Gen. 25:7-11), and later rabbinic tradition 'added the idea that he was born in a cave'.[251]

That tradition also located Moses' birth in a cave, developing the cryptic burial references in Dt. 34 into the notion that, from his *tomb-cave*, Moses would later be reborn for a future task (and see Chapter 11).[252]

Wright and others are mistaken when they accord historical status to the empty tomb tradition. It is a midrash, availing particularly - but not exclusively - of a *rebirth motif*, since 'Judaism knew, and was prepared to make use of, the idea that the funeral cave was also a womb of rebirth.'[253]

Rudolf Bultmann (d. 1976), probably the twentieth century's greatest New Testament scholar, advocated an extreme scepticism about the historical Jesus (criticised in *The Death of Jesus the Jew*), arguing that the worldview of the New Testament's authors necessitates *demythologization* if it is to be relevant to the modern world.

It is easy to misunderstand "demythologization". Bultmann was not attempting to eliminate myth from the New Testament. His purpose was to interpret it anew in a world where people do not attribute mental illness, for instance, to demons.

Bultmann, again contrary to some misguided interpretations, was anxious to ensure that the New Testament's message of salvation, as he understood it, was made available to everyone. His concern was to ensure that Christians did not find themselves in situations whereby their religious beliefs conflicted with the realities of their lived experience.

In a famous phrase, Bultmann says that *Jesus rose into the Kerygma* (the faith and preaching of the community), by which he also means that Jesus' resurrection was utterly inconceivable as an historical event (see below). The miracle of that *First Easter* resided in the disciples' ability to have moved beyond the catastrophe of the crucifixion to faith in the proclamation that *Jesus is Risen!*

Against Tom Wright, however, that proclamation was of an entirely subjective, not objective, nature. Bultmann nonetheless attributes value to the witness of the New Testament, maintaining that it encourages people to embrace lives of existential authenticity, by challenging them to "live in the now".

Bultmann understood the gospels to have been greatly influenced by Hellenistic mythology (in their understanding of Jesus as 'Lord' and 'Son of God', for instance[254]), but a strength of Fawcett's account, whilst not denying Hellenistic influences on the New Testament, is that it places centre stage the importance of Jewish mythology as a framework for interpreting the gospels. Pagan mythologies, contrary to conventional scholarly opinion, were largely alien to the evangelists.

What matters here is that myth is taken seriously as a vehicle for the communication of "gospel truths", providing we remain sensitive to Frederic Raphael's wise caution: '*Gospel truth* is an unacknowledged oxymoron.'

From the Greek, *mythos* can be translated as "legend" or "story". In both Jewish and Christian texts, the word carries negative connotations and, in the New Testament, it features only five times, most notably in the *Pastoral Epistles*, for example 2 Tim. 4: 3-4: 'The time is coming when people ..., having itching ears, ..., will turn away from listening to the truth and wander away to myths.' Such considerations do not mean, of course, that mythology is not presents in both Testaments.

With regard to the Old Testament, the *Creation Story* in Genesis 1 to 3 is an instance of *aetiological* myth (about "Origins"), and in the New Testament the account in Matthew's Gospel of Jesus giving the *Keys of the Kingdom* to Peter (16:13-20) has the character of a foundation myth, serving the purpose of providing legitimacy for those who, post-Easter, claimed authority for their leadership roles.

Myths are stories that are not meant to be taken as historical, but instead they can be described as occurrences 'that in some sense happened once, but which also happen all the time'.[255] The question to ask of them is not 'What happened?', but 'What do they mean?'

Whilst this is true, James D. Dunn points out that we need to ask ourselves a further question: 'What kind of myth is in the New Testament?' He maintains, and Wright would agree, that Bultmann's reduction of religious language in general and of resurrection-talk in particular to a *kerygmatic proclamation* fails to do justice to the conviction of St Paul, and of the four evangelists, that the resurrection says something by way of promise about the future as well as about the present, for both Jesus and believers.[256]

1 Cor. 15:12-34, referenced in the previous chapter and

with its citation of the risen Christ as 'the first fruits of those who have died' (v.20), appears to be directed against the view that resurrection hope is confined to the "now" of believers' experiences.

This perspective questions Bultmann's thesis, arguing that he abandons the historical affirmations about Jesus which, as Dunn interprets the data, the New Testament conveys by using mythological language, and thus he asks: 'What kind of myth?'

In other words, Dunn maintains that whilst the accounts of Jesus' death and rising from the dead may be couched in mythological language - the story in Mt. 27: 52-53, for example, of bodies rising from tombs and appearing to people in Jerusalem after the crucifixion and resurrection - it does not mean that *the resurrection*, in Bultmann's words, is 'utterly inconceivable as an historical event', thereby also disagreeing with Crossan, Sheehan, and Diarmuid O'Murchu (see below).

Mt. 27:52-53 reflects the belief, by no means universal yet popular in the first century, that a general resurrection of the dead would accompany the dawn of the messianic age: 'Martha said to him, "I know that he will rise again in the resurrection on the last day"' (Jn. 11:24; the reference is to Lazarus).

These two verses are not historical: they are a *distorted memory* (false recollections, see endnote 257). Apart from biblical literalists – fundamentalists, in effect – does anyone really believe that, after Jesus' resurrection, previously dead bodies were strolling about the 'holy city'?

And the preceding verse, Mt. 27:51 - about the tearing in two of the curtain of the Temple and an earthquake ('the rocks were split') - is a combination of midrash, religious propaganda and mythology.[258]

The reference to the Temple clearly alludes to its destruction in 70 by the Romans, which means that Mt. 27:51 was created sometime after the Jews' defeat in the Roman-Jewish War of 66 to 73.

Furthermore, this verse is not the record of a real event. The reason is that Josephus (d. 100, the Jewish historian who had played a leading role in the above war) had extensive knowledge of the Temple's workings, and he makes no mention of this catastrophe.

Matthew inherited the story from Mk. 15:38, and a central focus of Mark, notes Bart Ehrman, is that Jesus' death will establish a new relationship between God and humankind, by 'giving his life as a ransom for many' (Mk. 10:45).

A heavy curtain separated the "Holy of Holies" from the rest of the Temple, and the former was a special room at its centre where God was said to dwell. Once a year, on the Day of Atonement (*Yom Kippur*), the high priest (and he alone) would enter it, to offer *sacrificial atonement* for the sins of the people.

The supposed 'tearing in two of the curtain' is really a midrash on *Yom Kippur*, symbolising the claim that 'God has now come forth from his holy place, and people – all people – have access to Him', and no longer through sacrifice, priest(s) or temple cult.[259]

It is also an exercise in religious propaganda. The communities for whom Mark and Matthew wrote maintained that the destruction of the Temple complex (its area was vast – the *Court of the Gentiles*, for example, could have accommodated twelve modern football stadia) was God's punishment for most Jews having rejected the messianic claims attributed to Jesus, and "proven" by his resurrection.

The story of the curtain is a *distorted memory*, but one that was certainly "true" for those who believed that Jesus' death and resurrection had established a new relationship with God.

Mt. 27:51b, about the earthquake, is *another distorted* memory, constructed as a midrash and sourced from a number of 'Old Testament' passages, typically Is. 29:6 – 'Suddenly, you will be visited by the Lord of hosts, with thunder, earthquake and great noise'.[260]

These stories – of *raised bodies*, *a torn curtain* and *split rocks* – are mythological, in the sense that their purpose was to provide believers not with information but rather with a context for understanding how Jesus, crucified, was constituted *their* messiah, raised from the dead.

This is the kind of myth, to answer Dunn's question, to be found in the New Testament. The challenge of twenty-first century Christianity is to explore ways of rendering meaningful first century concepts and language in a world too easily influenced by the phenomenon of what Huston Smith has termed fact-fundamentalism.

Christianity's future, if it is to have one, will be decided by its ability to rise to this challenge, similar to how c. 95 the community for whom St. John's Gospel was produced had to make sense of these words attributed to Mary Magdalene: 'I have seen the Lord' (20:18).

Mary of Magdala, by some traditions identified with Mary of Bethany, (see Jn. 12:1-9; cf. Mk. 14:3-9) and according to the synoptic gospels one of the two Marys who went to the tomb early on Easter morning, is in the Fourth Gospel the first disciple to see the resurrected Jesus (having initially supposed him to be a gardener), who says to her:

Do not hold on to me, because I have not yet

ascended to the Father, ... to my God and your
God (20:11-18, abridged).

This passage is yet another instance of *distorted memory*, but its main context here, notes Pheme Perkins, is to ensure the Johannine community's understanding of the resurrection in relation to Calvary and the ascension: 'One is not to think of Jesus' resurrection as though he had returned to life and then later ascended into heaven. Rather, Jesus has passed into an entirely different reality.'[261]

For this evangelist, Jesus' crucifixion, resurrection and ascension to the Father constitute one event (see Jn. 12:32-33), establishing continuity of identity between his earthly and post-resurrection existence.

When Mary "sees the Lord", accompanied by the admonishment not to hold on to him, St John is drawing this "continuity of identity" to his readers' attention, for two reasons (we should bear in mind, as context, that this gospel gives us believers' reflections about Jesus, and not the words and thoughts of Jesus himself):

❖ By the time this gospel was compiled, Docetism – the belief that Jesus only appeared to have a human body – was advocated by some believers, and it posed a threat to developing (orthodox) Christology. Orthodoxy eventually triumphed at Chalcedon (451), in the claim that Christ is one person in two natures: human and divine. Jacques Dupuis SJ has neatly expressed this conviction by writing that 'Jesus Christ is God humanized, not man divinized. By not holding on to Jesus, Mary Magdalene is recruited in support of anti-Docetism, and suggestions that Jn. 20:18 reports her ipsissima verba are misplaced.

❖ The evangelist is anxious to have Mary's testimony anchored to Peter's and others' attestation that the tomb was indeed empty, thereby ensuring that belief in a 'fleshly resurrection', as Bart Ehrman expresses it, could not be dismissed as a story told by silly women (see Jn. 20:1-10; cf. Lk. 24:10-12).

Mary Magdalene's encounter with the risen Jesus also echoes the phenomenon of anangorisis discussed in Chapter 9, with reference to "Emmaus". Her vision reflects the "recognition scenes" redolent of Hellenistic literature of the era.

For St Paul, who had no knowledge of a death-resurrection tradition associated with a tomb, the same *fact*, contrary to what Tom Wright asserts, holds true for those followers of Jesus – Peter, for example – who knew him during his public ministry in Galilee, and the *vision stories* probably originated there, not in Jerusalem.

When John's Gospel anchors Mary Magdalene to the tomb tradition, we should understand this to be part of a wider apologetic agenda, for the simple reason that there may never have been a tomb: *DJJ*, agreeing with Dom Crossan, argues that Jesus' body was most likely consigned to a communal burial pit.

(The famous *Turin Shroud*, even if recent scientific findings – using an X ray scattering technique - can date it to first century Palestine, is not confirmatory of the claim that Jesus received a formal burial, despite Jn. 20:4-5 – 'Peter reached the tomb first ..., and saw the linen wrappings lying there'.)

What matters is that Mary believes in Jesus *only* when he appears to her, having first mistaken him to be the gardener who has removed the body from the tomb (see 20:14-16a).

Tertullian (d. 225), an early Christian and controversial apologist, recounted a bizarre story, perhaps derived from a Jewish source, that "Mary's Gardener" had removed the body because he was fed up with Jesus' disciples traipsing across his lettuce field to mourn at the tomb.[263]

Known as the *lettuce theory*, this legendary tale is nonetheless a reminder that legends about Jesus' resurrection are also a feature of the canonical gospels, and the account of guards placed at the sepulchre fits this pattern (see Chapter 7).

Are we really expected to believe that, as the first day of the week was dawning, when 'Mary and the other Mary' arrived to mourn at the tomb, 'suddenly there was a great earthquake; for an angel of the Lord, descending from heaven, came and rolled back the stone and sat upon it'? (Mt. 28:1-2)

This pericope continues by relating that the angel's 'appearance was like lightning, and his clothing white as snow' (v.3), going on to say that, in fear and shock, the guards at the tomb 'became like dead men' (v. 4: cf. 27:62-66).

St Matthew never intended such passages to be understood in a literal manner, and we do violence to these texts by imposing upon them the fact-fundamentalism characteristic of how some people interpret religious narratives.

There is much wisdom in Dom Crossan's well-known aphorism, worth repeating from Chapter 7:

> My point is not that those ancient people told literal stories and we are now smart enough to take them symbolically, but that they told them symbolically and we are now dumb enough to take them literally.

All four gospels have the women approaching the tomb as

dawn breaks, and John specifies that 'it was still dark' (20:1). The symbolism is clear, and Fawcett is certainly right when he argues that the darkness to light motif reflects mythological themes present in the culture(s) of the period.[264]

This scheme of thought is most famously represented in Genesis, where we are told that the Earth was covered in darkness until God separated light from darkness, calling the light 'Day' and the darkness 'Night' (1: 1-5, abridged).

In the New Testament, such mythology is very obviously at work in its four passion and resurrection narratives:

> The conflict between Jesus and the forces
> opposing him is aptly characterized by the use
> of these symbols. As his passion approaches,
> the power of the night increases, typified by
> the role of Judas in John's version of the Last
> Supper, where - after Jesus gives him a piece of
> bread – Judas is told to do quickly what he has
> to do, and the narrator concludes the account
> with this sentence: 'And it was Night'. (13: 21-30,
> abridged). Of this observation, George Steiner
> has said that Judas goes into a never-ending
> night of collective guilt: 'His exit is the door to
> the Shoah, the "final solution", proposed and
> enacted by National Socialism in the twentieth
> century. The authorities arrest Jesus under cov-
> er of darkness, during which the disciples flee
> into the anonymity of its powerful shelter. (Mk.
> 14: 43-51 and parallels). Finally, at the height of
> the day (noon), darkness came over the land
> until Jesus' death three hours later on the cross
> (Mk. 15:33-39; cf. Mt. 27:45-54).[265]

No more than in Genesis, however, the "darkness" on Golgotha is not powerful enough to extinguish 'the light', which is the hope of the *First Easter*: 'The light shines in the darkness, and the darkness did not overcome it' (Jn. 1:5).

We live in a world, Marcus Borg and Dom Crossan remind us, that has known "proper illumination" since only c. 1800, when a majority of the population in the West was able to afford candles, and electric light which facilitates typing this paragraph at 11.45 p.m. is still not readily available in many parts of the world.

For the ancients, the hours of darkness could be terrifying and it is little surprise therefore that light is an archetypal symbol throughout the Bible, having an important place in the celebration of Christianity's two major feasts: Easter and Christmas.

An entire book could be devoted to this topic but suffice to say that we see light symbolism present at Jesus' birth, his baptism, during his public ministry, at Golgotha and on that *First Easter*.

These accounts are often midrashic representations, typically how Is. 9:2, with its reference to people who walked in darkness having a great light shine upon them, has obviously shaped Lk. 2:29-33, where Simeon says this about the infant Jesus in the Temple. He identifies Jesus as having brought salvation to all peoples: 'a light of revelation to the Gentiles, and for glory to your people Israel' (v. 32).

At the transfiguration (Mk. 9:2-8; cf. Mt. 17:1-7, Lk. 9:28-36), where Jesus takes Peter, James and John up a mountain to pray, his appearance changes, in addition to Jesus' clothing becoming 'dazzling white'.

Moses and Elijah, respectively Judaism's premier lawgiver

and prophet who have already inherited post-mortem glory, join them there, symbolising the claim that Jesus is the fulfilment of messianic expectation.

Matthew's reference to Jesus' face 'shining like the sun' and the intense white of his clothing is once again a mythological representation of light symbolism.

This serves the purpose of reminding his audience that, even before the resurrection, Jesus was imbued with the light of God; and now, on the morning of the resurrection, the angel – with an appearance like lightning and clothing as 'white as snow' - serves a similar function.

It is significant that 'Mary and the other Mary' come upon this scene as dawn is breaking. They have been "in darkness", but now they walk "into light".

Their 'walk', of course, is *existential* and to interpret the narrative chronologically is to misunderstand it, just as those who interpret "on the third day" as linear time miss the eschatological significance of the epithet (see Chapter 5).

As Fawcett explains the scenario: 'It is still dark for them because they do not know that Jesus has risen', but forewarned, so to speak, by the story of the Transfiguration (Matthew, remember, has related that Jesus' face was 'shining like the sun'), the gospel's audience will know that the women are about to encounter Jesus as the risen Sun.[266]

['Sunday' probably takes its name from Mithrasism, the cult of a Persian sun-god, famous for killing a sacred bull whose blood formed the Earth and its inhabitants. He was also said to have been born in a cave, on 25th. December. And Mithraism's "first day" was known as 'Day of the Conquering Sun', see Chapter 1.]

Prior to Mary's encountering Jesus ('I have seen the Lord'), she says to the angels sitting where Jesus' body had been lying, 'They have taken away my Lord, and I do not know where they have laid him' (Jn. 20:13).

If this account is not historical (and it is not), then how to explain it? One explanation is that the entire Mary-Jesus experience is a midrash derived from the *Song of Songs*, (attributed to Solomon) in a chapter (3) known as *A Song of Love*:

> Upon my bed at night
> I sought him whom my soul loves;
> I called him, but he gave no answer.
> I will rise now and go about the city,
> in the streets and in the squares;
> I will seek him whom my soul loves.
> I sought him, but found him not.
> The sentinels found me,
> As they went about the city.
> 'Have you seen him whom my soul loves?'
> Scarcely had I passed them,
> When I found him whom my soul loves.
> I held him, and would not let him go ... (vv. 1-4)

The similarities are obvious: the above concluding verse, for example, clearly reflects Jn. 20:17, where Jesus tells Mary not to hold on to him; and incipient Docetism is its context in the gospel. (Islam promotes another Docetic belief: Jesus was confused with someone else; he did not die on the cross.)

The visionary experience behind this story and others like it (*Emmaus*, for instance) focuses on Jesus, but we should remember that, in the first century, many Jews had expected a general resurrection at the end of time (see Dan. 12:2), while other Jews denied the possibility of resurrection altogether (see Chapter 3).

The significance of this shift in focus from the general to the particular (during believers' lifetimes) was 'a major twist in the plot' and, in fact, 'off script altogether', in the words of Peter Enns, author of *How the Bible Actually Works*.[267]

He expresses this development by observing that, through Jesus, the future was brought into the present, as Paul tells it in Romans: 'If we have been united with him in death, we will be united with him in a resurrection like his' (6:5).

There are two possible explanations for the shift:

❖ Jesus truly rose from the dead, essentially in the manner advocated by Wright, Raymond Brown, Schneiders (see below) and the *CCC*.

❖ The power of his message was such that, after the crucifixion, Peter certainly (and others?) had a subjective experience of the risen Jesus, and this provided the *raison d'être* for the dissemination of his teaching, which soon thereafter spread to the Diaspora. In essence, this is a psychogenic argument for the resurrection; a consequence, perhaps, of the disciples' inner turmoil, and favoured by Sheehan, Bultmann and many other New Testament scholars.

It is interesting that Rabbinic Judaism, which emerged after the catastrophe of 66 to 73, asserts a general resurrection of the dead, contrary to the plain meaning of Torah, but – unlike Christianity – it has never appealed to appearances of dead individuals to verify such claims.

Once again, at the risk of labouring a point, it is visions, not an empty tomb (contra Wright), that lie at the back of the claim about Jesus' (particular) resurrection.

What is the "cash value" of these appearances?, to again

borrow a term from William James. What's their point? For Luke, exemplifying a typical response to this rhetorical question, they enable people to come to faith that Jesus really is the Christ (a title used 500 times in the New Testament): 'Was it not necessary that the Messiah should suffer these things and then enter into his glory?' (24:26)

As Bart Ehrman shows, if someone was buried in a tomb and later the corpse was found not to be there, 'this fact alone would not make anyone suspect that God had raised the person from the dead'.[268]

The "visions" that generated the disciples' faith would for them have been bodily manifestations, but *transformed/glorified*, as indicated by Lk. 24:26. Sr Sandra Schneiders IHM explains "glorified" in an engaging manner (redacted):

> A glorified body is not just a mortal body that glows in the dark. Glorification is a condition of bodiliness, which renders it not limited by space or time or causality as we typically experience it. The risen Jesus lives in God, in a glorified materiality which enables him to participate in our mortal reality at will, but free of its limitations, all of which are in some way related to human beings' mortality.[269]

Schneiders' presentation throughout her small book, which is very witty, concurs with that of Lohfink (see below), but a weakness they share (he more than she) is the failure to address adequately the extent to which the resurrection appearance stories have been shaped by the needs of the communities for whom the evangelists wrote.

And Schneiders is plain wrong to suggest that all of the

"events" associated with the death of Jesus could have been 'observed by anyone, believer or not', who was present at the time (p. 19 states explicitly that the crucifixion accounts are 'historical narratives').

With regard to Jesus' passion, readers are reminded again of the statement by *the Catholic Bishops' Conference of England and Wales*:

> 'It is necessary to remember that the passion narratives do not offer eyewitness accounts or a modern transcript of historical events' (see Introduction).

As *The Death of Jesus the Jew* argues, too many commentators persist in confusing the fact of Jesus' crucifixion with the accounts that were created later to explain it as an "atoning sacrifice", and the same (modified) principle applies to the gospels' post-resurrection stories.

The information we have about significant historical events is usually received third hand and rarely the accounts of contemporary observers who have witnessed or participated in them. This consideration clearly applies to our passion and resurrection narratives, the latter in particular.

If St Paul was able to operate without recourse to stories about *broiled fish*, and *finger(s) in a side*, then so can we. Schneiders, in fairness, points to the veracity of this observation, with her witty comment that 'the appearance narratives are not like traffic reports' (p. 18), and she does an excellent job of explaining how these stories, with the emphasis on "appearances", are the 'long form' of the original Easter proclamation.

It would be a mistake to interpret Jesus' glorified

appearances in the neo-Platonic sense of ongoing life without a body. "Visions", however, in this context mean only something that is "seen", whether they are really there or not.[270]

A distinction is drawn between *veridical visions* and *non-veridical visions*; the former means something that is really there (caused by God), and the latter denotes something that does not exist.

Those who favour Wright's position would say that Jesus really appeared to his followers: 'people truly met Jesus, alive again', constituting 'the original Easter proclamation'.

Crossan argues that the visions were in some manner hallucinatory, that is, sensory perceptions that have the compelling sense of reality, of true perceptions, but 'that occur without external stimulation of the relevant sensory organs'. These apprehensions are not only about "seeing" - they refer also to 'any other of the senses: hearing, feeling, smelling, and even tasting'.[271]

Gerd Lüdermann (d. 2021), adopting a naturalistic view of the resurrection, maintains that, when Jesus died, his body decomposed like that of any other dead body and, in consequence, 'Christian faith is as dead as Jesus'.[272]

Michael Goulder (d. 2010, the New Testament scholar distinguished for his work on midrash, who demonstrated how Matthew was an expansion of Mark, and how Luke in turn was a midrashic reworking of both Matthew and Mark), argued that supernatural explanations are unnecessary if we can identify suitable naturalistic ones, illustrated by this story (redacted):

> When, in 1588, the English fired upon the Spanish Armada and the cannon balls at first did not penetrate the enemy fleet, an English captain

shouted that this was because of "our sins". A natural explanation (relative proximity) was superseded by the religious one ("because of our sins"), rendering it obsolete. The same can be said of the disciples' visions: psychologically induced hallucinations, for example, best explain the resurrection appearances.[273]

Gerhard Lohfink, a Catholic priest, in *On Resurrection and Eternal Life* (see endnote 40), is very critical of all such interpretations, maintaining that Christian faith is most certainly not dead.

He concedes that the *Emmaus Story*, for example (see Chapter 9), is 'a literary consolidation of many such other appearances', whilst insisting nonetheless that Emmaus is based on a concrete historical experience (the name of one of the two disciples, Cleopas, is given).

Lohfink is on rather shaky ground here, for two reasons:

❖ If, as *The Death of Jesus the Jew* argues, Barabbas (meaning "son of the father") is a theological fiction having a propaganda function, then why should "Cleopas" be historical?

❖ He fails to contextualise *Emmaus*, which is best understood primarily as a *midrashic creation*, similar to how Matthew's and Luke's infancy gospels were compiled, in addition to exhibiting the characteristics of anangorisis, previously discussed. *Emmaus* reflects the story in Genesis of Abraham receiving and entertaining divine messengers who tell him that Sarah, Abraham's ninety year old wife, would have a son.[275] One way of identifying the midrashic connect between the resurrection and infancy narratives is to notice how Matthew, for example, employs two theological fictions, amongst others (most notoriously 27:25, a *text of terror*, to borrow a term from Phyllis Trible), in his gospel: *soldiers massacring children in Bethlehem and soldiers shaking, and becoming like 'dead men', on Easter morning* (2:16-18; 28:4). The *birth stories* are *Haggadic midrashim*; the *passion narratives*, however, do provide us with some historical data, but not to the extent advanced by Raymond Brown.

Lohfink is on firmer ground when he makes the observation that visions always have something to do with the subconscious mind, 'where so many things are stored: fears, longings, images of hope and past experiences', about which St Paul probably knew a thing or two (see Chapter 10).

From this consideration, Lohfink concludes that such phenomena are nonetheless veridical, because God 'and the Risen One himself' are the agents behind these experiences, in such manner that human beings' "actions" are not manipulated, thereby respecting their autonomy.[276]

His argument draws on the idea that 'God acts, always and without exception, through secondary causes', which is reasonable. It is a claim, however, that raises more questions than it answers.

The implications of this observation are beyond the scope of this volume, but suffice to say that behind Lohfink's position is partly an appeal to the *Cosmological Argument for God's Existence*, and it labours under the burden that, even if there is a necessary being, this does not mean that it is a conscious, moral entity in the manner conceived of by Lohfink and, of course, by St Thomas Aquinas (d. 1274). It is entirely legitimate to maintain that this being could be pure energy or a mathematical principle, and not the (*necessary, personal*) God of orthodox Christianity.

Notwithstanding, Lohfink performs a service to this dialogue by articulating what, in his view, Jesus' resurrection is *not* -

- ❖ that, in Jesus, the divine has broken through, or
- ❖ that his soul was freed from the body, and it has now 'risen aloft into the ether', or
- ❖ that, in Jesus, the immortal has conquered death.

When Jesus lived, all of these things could have been said, 'but they are precisely what Jesus' followers did not say: they were Jews, not Greeks'.[277]

Lohfink offers an interesting perspective on those who, in our modern world, are embarrassed about "visions", suggesting that it is a prejudice exhibiting 'pure cultural imperialism'.

Without naming him, this is a clear allusion to David Hume's famous dictum that 'a wise man proportions his belief to the evidence', regarding which he maintained that all religious statements should be committed to the flames, since 'they contain nothing but sophistry and illusion'.

(Richard Dawkins' opposition to religion(s) owes much to Hume's empiricism, and he would doubtless agree that 'metaphysics had never really existed – all that had existed was the delusion that nonsense was in some way very profound'.[278])

Hume (d. 1776), who proposed a version of pure scepticism (at best, we can establish probabilities) maintained that stories about miracles, including the accounts of Jesus' resurrection, 'abound chiefly among ignorant and barbarous nations' and, for this reason, it is irrational to accord them credence.

Lohfink takes exception to this assertion, arguing that 'historians and theologians can with good conscience accept that the Easter appearances really happened', whilst implicitly recognising that, like the Incarnation, this affirmation is the product of faith, since the *Easter Event* is a transhistorical reality available only to the believer.[279]

Hume, of course, can no more disprove such claims than Lohfink can prove them, yet their opposing views have the right to space in the arena of public opinion, an imperative championed by G.K. Chesterton (d. 1936):

> 'The believers in miracles accept them (rightly
> or wrongly) because they have evidence for
> them. The disbelievers in miracles deny them
> (rightly or wrongly) because they have a doc-
> trine against them.'[280]

Chesterton's own prejudice is evident here, and perhaps he would approve of a controversial saying attributed to Cardinal Manning (d. 1892), that 'dogma trumps history', but Alister McGrath makes a good point nonetheless when he says that 'a dogmatic belief that miracles cannot happen leads some people to refuse to take the resurrection seriously'.[281]

Hume never asserts that 'miracles cannot happen'. His point is that because they are contrary to our experience of the laws of nature they are intrinsically improbable. He is certainly right that miracles are unlikely to occur and that eyewitness testimony is far from reliable (Ehrman's point), but from this we cannot infer that it is always mistaken to believe in the miraculous.

Many criticisms have been made of Hume's 'take' on miracles, but for our purposes three will suffice:

- He assumes that the laws of nature are inviolable, but this does not rule out God's intervention in the world, as Christian orthodoxy understands His nature.

- The 'ignorant and barbarous nations' objection can be met by counter arguing that honest and rational witnesses have throughout history attested to genuine miracles. Cures at Lourdes, for example, may count against this objection.

- Hume maintained that 'claims of miracles occur in all religious traditions, thus nullifying one another', but this assertion can neither prove nor disprove the miracles of Christianity in general and that of Jesus' resurrection in particular. [282]

Lohfink and scholars who agree with him emphasise, in the words of Schneiders, that 'the Easter narratives are stories about Jesus himself, present bodily'.[283]

This matters, for two reasons, despite Thomas Sheehan considering them to be irrelevant (see Chapter 7):

- 'Bodily, Jesus is the great symbol of God, not as a representative of God but as Godself', by which Schneiders means that if, at death, Jesus had ceased to be a human being, then 'the Incarnation, God's becoming one of us that we might become one with God' could not have occurred. Only as a *body* 'could Jesus rise as himself, and this *bodliness* keeps us continuous with ourselves, 'even through death'.[284]

✧ The body is that dimension of our humanity both 're-lated to all creation and distinct from all else'. It symbolises individuality and at the same time our place in community, and at death 'the body is trans-symbolized so that what had made the person present now makes the person absent'. Jesus' body had similar experiences; but, in his resurrected state, this *glorified body*, unlike our post-mortem status, is now *re-present* in a special way, no longer impeded by physical barriers, 'as in his sudden presence among the disciples in a locked room in Jerusalem' (see Jn. 20:19).[285]

For Schneiders, what matters is this ability for Jesus to be recognizable whenever he chooses to be, even to people like St Paul who never met him "in the flesh", as this establishes for her the living presence of Jesus after his death: 'He cannot starve, be killed or grow old, because change has become irrelevant'.

Her emphasis upon Jesus appearing at will, but only to those (believers) he singles out, resembles how Moses and Elijah appear and disappear at the Transfiguration (Mk. 9:2-8 and parallels), suggesting that these visions are of a non-material nature and similar to how St Paul's visions seem to have been of Jesus transformed into a spiritual entity of some kind: 'what is perishable cannot inherit what is imperishable' (1 Cor. 15:50).

Schneiders never addresses adequately the consideration that Jesus' appearances were seen only by believers: *the famous 500*, for instance (see 1 Cor. 15:6). More to the point, however, how are ordinary people, not possessed of these post-resurrection abilities postulated of Jesus, able to see him?[286]

Is Schneiders important distinction, given below, between "physical" and "bodily" sufficient answer to this question? It may not be philosophically coherent.

Her treatment of the question makes it nonetheless incontrovertible, to paraphrase Karl Rahner (d. 1984), that "resurrection" does not mean a return to life in time and space (in our normal understanding of these categories); rather, it signifies the continuity of personal identity.

It is also clear from Schneiders exposition that post-resurrection abilities are possible by virtue of *Jesus' divine humanity*, 'which is bodily because it is human', and she goes on to clarify an issue that is frequently confused by many contributors to this dialogue:

> We need to learn how to think of bodliness not as equivalent to physicality but as our special way of being present. We are all "bodily as physical", so to speak; but physicality, as Jesus' resurrection teaches us, is not of the essence of human bodliness.[287]

In other words, one can *die physically* but be *alive bodily*, because *physicality*, whilst integral to *bodliness*, is subject to decay, change and death, and this allows Paul to say of Jesus: 'Death no longer has dominion over him' (Rom. 6:9).

This idea is articulated movingly at Requiem Masses: *life is changed, not ended (vita mutatur, non tollitur)*.

Jesus' *glorified bodliness* produced the phenomenon known as a *saturation event*, that is, the *First Easter*. It was so unexpected, overpowering and without precedent that 'no one knew what to say or do, how or what to describe, what it meant or means'.[288]

In Schneiders' words, people were "blown away" by the *Easter Experience*, suggesting that it is best understood through the "prism" of 'a phenomenologically based literary approach rather than a historical-critical one', meaning that *forensic* examination of the gospels' resurrection narratives can take us only so far in our study of this *Saturation Event*. [289]

She has a point (see endnote 289), and not least because her *phenomenological approach* seemingly answers Wright's insistence that belief in the empty tomb is a necessary condition of Jesus' resurrection, but this consideration does not remove the need to evaluate critically the nature of the appearance stories themselves.

(Vermes, it should be noted, makes the good debating point that *the empty tomb* tradition must be early, on the grounds that 'if the story had been manufactured by the primitive church to demonstrate the reality of the resurrection of Jesus, one would have expected a uniform and foolproof account attributed to patently reliable witnesses'[290])

Ehrman identifies a key question that is often neglected in the discussion: 'Why do we have such a strong and pervasive tradition that some of the disciples doubted the resurrection, even though Jesus appeared to them?'[291]

Mt. 28:17, for example, relates that "the eleven" (Judas had supposedly died by then) had a vision of Jesus, but some of them "doubted" (see also Lk. 24:10-11, 37-43; Jn. 20:1-10, 20, 24-28; Acts 1:3).

Some commentators suggest that 'if the disciples had merely had visions, it would make sense that there was considerable doubt about what they had seen' , but there are two problems with this proposal:

- ❖ If Schneiders is right, Jesus' resurrected body was in some way material, but not crudely, "physical" and able to interact with 'all that we mean by matter in this world'; that is to say, the appearance stories are about Jesus himself, present to the disciples in bodily form, and she explains the discrepancies in the accounts by postulating 'they are a warrant of credibility about the witnesses and their witness' (p. 33).

- ❖ People who have these experiences 'tend *not* to doubt what they have seen'; indeed, continues Ehrman, a prominent characteristic of the phenomenon is that the recipients insist, sometimes vehemently, that the visions are real, 'not made up in their head' (p. 191). The myriad sightings of the Virgin Mary from Knock to Medugorje and the claims made by those who have seen UFOs are testimony to this fact.

A tentative solution to the conundrum is that three or four people (Peter, Mary Magdalene and Paul, for example) had visions of Jesus after he died, and most of their associates believed them, but others did not, and it is this scenario that we find represented in the gospels.[293]

This suggestion, in addition to explaining the "doubt tradition", may also illustrate how, as the stories of the appearances were told again and again, embellishments crept in, and some stories would have been made up, as the apocryphal *Gospel of Peter* demonstrates (see below).[294]

These 'embellishments' led to accounts of all of the disciples (and others) having seen the risen Jesus, but it must be emphasised that such innovations were a natural development; they were not exercises in deception.

Studies have shown, contrary to the position adopted by Tom Wright and like-minded others, that oral traditions (including those claiming to incorporate eyewitness accounts of the risen Jesus), involve people remembering 'all sorts of things, some of them in vivid detail, even though they never happened at all'.[295]

This data supports indirectly Kathleen Corley's thesis outlined in Chapter 6. It also reinforces the claim that hearsay information can easily distort eyewitnesses' memories, with particular regard to happenings of 'a highly dramatic nature, which almost by necessity evoke strong and detailed visual imagery'.[296]

The observations about *saturation events* reflect this description of "dramatic happenings"; but, for Schneiders, 'the accounts of the bare facts never changed much after the first reports' (p. 31), suggests that the 'detailed visual imagery' cannot be stories about an event that grew in the telling. Her deduction is almost certainly wrong (see *Gospel of Peter*, below).

Another problem is that the reference to 'first reports' seems to focus on the gospels' narratives, ignoring the consideration that the *three day tradition*, as previously noted, is an eschatological, not chronological, category.

Failure to recognise this important distinction, notwithstanding the insistence by Raymond Brown that 'Christians believe in Jesus, not in a tomb', continues to bedevil studies of Jesus' resurrection.

The best documented instance of people having recollections of things that never happened are stories about "UFO abductions", which have been studied by John E. Mack (a psychiatrist lecturing at Harvard Medical School) and Susan Clancy Ph. D., whose book is *Abducted: How People Come to Believe They Were Kidnapped by Aliens.*

Their conclusion is that "memories" of abductions are social constructs, that is, 'the culture we live in and experience makes it possible for people to think aliens have temporarily carted them off'; and it is interesting that, prior to c. 1962, there were hardly any accounts of such phenomena, the period when television and film began to feature stories of alien invasions.[298]

Clancy shows how the power of suggestion can sometimes become a "memory" that generates its own reality, arguing further that, when the vivid imagining of an event is discussed in the presence of authority figures, they 'become that much more cemented in the brain'.[299]

In a fascinating, if very odd, study known as *Do You Remember Proposing Marriage to the Pepsi Machine?* (2006), the purpose of which was to ascertain the extent to which, if at all, *imagining* a ridiculous experience could later give rise to *remembering it*, researchers found that 'imagining events can lead to the development of false memories for those events'.[300]

This research (see endnote 300), strange though it may seem and when taken in conjunction with other factors, suggests that supposed eyewitness accounts in the New Testament are not particularly reliable, a position rejected by Richard Bauckham.

In his Jesus and the *Eyewitnesses* (JE), Bauckham - whilst acknowledging that editorial processes have been at work - insists that the gospels in general and the resurrection narratives in particular are 'highly reliable reports of what Jesus said and did'.[301]

His argument is not persuasive, for these (summary) reasons:[302]

- ❖ It largely ignores the findings (going back more than 100 years) of reputable scholars in the field of memory research, having a too optimistic appraisal of people's memory recall.

- ❖ *JE* disregards the important considerations **a**) that Jesus' initial followers, uneducated Aramaic speakers, were in no position to "record" the events of his life that we now have recounted in Greek, and **b**) that the earliest known references to Jesus come not from the "historical" gospels, but from St Paul. We too easily overlook the implications of the fact that he, our first *Christian writer*, 'is the closest thing we have to a surviving author who was an eyewitness to the life of Jesus' (see Gal. 1:18-20), and what Paul tells us about the historical Jesus could fit on the proverbial postage stamp, beginning with the datum that Jesus was 'born of a woman' (Gal. 4:4).[303]

It is understandable to think that even if Paul provides us with little information about Jesus, the gospels do a better job, but this is not the case.[304]

They exhibit similar problems. Many books have been written about this question, but for our purposes two observations will suffice, pertinent to the resurrection narratives:

- ❖ As we have seen in Chapter 6, St Mark's Gospel ended originally at 16:8, with the women (having been told about the resurrection) fleeing from the tomb, and saying 'nothing to anyone, for they were afraid'. In the twelve verses that follow (most of which are a pastiche on the endings of Matthew and Luke), verses 17 and 18 - the strange ones about believers in Jesus' resurrection being able to cast out demons, speak in foreign tongues, pick up snakes and drink poisons safely - are *forgeries*. Jesus (*my name* is referenced) never spoke these words. They are a fabricated pericope inserted into the biblical text by a later scribe, recopied over the years, and most famously preserved in the *King James Version* (*KJV*, 1611). [305]

✧ Careful study of the (three) synoptic gospels shows that Jesus did not attribute much importance to "resurrection". His preference was to speak of the hereafter 'more in terms of eternal life than of re-awakened dead bodies'.[306] In Jewish thought of the time, there was no expectation that the messiah should die a sacrificial death and rise again, no more than it is a contemporary expectation, contrary to what movements like *Jews for Jesus* claim. Jesus and his followers were not therefore 'preconditioned by tradition or education to look forward to a *risen Christ*; so the first narrators of the Jesus story had no pattern to follow when they tried to explain what happened to their deceased and buried teacher'.[307] If this deduction is right (see 'Hick', below), then the prophetic sayings attributed to Jesus about his death and rising again (Mk. 10:33-34, for example) cannot be historical. In other words, as with Paul, they too provide us 'with little information about Jesus.'[308]

This conclusion is validated by the arguments outlined in Chapter 5, with particular regard to Fawcett's brilliant account of the *third day tradition*.

And *The Death of Jesus the Jew* (Chapter 3) provides further *evidence* for this inference, based on the assumption that the *Triumphal Entry* (Mk. 11:1-11 and parallels[309]) reflects a historical kernel.

If so, then Jesus probably knew he would be crucified, but this is a far cry from claiming that 'some kind of preternatural knowledge enabled him to predict the circumstances of his own death, a presumption underlying liturgies of the Eucharist' (p. 41), and the position advocated by Tom Wright.

Another reason for thinking that Mk. 10:33-34, which relates how the Son of Man will be condemned to death 'and after three days rise again', cannot be Jesus' *ipsissima verba* has to do with the disciples.

The "prophecy" is addressed to them, but – as Vermes observes – not a single one recalls it during the crucial time between that Friday and Sunday (notionally, 7th to 9th April 30 CE), 'or even later when the resurrection became the central topic of the preaching of the primitive church'.[310]

In the light of these considerations, the conclusion is indubitable that 'the announcements concerning the resurrection of Jesus are later editorial interpolations', and often accompanied by bumbling attempts to explain away the disciples' failure to remember the "prophecies".[311]

Peter, for example, refuses to believe Jesus and rebukes him (Mk. 8:32b), and the other apostles are presented as dimwits, unable to understand "resurrection": 'They kept the matter to themselves, questioning what this rising from the dead could mean' (Mk. 9:10).

Every first century (Palestinian) Jew knew the meaning of "resurrection", even if many of them rejected the idea as preposterous (see Chapter 2), so there can be little doubt that what we are seeing here is an excellent illustration of a practice as common then as now: *spin*.

The concept of general resurrection was gradually achieving dominance by the time of the Second Temple's destruction in 70, but the distinctive nature of the claim made about Jesus is that his *bodily resurrection* brought into the present what had been anticipated as a future event.

In this regard, it marked a departure from normative Jewish expectation, and whilst Vermes acknowledges that "resurrection" would have been understood as "bodily" (in a manner somewhat like Schneiders' explanation), he insists nonetheless that, for Peter and Jesus' immediate followers, *the resurrection as saturation event*, would have been experienced by them as the consequence of the outpouring of the Holy Spirit.

Acts 2 is an account of *The Coming of the Holy Spirit*, where Peter declares that God raised Jesus from the dead and, exalted at His right hand, he received from the Father the promise of the Holy Spirit, now poured out over the disciples at Pentecost (vv. 1, 24, 32 and 33).

The consequence of this experience is that the disciples were empowered to act as Jesus' witnesses by performing charismatic deeds, typified by the 'fabricated pericope' (Mk. 16:17-18; cf. Acts 10:34-43) examined above, which doubtless has a historical memory behind it, for the simple reason that there was certainly extensive *missionary outreach to the Diapora* by the time Luke-Acts and the Gospels of Matthew and Mark were circulated.

The famous account of *tongues of fire* and the apostles' ability to speak in the native language of 'devout Jews from every nation under heaven living in Jerusalem' (Acts 2: 2, 5-13) clearly echo this empowerment.

They reflect what is probably a genuine memory of 'the freshness and lack of sophistication of the original Jewish followers of Jesus before Paul conquered the intellectual high ground ... and exported his ideology to the non-Jewish world'.[312]

Their *inspirational context*, of course, was Jewish and Luke (author of Acts) provided a framework for understanding Jesus' resurrection against the background of King David's reign (d. c. 970 BCE), the writer according to tradition of Ps. 110, where *Verse 1* talks of God saying to the messiah, 'Sit at my right hand ...'[313]

In Acts, Peter quotes it by way of substantiating the claim that, in Jesus, the prophetic character of the verse is fulfilled.

Ps. 110:1, therefore, is a kind of proof text for the resurrection and, when taken together with 16:10 - 'you will not abandon my soul to Hades, nor let Thy Holy One see corruption' - Luke succeeds in presenting Jesus' resurrection as a *predestined act*, one that almost 1,000 years earlier had been foretold by *David the Prophet*.[314]

Passages such as these, against the background of the story about Elijah reviving the son of the widow of Zareph (1 Kings 17:17-24) and the likelihood that Jesus' disciples may have thought of him as *Elijah Resurrected* (see Mk. 8:27-30), could infer a matrix for the *midrashic development* of a tradition moving from belief in a general resurrection to one associated with an individual - Jesus.

It should be remembered, however, that we must never separate the *particular* from *the general* – Christ's resurrection, for St Paul, accomplishes the general resurrection of all humanity: 'If there is no resurrection of the dead, then Christ has not been raised' (1 Cor.15:13 and see below).

Vermes himself does not suggest the above inference, but he notes that in popular prophetic Judaism 'the phenomenon of resurrection, the restoration to life of a person recently deceased, in no way appeared to be out of place.'[315]

BJJ has shown how Matthew's infancy gospel serves the purpose of presenting Jesus as the *Greater Moses* (also the theme of *The Sermon on the Mount*), and is it possible that the accounts of Jesus' bodily resurrection are really (at least in part) about this greater *than another theme*?[316]

Moses, for example, dies before reaching the Promised Land, and of him Deuteronomy says: 'Never since has there arisen a prophet in Israel like Moses, whom the Lord knew face to face' (34:10), but of Jesus the New Testament says that 'he deserves a glory greater than Moses' (Heb. 3:3).

The oral traditions behind the gospels (Mk. 16:1-8, for example, with its account of the *empty tomb*) would have reflected this idea, and it is not inconceivable that Jesus' disciples, following the trauma consequent upon the death of their charismatic leader, could have seen personified in him the qualities attributed to Enoch, Moses, Elijah, Elisha, and even Isaiah.

This *personification* manifested itself in visions of Jesus raised from the dead, and it is no accident that Elijah is referenced at Jesus' crucifixion, since he was expected to announce the advent of the messianic age (see Mk. 15:33-36 and Mt. 27:46-50; cf. Mk. 9:1-13.)

In addition, Rabbinic Judaism attested the post-mortem exaltation of Moses and Isaiah (two of Jesus' *sainted predecessors*), on the pattern of Acts 7:55; the context is the *Stoning of Stephen*:

> Filled with the Holy Spirit, he gazed into heaven
> and saw the glory of God, with Jesus standing at
> God's right hand.

St Luke's account of *Jesus' Ascension* (24:50-53; cf. Acts 1:3-11) also echoes this exaltation imagery, going "one better" than Moses' encounter with God on Sinai (Ex. 34:29), and it probably also alludes to a description in Livy (d. 17 CE), the Roman historian, of 'the ascension of the emperor to heaven'.[317]

Jesus would thus be *a prophet in Israel truly greater than Moses* (and, in the Diaspora, *greater than Caesar*) because his exaltation means that 'we too might walk in newness of life' (Rom. 6:4).

Tomb traditions reflect this phenomenon: 'Mark 16:1-8 intends to surpass those *sainted predecessors* by escalating from "no tomb" for Enoch and Elijah to "unknown tomb" for Moses, to "empty tomb" for Jesus.'[318]

As with the gospels' two accounts of Jesus' birth (exercises in *haggadic midrashim*, providing us with no historical or biological information), the "empty tomb" is also a midrash; its aim to promote the claim that, with Jesus, someone greater is here, to paraphrase Heb. 3:3.

These observations reinforce a central theme of this book: there was no "empty tomb", for the simple reasons that a) there was no formal burial in the first place and, b), the "empty tomb" is typical of the fact that stories of *saturation events* grow in the telling.

The "empty tomb" is a mythological (and midrashic) way of contextualising, years later, the original *Easter Moment* associated with visions: *He appeared first to Cephas, then to the twelve* (1 Cor. 15:5).

We should not impose our agendas upon the evangelists; to paraphrase Aristotle (in a very different context, of course), their concern was more poetical than historical, for poetry relates to the universal, and history to the particular.

A difficulty with our fallible attempts to interpret the meaning of Jesus' resurrection is that, especially in the West, the emphasis for 2,000 years has been on 'the particular', but Paul who, as indicated above, provides our first recorded witness to it, insists that its significance cannot be divorced from 'the general resurrection of all humanity'.

This universal approach is prominent in the Eastern (Orthodox) Church (see endnote 318). It has the advantage of providing us with a more holistic understanding of Easter. The word probably derives from the Anglo-Saxon cult of 'Eostrae', goddess of spring and fertility.[321] This approach may better conform to how *Cephas* ('Peter') understood his vision of the risen Jesus, as one for whom it was impossible to be held in the power of death (see Acts 2:22-24).

Vermes is likely right when he says that it is impossible to establish the stages, beginning with despair followed by hesitant belief, which led to the conviction that Jesus had been raised from the dead.

But, for Vermes, Peter's claim that Jesus was no longer 'held in the power of death' points to 'the metamorphosis of the apostles', confirmed by 'the efficacy of their charismatic healing', in the name of the risen Jesus. This is 'the genuine miracle of Easter'.[322]

In other words, Jesus - crucified and dead - rose in the hearts of the disciples who had loved him, and this conviction was validated by their visions of him.[323]

These visions, and these alone (not the "empty tomb", regardless of what Tom Wright argues, persuaded them that Jesus had been raised from the dead.

Given their (apocalyptic-eschatological[324]) understanding of 'the general resurrection of all humanity', it should be no surprise that Peter and others would have seen that process beginning in the person of Jesus, the *crucified messiah* restored to new life, a belief pithily expressed by St Paul: 'Christ has been raised from the dead, the first fruits of those who have died' (1 Cor. 15:20).

Had there been no *Maccabaean Uprising* in 166 BCE (see Chapter 4), these convictions would never have come to fruition (what nowadays we term "martyr theology" was current in the first century), and there would have been no appearances of Jesus to 'Cephas, then to the twelve, and to more than five hundred brothers and sisters at one time' (1 Cor. 15:5-6).

Were these appearances *veridical*? In the manner postulated by Schneiders, did Peter and 'the twelve' really see Jesus? Or are visions *nonveridical*? What Paul wrote about Jesus appearing to him may not be a genuine memory, but instead a function of his imagination; that is, he *visualised*, he did not *see* Jesus, in the sense of the ordinary meaning of the verb 'to see'.

For Tom Wright, as we have seen, the visions are veridical: 'Enormous forces in our culture are determined to deny Jesus was raised from the dead. And, over and over again, they use arguments which can be shown to be invalid.'[325]

Gerd Lüdemann, as previously noted, disagrees: 'Christian faith is as dead as Jesus'; for him, no empty tomb means no resurrection, arguing that the entire Christian enterprise is redundant. With Sheehan, he agrees that the visions are nonveridical, the product of psychological factors (see Chapter 9).

Sheehan nonetheless questions Lüdemann's conclusions, and also Wright's implication that there is a conspiracy of intellectuals to suppress the truth about the resurrection. This latter claim is risible.

Lüdemann makes the error of thinking that Christianity is a completely false interpretation of Jesus' life, but Sheehan maintains that it is "true", in the sense of promoting what the Greeks called "living well", and what many contemporary believers now term *orthopraxis*: an emphasis away from beliefs about Jesus to imitating him.

Doing Christianity adopts this approach. For Paul Higginson, 'Jesus spoke in parables, not theological jargon', by which he means that Christianity is primarily 'a way of living, not a way of believing' (p. 12).[326] 'Law' is a poor translation of 'Torah', which is better rendered 'teaching' and 'way of living', which is how this famous verse should be interpreted:

> Do not imagine I have come to abolish the Law
> or the Prophets. I have come not to abolish but
> to complete them. (Mt. 5:17)

We are so accustomed to the language of *believing in the resurrection* - 'On the third day he rose again in accordance with the Scriptures' (*Nicene Creed*) – that we can easily miss how Jesus was concerned with the afterlife mainly to the extent that it impacted on people's lives in the here and now:

> When the Son of Man comes in his glory, ...
> he will put the sheep at his right hand and the
> goats at the left. ... Then the king will say to
> those at his right hand, 'Come, you that are
> blessed by my Father, inherit the kingdom
> prepared for you ..., for I was hungry and you
> gave me food, I was thirsty and you gave me
> something to drink, ... I tell you, just as you did
> it to one of the least of these ..., you did it to
> me. Then he will say to those at his left hand ...,
> depart from me into the eternal fire prepared
> for the devil and his angels. ... These will go
> into eternal punishment, but the righteous into
> eternal life. (Mt. 25:31-46, abridged).

It is clear that, for Jesus, he viewed the afterlife in terms of rewards and sanctions, but his understanding of *Gehenna* ('Hell') and 'eternal punishment' refers not to some 'underworld of fiery torment', but to the notion of annihilation, not torment.[327]

From this observation, which can be a surprise to many Christians, it seems that only the righteous (those at *his right hand*) will experience resurrected life, because those *at his left hand* have simply ceased to exist: 'for them, there would never again be any hope of life', writes Bart Ehrman.

Our traditional images of heaven and hell are later developments and not part of the message of the historical Jesus, the main focus of which is on the Kingdom of God (a Pharisee term), which has a twofold meaning: *a future state of affairs* (Mk. 1:15) **and** *the present reign of God* (Lk. 17:21).

That Kingdom, *present* and *future* reign of God, is characterised by what Diarmuid O'Murchu refers to as the *empowerment of love*, and that empowerment is manifest in the imperative to love others: 'Love your neighbour as yourself' (Mk. 12:31; cf. Mt. 5:43-44, a paraphrase of Lev. 19:17-18).

This imperative achieves its quintessential expression in *the Parable of the Good Samaritan* (Lk. 10:25-37), concluding with an injunction: 'Go and do likewise', meaning to provide assistance to the needy.

The same theme permeates the Johannine passion-resurrection narrative, represented in Chapter 21 (a probable addition to the gospel) by Peter's encounter with the risen Jesus (vv. 15 to 19).

The triple question addressed to Peter undoes the three times he denies Jesus before the high priest (18:12-27), with Jesus asking, 'Simon, do you love me?' Peter replies, 'Lord, you know that I love you', and Jesus answers with 'Feed my sheep'.

We have already seen above one interpretation of the *Parable of the Sheep and Goats* (some commentators argue that Matthew is not referring to acts of mercy in general, but to ones of which Jesus' disciples have an entitlement), and this exposition applies also to the 'Feed my sheep' of John, with the additional point that the sheep metaphor appears to relate to the development of *ecclesial offices* in the early Jesus movement, c. 100, as Pheme Perkins suggests.[328]

What is evident about this development is that visions of the post-resurrection Jesus (veridical or not) are concerned with pastoral care of the flock, echoing a key theme of the ministry (see Jn. 10:3-4 and 17:9-12, to give two illustrations), and Higginson is probably right to emphasise Jesus' ministry as primarily an exercise in *orthopraxis*, a position shared with one of Judaism's most famous rabbis, Hillel, and the grandfather of Gamaliel at whose feet St Paul claimed to have been taught (see Acts 5:35-39):

> Do not do unto others what you do not wish to
> be done unto yourself.

Sheehan would endorse Higginson's sentiments, but he goes further, to say that 'all religious doctrines are mythical'.[329] In this context, 'mythical' encompasses the view that Jesus' body remained in its grave, regardless of whether this was a tomb or communal pit.

Schneiders would question the claim (as does Higginson), arguing that 'Jesus is alive personally', insisting that the focus of faith 'is not the ongoing influence or example of someone who once lived, like St Paul, and is no longer among us'.[330]

In case of any doubt, she writes: 'Christian faith does not merely affirm that Jesus is alive with God, nor simply that in some way he is still with us'. The affirmation is that 'Jesus is bodily risen ..., he can be seen, heard touched.'[331]

As already indicated, there are problems with appeals to the *seen, heard and touched argument*, and there is a sense in which this entire debate can generate more heat than light.

Schneiders describes the *First Easter* as a *saturation event* and, for her, its reality continues to be available to us; but it might be better to compare it to another *saturation event*, some fourteen billion years ago: the *Big Bang* (the concept was first proposed in the 1920s by Georges Lemaitre, a brilliant mathematician and Catholic priest).

This *originating event*, a *primordial explosion* (lasting a trillionth of a trillionth of a second), 'is not available to us except by guesswork and theory'. And just as scientists interpret it by reading the effect that is our world back to that *unimaginable moment of the Big Bang*, Richard Holloway remarks that theologians read back from the effects of *The First Easter* on the disciples to hypotheses explaining *that first saturation/ emerging event*.[332]

The Resurrection of Jesus the Jew addresses these hypotheses in detail, but Holloway suggests that the complexities of *resurrection research* may be reduced to two considerations:

- ✦ the originating, mythical resurrection, the big bang as it were, that ignited the Christian movement, and
- ✦ the effectual resurrection, 'which is the continuing impact of Jesus upon history'[333]

Not everyone will agree with his first classification, but there can be no doubting the validity of Holloway's second point, noting that 'the interesting thing about the resurrection is not what was claimed, but who made the claim'.

He is referring to how the disciples had deserted Jesus (see Mk. 14:50 and parallels), but later they 'somewhere found the courage to proclaim the meaning of his life; and that transformation, that turnaround, is what we mean by resurrection'.[334]

Bultmann, as noted, famously said that 'Jesus rose into the kerygma', that is, into the faith and preaching of the first believers. For Holloway, that hope is alive today, manifest in the heroic example of Christians like Dietrich Bonhoeffer, Martin Luther King and Archbishop Romero, challenging us 'to join with others to bring new life to human communities that are still held in the grip of death'.

'Death' is capable of diverse interpretations: existential (Holloway, above) and otherwise. St Paul saw it as the last great evil to be destroyed, having entered the world because of sin, but Christ's sacrificial crucifixion and resurrection have 'destroyed death forever' (1 Cor. 15:26; cf. Rom. 6:23).

Having addressed the problems attendant upon traditional interpretations of the death-resurrection narratives and agreeing in essentials with Holloway, Diarmuid O' Murchu remarks that death is neither a limitation or an evil, but instead 'a necessary good, an evolutionary, God-given imperative, for the development and flourishing of all life-forms'.[335]

He further maintains, rightly and with particular regard to St Paul's theology, that even a superficial knowledge of the gospels shows that Christians have exaggerated the significance of Jesus' death, to the point of distorting 'the empowering and liberating praxis of his life', an insight that also informs, without defining, Higginson's *Doing Christianity*.

Sandra Schneiders makes the important comment that 'the Incarnation, as opposed to the historical event of Jesus' life, is a transhistorical reality, available only to faith'.[336]

O'Murchu, paraphrasing Pope Benedict XVI (d. 2022) and echoing *saturation language*, observes that the resurrection constitutes a critical leap into 'a totally new evolutionary dimension'.

Unlike Schneiders and the pope, however, he extends the evolution metaphor to embrace the requirement for a new Christian paradigm, one which is no longer hampered by its current anthropocentric and patriarchal limitations, and is rid - once and for all - of its flawed *disaster-rescue theology* represented by the doctrine of *Original Sin* (see endnote 337).

For O'Murchu, "incarnation" did not begin with Jesus, 'nor should it be reserved to the Christian understanding of faith, which seems to be Schneiders understanding of this 'transhistorical reality, available only to faith'.

It began *seven million years ago*, in East Africa, since when 'the divine creativity was fully at play', and it is hardly credible that 'God was looking down the timeline, deciding to birth forth a new life-form', while at the same time having second thoughts about it, and then waiting seven million years before this new life-form could be 'declared saved'.[337]

O'Murchu continues by challenging us to recognise that such a construct 'is so convoluted that it seems to me no sincere religious believer would take it seriously', for the reason that 'it fails to honour the grand time scale of God's creative spirit' (*Incarnation: A New Evolutionary Threshold*, pp. 82 and 168).

'Spirit' should now be understood in terms of new scientific horizons (with particular regard to *Quantum Physics*), and these enable the perception that, long before Jesus, God's revelation was at work for billions of years before the existence of human beings and religion, through which people are invited to be co-creators, not masters, in an evolving process, one that celebrates the *Great Spirit's* presence in our world.[338]

This *Cosmic Spirit* enabled the disciples to realise *Kingdom Values* here on Earth: 'The Kingdom of God is close to hand, repent and believe the good news' (Mk. 1:15).

Against this background, O'Murchu understands Jesus' resurrection as God's vindication of that *Kingdom Vision*. Like Thomas Sheehan, he affirms that we do not know what happened to Jesus after his death, and at one level it doesn't matter, because – in Sheehan's words – 'Jesus is not the object of the message he preached'.[340]

Indeed, contrary to how the churches portray him, Jesus' mission was to be replaced by the *Kingdom Values* he espoused, a truth encapsulated by Dietrich Bonhoeffer in his famous *Letters and Papers from Prison*, where he championed this easily misunderstood quotation: 'God would have us know that we must live as men who manage our lives without Him' (16th July 1944).

O'Murchu acknowledges, however, that for Tom Wright (and others) what happened to Jesus matters a great deal, but he maintains that the essence of the meaning of the resurrection is 'to capture anew the full cosmic scope of God's radical presence in our midst', a reality probably first proclaimed by women and only later accepted by men.[341]

The inference is that 'angelic figures, empty tomb scenarios and various appearances' serve the purpose of 'giving hope and meaning to Christians especially in times of persecution'.[342] We can discern in this observation the close link between the *Maccabaean Rebellion* and resurrection belief, though O'Murchu himself does not develop the connection.

Emphasis on supernatural scenarios associated with the resurrection is a distraction, O'Murchu argues, from the primary aim of Christian faith: the empowering of people to establish *Kingdom Values* 'in our cosmic home'.[343]

Only when Christians take seriously this imperative can they hope to understand what 'the mystery and meaning of resurrection are all about', and in the process rid themselves of a *Creation-Fall-Redemption* paradigm that has run its course, even if 'millions of Christians still adhere to it to one degree or another'.

Paschal Paradox, O'Murchu's affecting autobiography, describes how his understanding of God had been 'gradually released from the tomb', to encompass a more authentic (evolutionary) paradigm, one which in respect of the resurrection focuses not on what may have happened to Jesus but concentrates instead on 'linking it with life rather than with death'.[344]

Regarding his own death, O'Murchu remarks on p. 72 that the energy of his embodied existence will go elsewhere, 'since according to the laws of physics energy is never wasted', commenting that where it goes 'I don't know, and why do I need to know?'

He argues that, for too long, Christian theologies of death have focused on this *need to know*, but the challenge is to recognise that 'we make our own heaven or hell right here in front of our eyes', insisting that believers should no longer project their own anxieties onto 'a divine scapegoat on a cross'.[345]

O'Murchu appears to embrace Panentheism which maintains that all things are in God: 'In him, we live and move and have our being' (Acts 17:28). It does not identify the world with God (Pantheism), but claims that the world is ultimately dependent upon God.[346]

Leaving aside the possibility that his account of God's relationship with the world could be confused with a sophisticated version of *Intelligent Design*[347], it has two important merits:

- ❖ Notions pertaining to Christian revelation, as traditionally understood, are no longer fit for purpose, and

- ❖ O'Murchu's linking of Jesus' resurrection with life rather than with death facilitates a shift in focus away from "visions" to what Harry Williams, in *True Resurrection*, calls 'the logic of hope'. He suggests that all efforts to pin down the resurrection are rather like 'nailing jelly to a wall'. What matters is not the "evidence of visions", but a willingness to recognise that 'we ourselves are agents of resurrection'.

In the light of these considerations, a lived experience of "presence", and not arguments about the veridical or non-veridical status of visions, is what counts.[348]

This resurrected presence of Jesus, through *sacrament, word* and *other means*, remains available to believers today, and it must have been the *originating experience* of the disciples that *First Easter*: 'Were not our hearts burning within us while he was talking to us on the road?' (Lk. 24:32)

Modern people, if they believe in the afterlife at all, typically understand the *continuity in discontinuity* of their deceased loved ones in terms of the soul outliving death, but the writer of the Road to Emmaus was depicting the beliefs of first-century apocalyptic Jews, and for them this entailed a resurrection from the dead.

Their experiences of Jesus' resurrected life would have been understood in the context of their own deeply held convictions: 'Jesus had been bodily raised from the dead'.[349]

Schneiders interprets this to mean that, in death, if Jesus had ceased to be his bodily self, he would not have been a human being, and then 'what we call the Incarnation (God's becoming one of us) would have ceased', because Jesus is 'the great symbol of God, not as a representative of God, but as God-self'.[350]

She is certainly right to affirm that 'bodiliness is what keeps us continuous with ourselves no matter how much we change over time', because 'no one else is me, and I am not anyone else', but there is a circularity to this argument, in the sense that Schneiders maintains Jesus' resurrection to be a function of 'the One in whom our humanity participates in Trinitarian life and which makes that Trinitarian life present to us' (p. 40).

Her argument is susceptible to a criticism made long ago by Matthew Tindal (d.1733):

> It's an odd jumble to prove the truth of a book
> by the proof of the doctrine it contains, and at
> the same time conclude these doctrines to be
> true because contained in that book.[351]

Schneiders is making a case not on the merits of resurrection thinking current in the first century but with regard to how later generations interpreted it, culminating in the definition at Chalcedon (451), and the fifth century was a very different context from that of the apocalyptic-eschatological worldview entertained by Jesus and his discipleship group.

The (original) Ebionites, for example, and arguably best representative of Jesus' actual teachings, had no problem claiming both messianic and resurrection status for him, whilst at the same time rejecting belief in the virginal conception and most of St Paul's other teachings. James, the brother of Jesus, was probably their leader.[352]

Furthermore, Schneiders' inference draws on the claim

that 'Jesus and his first disciples thought that the issue of his bodily resurrection was critical to Christian faith'. Did he? Did they?

Apart from the fact that there was no "Christian faith" at the time (we should avoid the temptation to read later views into earlier times), it is also the case, contrary to popular belief, that "resurrection" played a minor role in Jesus' teaching, a perspective almost certainly shared by the disciples during his lifetime.

It must be emphasised, however, that whilst Jesus and his followers (unlike the Sadducees) would have taken for granted the notion of an afterlife, they would not have subscribed to Plato's account in *Phaedo* of the body-soul relationship, where Socrates, in the company of friends, prepares himself for immortality.

Phaedo recounts the West's second most famous story of a noble demise (*The Death of Socrates*). Plato invites the reader to view death with the same equanimity shown by Socrates when he drank the hemlock for the "crime" of having *corrupted the minds of the youth of Athens*.

And, contrary to some recent speculation, reincarnation was not part of the horizon of the Jesus movement, but John Hick is probably right to note that, though incompatible on the surface, the two doctrines are variations of a common view that human beings survive death as embodied beings.[353]

Hick, in an interesting observation, remarks that whilst the two concepts disagree with the Platonic notion of disembodied souls, 'the reincarnation doctrine affirms repeated resurrections of a particular kind'.

When we hear or read the word "resurrection", however, the understandable response is to dress it, so to speak, with distinctive "body imagery" in the manner defended by Schneiders and Wright (and implied by Higginson), but there is no good reason to infer that the disciples would have thought exclusively in this manner.

We make the assumption because of our familiarity with the gospels' resurrection narratives, but if instead we focus, again, on the *originating visionary experience(s)*, as recounted by Paul, then it is entirely credible, Hick suggests, that the manifestations of Jesus after his death would have been associated with "resurrection", since the concept was familiar to the disciples, and there would have been a natural progression in their minds from 'We have seen the Lord' to 'God has raised Jesus from the dead', culminating in the gospel stories as we now have them.[354]

The point here is that Jesus' disciples 'believed in life after death before and independently of his resurrection', and in this sense there was a pattern to follow when they tried to make sense of his crucifixion; but one, as remarked earlier in this book, that applied it to a new set of circumstances: belief in a resurrected messiah.

In other words, the visions were not a consequence of the "empty tomb" ('Jesus ... is not here. Look, there is the place they laid him', Mk. 16:6); rather, they were the cause of the empty tomb tradition, made possible because the disciples already had a conceptual framework - "resurrection" - around which legendary materials were able to develop. *The legendary motif* became more pronounced (and exotic) as time went on, as shown by the *Gospel of Peter* (see below).

This explanation makes sense in respect of the further consideration, argued in *The Death of Jesus the Jew* and again in this volume, that Jesus was not accorded a formal burial; indeed, the burial accounts in the gospels are midrashic-legendary creations designed to flesh-out, as it were, *the originating visionary experience(s)*, which took place in Galilee, not Jerusalem: *Go, tell his disciples and Peter, you will see Jesus in Galilee* (Mk. 16:7, paraphrase).

Luke's situating of resurrection appearances in Jerusalem[155] is therefore an exercise in *theological spin*: 'Jesus had to die in Jerusalem and nowhere else', as Thomas Fawcett explains it (see earlier chapters), because in Jewish mythology that city (*Rock of Zion*) symbolised a link between heaven and earth.

The disciples' visions, veridical or otherwise (something can be seen, there or not), thus serve the purpose of demonstrating that Jesus is the new and definitive link between heaven and earth: 'I am ascending to my Father and your Father, to my God and your God' (Jn. 20: 17b; cf. Lk. 24:50-53).

In Riverstick (Ireland), a tiny village on the road between Cork Airport and Kinsale, its Catholic church has a huge, concrete cross to the left of the main entrance, impossible to miss and pointing (somewhat belligerently) to the sky.

It always reminds me of the above words addressed to Mary Magdalene and of these verses (38-42) in the apocryphal Gospel of Peter (GoP, written c. 125[356]):

> During the night on which the Lord's day
> dawned, while the soldiers stood guard ..., a
> great voice came from the sky ..., and two men,
> very bright, descended from it and drew near
> to the tomb. The stone cast before the entrance
> rolled away by itself and moved to one side; the
> tomb was opened and both young men entered.
> When the soldiers saw these things, they woke
> up the centurion and the elders ..., and as they
> were explaining what they had seen, three men
> emerged from the tomb, two of them supporting

the other, with a cross following behind them.
The heads of the two reached up to the sky, but
the head of the one they were leading went up
above the skies. And they heard a voice from
the skies, 'Have you preached to those who are
asleep?' And a reply came from the cross, "Yes".'

GoP goes on to relate that the soldiers and their centurion proceed to a meeting with Pilate, in the company of some Jewish elders, where they impart the information that Jesus 'actually was the Son of God' (v. 45, echoing Mk. 15:39).

Pilate's reply, 'I am clean of the blood of the Son of God; you decided to do this', is a continuation, about forty-five years later, of the libel of Mt. 27:25, ('His blood be on us and on our children'), which was itself a response to the infamous scene of Pilate washing his hands in front of the crowd (v.24, a midrash based on passages from the Old Testament[357]).

Neither gospel is providing us with an account of historical events, but with an exercise in political and religious propaganda arising out of the circumstances prevailing after the end of the (first) *Great Jewish-Roman War*.

We should not be surprised that GoP failed to be included as an authorized "fifth gospel" (it's almost complete "nonsense"), but what it does show, following Hick and with regard to the resurrection, is that, as time passes, stories develop in the telling.

No sensible person will argue that the soldiers' *visions* in 'Peter' are of a veridical nature, but what distinguishes that judgement from, say, the claim that Paul's vision was of a different order? Are we dealing here with a difference in degree or a difference in kind?

Dom Crossan, who also observes that the emergence

of the three men from the tomb mimics the procession of Roman emperors, would argue 'difference in degree', but one that nonetheless affirms, in faith, 'the continued presence of absolutely the same Jesus in an absolutely different mode of existence'.[358]

Wright and Schneiders opt for 'difference in kind', based in part on the obvious point that *GoP*, unlike the canonical gospels, provides a description of the resurrection, but more particularly because Jesus' post-mortem 'different mode of existence' pertains to him in a unique manner (*bodily continuity in discontinuity*). In other words, it is not merely a function of the disciples' perception, however we are to define that perception.

It is my view that, in context, the entire Jerusalem tradition (of burial, rolling stone, angels etc.) is a secondary one, representing legendary accretions imbued with midrashic characteristics; that it arose from *Christophanies* - the appearance stories proclaimed originally by Paul in 1 Cor. 15:3-7.

Insofar as an impartial assessment of *evidence for Jesus' resurrection* is possible (it is not), the honest conclusion should be that whether one opts for the Crossan camp or the Wright party, nobody should be denied the appellation 'Christian' on the basis of their choice.

There is much food for thought in an observation made by Harry Williams (d. 2006), in *True Resurrection*:

> There can be no evidence for miracles, if by "evidence" we mean the public exhibition of some change in the world observed as external reality: the change comes to the observer, not to what is observed. It is not a case of saying, 'Look now at that!' The testimony to miracle can only be,

'Whereas once I was blind, now I see'.

He is, of course, paraphrasing a famous verse, '12', in St Paul's beautiful 1 Corinthians 13 (and the song *Amazing Grace*) , which concludes with 'And now faith, hope and love abide, these three, and the greatest of these is love' (v. 13).

The implications of Williams' position would necessitate a small book in its own right; but suffice to say, with Alfred, Lord Tennyson (d. 1892), that *there is more faith in honest doubt than in half the creeds; and the creeds serve Love*, I would add.

Or, to express this idea another way: Are the differences between Crossan and Wright 'minor'? Do our theological arguments miss the mark? Chapter 12 will return to this question.

Williams makes another comment, to the effect that inability to resolve our theological differences, 'minor' or 'major', are sometimes akin to a man dying of thirst by a mountain stream because he cannot find the water tap. Williams had a point.

In 1930, Sigmund Freud (d. 1939), in his essay *Civilization and its Discontents*, examined the phenomenon of the *narcissim of minor differences*.

Richard Holloway explains it by saying how Freud had noticed that 'our most likely scapegoats are neighbours or associates who betray marginal differences from us, onto whom we can fix reasons for our suffering, and this is why some of the grimmest conflicts in history have been between communities that lived peacefully alongside each other for years, till some aggrieved person exploded a real or metaphorical bomb that blew apart centuries of tolerance'.[359]

Freud was writing in the context of the Nazi threat, which he thought, disastrously, could be contained as 'a relatively harmless satisfaction of the inclination to aggression' (Holloway).

The commemoration of that *First Easter Day*, notionally 9th April 30, would in time have explosive consequences for Jewish communities that, for centuries, had lived in relative peace alongside their Christian neighbours.

This "peace", in the last decades of the nineteenth century and into the twentieth, was undermined by church periodicals, affiliated newspapers and formal pronouncements, regularly promoting "true anti-Semitism", contributing to a "perfect Catholicism" (see chapter 12).

They made an insidious contribution to the rise of popular anti-Semitism, a development harnessed by the Nazis for their own evil purposes, culminating in the extermination of six million Jews. The legacy of their crimes affects the Christian narrative down to our time. These and related considerations, pertinent to *The Resurrection of Jesus the Jew*, will occupy us in the closing chapter of this book.

—

CHAPTER 12

The First Easter and the Anguish of the Jews

*'The Jewish faith has been superseded
by the teachings of Christ.'*
Pope St Pius X

At the height of the *Dreyfuss Affair* (the notorious wrongful conviction of a Jewish officer for allegedly passing military secrets to Germany and later exonerated), readers of *L'Osservatore Romano* (LR) were informed that:

> The Jewish race, the deicide people wandering throughout the world, brings with it the pestiferous breath of treason. (December 1897)

Sixty-eight years later, the same *Catholic daily*, de facto mouthpiece of the Vatican since 1861, reported this statement:

> The Church ..., mindful of her common patrimony with the Jews, and motivated by the Gospel's spiritual love and by no political considerations, deplores the hatred, persecutions

and displays of anti-Semitism directed against
the Jews at any time and from any source.
(Vatican II, October 1965)

How to explain this *volte-face*? It is largely the result
of Christians reflecting on the theological legacy of the
Holocaust and its causes.

The Shoah reminds us, to paraphrase Viktor Frankl
(d.1997), psychiatrist and Holocaust survivor, that in this
world there are essentially two kinds of human beings: the
"race" of the good person and the "race" of the bad person.

Against the background of pogroms in Russia, during the
1890s, an LR journalist wrote that Jews were responsible for
them, arguing, incredibly, that French, Russian and Austrian
anti-Semitic movements were the work of "cosmopolitan
Judaism".[360]

At the same time, *LR* devoted a series of articles to drawing a distinction between *good (kind) anti-Semitism and bad
anti-Semitism*, a theme that was to appear regularly in Church
publications into the early twentieth century.[361]

Good anti-Semites were 'sober, thoughtful Christians', re-
acting to the supposed dominance of Jews in public life, with
particular regard to the financial sector.

Bad anti-Semites, on the other hand, were a discredit to
'true, Christian anti-Semitism'; they represented a 'new
form of anti-Semitism', one that was 'an artificial form of
Judaism itself'.

This absurdity was predicated on the basis of the Jews
themselves having organised the above-mentioned pogroms,
rendering impossible the good intentions of *kind and true
Christian anti-Semites*.[362]

Lest there be any room for doubt, the Vatican daily (1st

July 1892) declared that:

> True anti-Semitism is and can be in substance
> nothing other than Christianity, completed and
> perfected in Catholicism.

These shocking pronouncements are indicative of a wider culture of anti-Semitism (*history's longest hatred*) prevalent at the time, which was by no means confined to Catholicism, but they are nonetheless egregious examples of a phenomenon that, by the late nineteenth century, had become deeply embedded in the *Christian psyche*: the arrogant belief that it was in every way superior to Judaism.

The phrase *perfected in Catholicism* is also redolent of this hubris, coming, as it did, twenty-two years after the (limited) definition of papal infallibility at Vatican I (1870). The background was the *Syllabus of Errors* (1864). It excoriated the beliefs that people are free to embrace and profess their religion of choice, and that popes should reconcile themselves to, 'and come to terms with, progress, liberalism and modern civilization'.

William Gladstone (d. 1898), British prime minister at the time, and Abraham Lincoln (d. 1865) were both scandalised by the *Syllabus*; and of the bishops' failure at Vatican I, it has been described by Peter de Rosa as 'a wonderful metamorphosis – shepherds had turned themselves into sheep' (see endnote 1).

Vatican II performed another spectacular *volte-face*, this time on the notorious Syllabus, by decreeing that:

> No one is to be restrained from acting in accordance with their religious beliefs, whether

privately or publicly, whether alone or in association with others, ... since 'the right to religious
freedom has its foundation in the very dignity
of the human person, as this dignity is known
through the revealed Word of God and by reason itself'. (December 1965)

Pius IX (d. 1878), *pope of the Syllabus and of Vatican I* and
the longest reigning pontiff to date, must have been spinning
in his grave when these declarations were made.

Yet Vatican II, anxious to safeguard a particular understanding of (propositional) Christian revelation, insists that
Jesus personally had commissioned St Peter and the other apostles 'to propagate and govern the unique Church of
Christ', and 'although many elements of sanctification and
of truth can be found outside of her visible structure', these
are 'gifts properly belonging to the Church of Christ', and
possessed of 'an inner dynamism towards Catholic unity'.
(November 1964)

Leaving aide the virtual historical certainty that Jesus
never commissioned (let alone "ordained") anyone, such
passages, for all their later *ecumenical spin*, exhibit a redundant Catholic imperialism, more at home in the nineteenth
century than in the post-Vatican II Church.[363]

Pope St Pius X (d. 1914), who succeeded Leo XIII (d.
1903), would also have been spinning in his grave regarding
the above initiatives: efforts to accommodate 'progress, liberalism and modern civilization', which ran counter to these
words he addressed to Theodore Herzl (d. 1904, founder of
modern Zionism):

'The Jewish faith was the foundation of our

own, but it has been superseded by the teachings of Christ and we cannot admit that it still
enjoys any validity.' (26th January 1904. In 1994,
the Vatican recognised the state of Israel)[364]

A clearer endorsement of supersessionism it would be
hard to find, a prejudice shared by Rafael Merry del Val (d.
1930), Pius' secretary of state. This English-born cardinal of
Spanish aristocratic descent had another, very peculiar, claim
to fame.

A relative, 700 years earlier, was Dominguito del Val, a six
year old child revered in Spain 'as a martyr and a saint'. In a
1933 biography of the cardinal, the story was told of the boy's
crucifixion on Good Friday 1250 by Jews, 'out of their hatred
for the Catholic religion'.[365]

Known as the *ritual murder* charge, instances of this *blood
libel*, emanating from the notorious and unhistorical Blood
Cry of Mt. 27:25 ('*His blood be on us and on our children*'), have
been a feature of Christianity's anti-Jewish polemic from as
early as the twelfth century (and probably earlier), when, at
Easter 1144, a twelve year old boy, *William of Norwich*, was
allegedly slain by local Jews.

Dangerous fantasies of this kind still circulate in our time,
propagated by anti-Semitic conspiracy theorists, especially
(but no longer exclusively) in the Arab world.[366]

At the core of the *blood libel* is the fake claim, disseminated
by thousands of Catholic-owned newspaper accounts at the
end of the nineteenth century and into the early years of the
twentieth, that Judaism required its adherents 'to capture
Christian children, mutilate and torture them as painfully as
possible, and then drain them of their blood'.[367]

According to these publications (*Civiltá Cattolica*[368], for example), the blood was needed for ritual purposes, 'from the making of Passover matzah to marriage celebrations'.

In 1899, Merry del Val, bizarrely considered an expert on the blood libel owing to his tenuous connection with little Dominiguito, was tasked by the Holy Office to investigate claims made about it in a book, *The Mystery of the Blood Among the Jews*, authored by a Catholic priest and notorious French anti-Semite, Henri Desportes.

At the end of July the following year, the cardinal inquisitors of the Holy office, with the approval of Leo XIII, concluded - to the dismay of Cardinal Vaughan (d. 1903), leader of England's Catholics – that no declaration of Jews' innocence regarding the *blood libel* could be made by the Vatican.[369]

In making their judgement, the inquisitors no doubt considered themselves to be *good anti-Semites*, since – as David Kertzer remarks – to formally repudiate the *ritual murder charge* would have also required them to abjure the cult of St Simon of Trent.

His young, mutilated corpse was found on Easter Sunday 1475, another alleged victim of the *blood libel*, like Dominguito, and the cult devoted to Simon was formally recognised by the Holy See.

Catholics as recently as the opening decades of the twentieth century were encouraged to accept as fact the scurrilous and dangerous *blood libel accusations*, a libel repeated again and again in the pages of *Civilitá Cattolica*, the influential Jesuit publication, founded 1850, and considered to reflect the Vatican's perspectives on the issues of the day.

Fr Edward Flannery, in *The Anguish of the Jews* (1965), comments that, as far back as the seventeenth century in Poland, the Jesuits had earned a reputation for anti-Semitism, and they had also excluded candidates of Jewish ancestry from

the Order (a policy long rescinded), but that this reputation 'was but an aspect of their stout defence of Catholicism
against any and every agency they considered a peril'.[371]

Flannery's seeming words of exculpation have been
echoed more recently by Pope Francis, himself a Jesuit, when
he addressed the staff of *Civilitá Cattolica*, by noting that formerly it had been 'harshly combative, in tune with the general atmosphere of the time', but that its contemporary task is
'not to build walls, but bridges ..., to establish dialogue with
people ..., and to dialogue it is necessary to lower defences
and open doors'.[372] Francis' pontificate insists upon a *compas-
sionate language of faith*.

That 'general atmosphere of the time' was defined in
terms of official Catholicism's response to the supposed
threats from 'progress, liberalism and modern civilization',
typified by its paranoid reaction to the gradual assimilation
of Jews into public life, following the final collapse of the
Papal States (1870) and the emergence of democratic gov-
ernments in European states.[373]

A significant feature of that 'paranoid reaction' was the
widespread belief, by no means confined to defenders of the
Vatican status quo, that Jews were engaged in a conspiracy to
be masters of the world, a delusion fomented by a notorious
hoax: *The Protocols of the Elders of Zion*.[374]

Conspiracy theories, since the advent of the Internet and
its ability to produce "deep fakes", have become an endur-
ing and sometimes dangerous feature of modern life, but the
phenomenon was also present in the first century.

In St John's Gospel, immediately following Jesus' raising
of Lazarus from the dead, the story is related of the Pharisees
and chief priests gathered together in council plotting to
murder Jesus. It is part of the section where Caiaphas utters

the infamous pronouncement, 'It is better to have one man die for the people than to have the whole nation perish' (see 11: 49-57).

Historians have long noted problems with this gospel component (the words attributed to Caiaphas, for example), but what is noteworthy is that *a resurrection theme* is here the prelude to Jesus' arrest, trial(s) and crucifixion, and in the preceding section we are told that Lazarus had been four days in his tomb (11:17).

The *four days theme* may allude to the Zoroastrian belief that the spirit endured beside the body for about ninety-six hours; but the *three days theme*, examined in Chapter 5, is typically a Jewish idea, symbolising belief in a general resurrection at the end of time, a concept developed later in the Talmud, the most important works(s) of the rabbis, dating from the late fourth century but including material from much earlier times.[375]

It is hardly likely that resurrection belief was a motivating factor behind Jesus' death. The consideration, however, that the evangelist implies as much (writing some sixty-five years after Golgotha) is strangely characteristic of beliefs about *Jewish conspiracy theories* going back to the first century, and they remain in evidence to this day, exemplified by the phenomena known as *Qanon* and the *Dark Web* (see below).

John's account of the plot hatched by 'the Pharisees and chief priests' is clearly an exercise in propaganda and apologetics, reflecting the need to deflect from the Romans, and onto "the Jews," primary responsibility for Jesus' death.

This idea, in various forms, was a recurring theme of both "official" and popular Catholic press coverage from the 1840s, which is the context for Pope Gregory XVI declaring that 'the Jews are a nation of deicides and blasphemers'; Christianity's 'sworn enemies'.[376]

Gregory's pronouncement, to our ears, is shocking, but it is typical of what most Christians of that era believed. And more to the point, its false representation of "the Jews", echoing passages in the New Testament, anticipated how, by the 1930s, popular Catholic anti-Semitism had nurtured support for Fascism, which in turn explains the Church's weak response to the terrors unleashed by Hitler and Mussolini.[377]

Racial hatred and a maniacal drive for world domination were key factors motivating the Axis powers during World War II. Christian prejudice had attributed these same repulsive dispositions to Jews, supported by the ludicrous claim that the Talmud encouraged *the* Jewish compulsion to take over the world, since all Jews were allegedly the 'sworn enemies' of Christianity.

QAnon, in our time, is *a conspiracy theory of everything movement* for the continuing dissemination of this vile claptrap, as well as providing a platform for the spreading of disinformation (material shared with the purpose of deception) regarding Covid-19 and the vaccines developed to fight it.

[Its *vaccine agenda* should not be confused with legitimate concerns pertinent to the study of side effects and related issues affecting the world-wide vaccination programme; see O' Murchu, *Beyond the Pandemic: Spiritual and Ecological Challenges* (Orbis, 2022).]

Q came to prominence following a cryptic remark, 'it's the calm before the storm', by (then president) Donald Trump in 2017, and after the attack of 6th January 2021 on the U.S. Capitol it soon became 'an international news curiosity', but even before then it had exerted its baleful influence on the Republican Party.[378]

Contributors to Q, in addition to promoting the lie that

Trump won the 2020 election, endorse contemporary versions of anti-Semitism. They refer to the murder of six million Jews during the War as "holohoax", with one post declaring *The Protocols of the Elders of Zion* to be 'pretty accurate, whether a forgery or not'. Q also depicts wealthy Jews as a protected group, scheming among themselves in cliques to amass riches and destroy those who oppose them, as well as espousing a modern version of the *blood libel* charge, centred on Adrenochrome, a chemical substance used to aid blood clotting.[379]

This compound, suggest *QAnon conspiracy theorists*, is a super drug extracted from the adrenal glands of young, living children, with the aim of conferring eternal life upon its consumers.[380]

Other Q *enthuasists* describe andrenochrome as 'the drug of the elites', sold on the black market and extracted from tortured youngsters, enabling famous people like Bill and Hilary Clinton to be child-blood drinkers, a ritual practice supposedly also indulged by many Jews.

Thousands of American children were said to have been kidnapped to facilitate these abhorrent rituals, and on television (2020) one mother 'claimed that her daughter had been kidnapped and ritually murdered to obtain andrenochrome'.[381]

This woman, almost 800 years after the appearance in 1144 of the *William of Norwich Blood Libel*, exemplifies the extent to which *history's longest hatred*, anti-Semitism, continues to pollute our religious and political discourse, failing to be 'a proclamation of liberation from death in the here and now'.

A particularly egregious example of this phenomenon is *Holocust Denial*, "holohoax", in the Q *lexicon*, a perfidious deceit not limited to *Qanon* believers, and one that brings dishonour upon our fragile humanity; for 'hostility and hatred directed against Judaism are in complete contradiction to the Christian vision of human dignity' (Pope John Paul II).[382]

Readers, at this point, may be questioning the relevance of much of this chapter to Jesus' resurrection. Its significance, after Auschwitz, is that Christians can witness authentically to their own faith tradition only if they honour unconditionally the religion of Jesus, a theme at the heart of this trilogy: *The Birth of Jesus the Jew*, *The Death of Jesus the Jew* and *The Resurrection of Jesus the Jew*.

And belief in his resurrection cannot have a privileged status removed from the effects of centuries of anti-Jewish teaching and practices sanctioned by the Church, outlined here and most particularly in *DJJ*.

Jews who undertake purposeful dialogue with Christians are very conscious of this history, one that Christians either ignore or play down, often drawing contorted distinctions between "unchanging doctrines", "teaching" and "popular beliefs".

In the words of William James, previously referenced, what matters ultimately is a religion's "cash value", and mainstream Christianity is now running out of its *currency reserves* in that area, increasingly prone to the allure of competing, potentially dangerous, fundamentalisms.

There never was, and there never will be, *good Christian anti-Semitism*. The concept is an outrageous and dangerous oxymoron, and it originated from New Testament passages such as these:

❖ 'You are from your father the devil, and you choose to do your father's desires. He was a murderer from the beginning ..., he is a liar and the father of lies' (Jn. 8:44, dated to c. 97).

❖ 'You suffered the same things from your own compatri-
ots as they did from the Jews, who killed both the lord
Jesus and the prophets ..., they have constantly been fill-
ing up the measure of their sins; but God's wrath has
overtaken them' (1 Thess. 2:14-16, abridged and dated
to c. 50).

Excerpts of this kind contributed to the development
of *bad Christian anti-Semitism* and the Holocaust deniers
of our time - like John's Gospel long before them (but in a
very different context) - promote a false narrative: that Jews
(and myriad others) are lying when they point to the ashes
that spewed from the chimneys of the death camps, 'to fall
nameless and graveless over a continent that had become a
graveyard.'[383]

(And see endnote 379, where Fintan O'Toole describes
anti-Semitism as 'hard-core racism'.)

For these and other reasons, Holocaust deniers must
be named for what they are: malicious heirs to those who
propagated older myths about the ritual murder of Gentile
children and farcical conspiracy theories of Jews plotting to
dominate the world, execrable slander-libels now resurrected courtesy of *QAnon* and similar purveyors of insidious disinformation. "Deniers" seek to make reason hostage to a particularly odious ideology, to paraphrase Deborah Lippstadt,
author of *Denying the Holocaust: The Growing Assault on Truth
and Memory*.

As Gill Seidal observes, 'those who today are denying the
reality of the Holocaust are not harmless cranks, like believers in a flat earth, or like those who claim to be visited regularly by extra-terrestrial beings'.[384]

The world, she notes, is 'a brighter place' thanks to the

amusing and quirky eccentricities of "flat-earthers"; but those who, in the face of overwhelming evidence to the contrary, persist in denying the Holocaust have allied themselves with evil forces in our society, but *light shines in the darkness, and the darkness will not overcome it* (Jn. 1:5, adapted).

In the Fourth Gospel, "light" is a recurring theme, typified by the evangelist having Jesus say, 'I have come as light into the world, so that everyone who believes in me should not remain in the darkness' (Jn. 12:46).

This verse is part of a section (12:44-50) where, at the end of his public ministry and alluding to Deuteronomy, Jesus implies that those who refuse 'to heed the prophets sent by God are condemned', and they will not inherit eternal life.[385]

By the time this gospel was written, perhaps as long as fifty years after 1 Thessalonians (our first New Testament writing), a tradition that "the Jews" had killed Jesus had become firmly entrenched.

We see its embryonic form represented in the passage given above (1 Th. 2:14-16), a calamitous and gross distortion of historical truth that has persisted down the centuries and championed by *L'Osservatore Romano* as recently as 1897 (and later), by its references to *this deicide and treacherous people*. Holocaust deniers peddle similar untruths, ostensibly for very different reasons.

The remote causes, however, of such distortions, regardless of who promotes them, may be traced back to what has been called the *New Testament's texts of terror* (see Foreword), of which 1 Thess. 2:14-16 is a notorious example.

Scholars debate its provenance, with one explanation being that it is an interpolation. The two verses can be removed from the letter without affecting its flow and overall meaning, but – as Amy Jill Levine notes – even if Paul was not their author, we must deal with the anti-Jewish nature of the text as it now stands, 'since what one intends and what another hears are not always the same thing'.[386]

What matters is that 1 Thessalonians generally reflects an apocalyptic worldview, that is, one in which, as the end-time approaches, humanity is divided into those who have the correct belief (*orthodoxy*) and those who are damned because of their *heresy*.[387]

It is against this background that we should understand the earliest known reference to the resurrection, where Paul praises Gentile converts for turning away from idols, 'to serve a living and true God'; the same God who raised Jesus from the dead (1:9-10, abridged).[388]

Verse 10 concludes with this clause: 'Jesus, who rescues us from the wrath that is coming'. It is a midrash on Ezekiel 38:18-23, which addresses how God's righteous anger and deliverance will be manifested at the end-time. This conviction is now applied to the resurrected Jesus as God's agent, validating Paul's belief that Jesus is the messiah.[389]

Chapter 10 has shown how, for St Paul, *Adam's faults* are redeemed through Jesus: 'God proves his love for us that while we were still sinners Christ died for us' (Rom. 5:8). He affirms the same idea in 1 Thessalonians, using the language of "rescue" and "wrath", and later developed (in)famously by St Augustine's notion of *Original Sin*, with its concomitant notion that *it* is transmitted through the "seed of Adam", indicating that – one way or another – humankind 'is in a state of alienation from God'.[390]

It was almost certainly Paul who established this distinctive relationship between "resurrection" and "universal rescue", thereby constituting Jesus as a quasi-divine figure, but it is very unlikely that Jesus' original discipleship group

– who on the whole were Jews influenced by Pharisaism – would have made this identification.

They nonetheless read some kind of sacrificial meaning into Jesus' death and resurrection (hence the *Last Supper* narrative, which does not report an event in real time[391]). That significance they conceived in terms of Jesus' presumed messianic status, which complemented the belief in his resurrection within the template of first century Jewish thought. "Sin", however, would not have been a determining focus of that matrix, in the manner that it became so integral to Pauline Christianity.

Christians seldom appreciate that normative Judaism has a rather different understanding of sin to the one promoted by Paul. Unlike him and the Church which he effectively founded, it has never subscribed to the concept of *fallen human nature, the negative anthropology* that people are born in a state of estrangement from God. In this regard, to paraphrase Amy-Jill Levine, Judaism has no need of a *rescue-intermediary theology* centred on the person of Jesus as a saviour figure.[392]

For Jesus, sin was about transgressions against God and neighbour - 'Hear, O Israel: the Lord our God, the Lord is one ..., and you shall love your neighbour as yourself. There is no other commandment greater than these' (Mk. 12:29-31). He never subscribed to the belief that sin is somehow rooted in human nature.

That idea originated with Paul, as a midrash of sorts on the Hebrew word *het*, meaning 'to miss' or 'to fail'. If, as noted above, the terms *good anti-Semitism* and *bad ani-Semitism* are dangerous conceptions, an argument can also be made that *St Paul's midrash on sin*, grafted onto belief in the resurrection of Jesus, has had some appalling (unintended) consequences.

When Paul wrote 1 Thessalonians, famous for its "trumpet blast" to accompany the Lord's return (4:16), he thought he would have been alive at Jesus' second coming, and in his last known letter – Romans – its recipients were assured that 'salvation is near', for 'the night is far gone, the day is at hand' (13:11-12).

Paul was mistaken, of course, but his conviction that Jesus had been raised from the dead nonetheless confirmed his apocalyptic worldview that the Kingdom was about to irrupt into history; and, whilst Jesus confined his ministry to Jews, Paul (probably unaware of this restriction) promoted his mission in the Diaspora.

For him, faith in Christ enabled Gentiles to repudiate their former sinful ways: Jesus' crucifixion and resurrection defeated the hold sin and death had over humankind.

Rejected by mainstream Judaism (even if, like Jesus, he lived and died a Jew), the words below, attributed to Paul at Corinth, and written after his death, typify how by c. 90 the nascent Jesus movement was moving inexorably away from the parent religion (up to this point, it may have remained a more or less tolerated sect within Judaism):

> Your blood be on your own heads! I am
> innocent.
> From now on, I will go to the Gentiles (Acts
> 18:6b; cf. 13:46 and Mt. 27:24-25[393]).

The wording, given the subsequent Jewish-Christian relationship is, to say the least, unfortunate. But it illustrates how an anti-Jewish tradition, first recorded in 1 Thessalonians and later appropriated by the Gentile Christianity St Paul founded, led in time to the racial anti-Semitism of the nineteenth century, which paved the road to Auschwitz. And it endures to this day in the loathsome new phenomenon of Holocaust Denial, be it "soft" (minimising the extent of the Shoah) or "hard" (Jews have fabricated it).

Today's anti-Semitism is "new" only because 'the modern advocate of Jew-killing is likely to be scrupulous in denying that he is in fact an anti-Semite'.[394]

When Paul wrote of Jesus rescuing the believers of Thessalonica from 'the wrath that is coming', he had no way of envisaging how - 2,000 years later - his fellow Jews might view that pronouncement, millions of whom, within living memory, having witnessed an *apocalyptic wrath* of a very different order: the systematic attempt, at the heart of a *Christian continent no longer Christ-like*, to murder by gas, bullet and fire the descendants of *Jesus the Jew*.

Christians cannot go behind Auschwitz and undo the centuries' long *teaching of contempt* that was its seedbed. That background provided the Nazis with historical precedent of Jews being confined to ghettos, barred from dining/recreational areas, made to wear the yellow star and discriminated against in law (the notorious "race defilement" statute, for example), to name but some of the many decrees enforced against them.

Laws are windows into a society's values, to paraphrase Harry J. Cargas, and the Third Reich succeeded in establishing a culture in which the law, no longer serving the interests of justice, became an instrument of totalitarian oppression, exemplifying these famous words of Raul Hilberg (d. 2007):

> The Nazis did not discard the past; they built upon it.

They did not begin a development; they completed it.

Claims that the Nazis were the enemies of Christianity as
much as they were of Judaism necessitate careful and sensitive evaluation, and not least because National Socialism was
the agency for implementing, albeit in uniquely evil ways,
prejudices long embedded in the social fabric of Christian
Europe.

Indeed, some commentators have argued (mistakenly, in
my view) that Nazism arose from Christianity as a "natural
development", a position adopted in the light of one interpretation of Hilberg's *The Destruction of the European Jews*.
Nonetheless, there remains food for thought in Elie Wiesel's
remark during a television interview, that 'Christianity died
in Auschwitz'.

For Sandra Schneiders, the *bodily* resurrection of Jesus, as
Saturation Event, is of universal significance.

Her belief may or may not be true, but what is indubitable is that another *saturation event*, the systematic attempt
to exterminate the Jews of Europe, is *the Event* of universal
significance that will forever more determine how Christians
respond to this question, placed on the lips of Jesus after his
death and resurrection:

Who do people say that I am? (Mk.8:27; cf. Mt.
16:13-20)

Our task now, eschewing all forms of religious fundamentalism (especially the anti-Semitism of the Christian Right)
and political totalitarianism, is to journey beyond the death
camps - together with their survivor-victims - and shape, if

possible, a different future. This endeavour will entail not only an improved Christian theology of Judaism, but 'a revision of Christian theology altogether'.[395] That undertaking, in the shadows cast by the Holocaust, is enormous, and it will not be completed in my lifetime, if ever.

It is all the more daunting when we realise, again paraphrasing Diarmuid O'Murchu, that the religions of today are heirs to a long patriarchal tradition of *will-to-power*, contaminated by a prolonged evolutionary phase of domination, control and violence, which nowadays is typically mirrored in, and camouflaged by, theological dogmatism and obfuscation.[396]

Hans Küng was so right to have insisted that without peace between the religions there can be no peace amongst the nations, an apposite adage when the current Israeli-Hamas War is clearly underpinned by unnamed religious ideologies.

The use of precise language (how "genocide", is interpreted, for example) is a casualty of this conflict, but it remains an imperative always to call out atrocities of war for what they are and, at time of writing, Israel's response to the heinous attack of 7th October 2023 has assumed a character wholly disproportionate to its legitimate aim to rid the region of the Hamas terrorists who seek to eliminate Israel, but *ends never justify means.*

There are dangerous political and religious fundamentalists on both sides of this appalling conflict, promoting "more violence the better", because that is how their "God" will supposedly deliver the outcome they want.

"Dialogue" is more urgent than ever, an invitation to all people of goodwill to

- recognise with utter honesty the atrocities of the past
- acknowledge that we cannot change the past, but that

it is possible, to paraphrase the late Fr Gabriel Daly (d.2023), to risk a new future, other than the one imposed by the past or by memory

❖ accept, with humility, the need for reconciliation and forgiveness, based upon genuine respect for the other, in recognition of the fact that 'the peoples of the world have not yet learnt that one piece of ground is no more and no less sacred than any other and that descent does not confer superiority or spiritual authority' (Thomas Fawcett).

In furthering these endeavours, to return to the rhetorical question asked towards the end of Chapter 11 regarding the differences between Crossan and Wright: 'Yes', how we understand *The Resurrection of Jesus the Jew* is of minor significance in light of the greater challenge now ahead of us: the imperative to reimagine the entire Christian narrative and how that regenerated vision will challenge societies now facing the menace of so-called *alternative realities*.

To paraphrase (newly-created) Cardinal Timothy Radcliffe OP, we cannot afford the luxury of entertaining "your truth" and "my truth", at the cost of losing touch with truth itself.

Tim Crane, in *The Meaning of Belief*, observes rightly 'how utterly different the religious impulse is from science or any other epistemic endeavour', and that comprehensive accounts of how religion functions in today's world must take seriously this difference.[397]

What Crane says of religion(s) in general applies in particular to our study of Jesus' resurrection, and he quotes with approval a famous statement of Alfred North Whitehead, mathematician and theologian (see endnote 346), adapted here:

> Resurrection is the vision of something which
> stands beyond, behind and within the passing
> flux of immediate concerns; it is real, and yet
> waiting to be realised; something which is a
> remote possibility and yet the greatest of present
> facts; something that has meaning and yet eludes
> our understanding; something which is the ulti-
> mate ideal, and perhaps a hopeless quest.[398]

Whitehead's reflection will never satisfy those, like Tom Wright, who insist that the *First Easter* is about something that happened to Jesus independently of the effect that his life had on the original discipleship group, but for a moment let us indulge a thought experiment.[399]

Suppose that Paul never had a *temper tantrum* ('I will go to the Gentiles'), that at the *Council of Jerusalem* (see Acts 15) he and James, the natural brother of Jesus, had agreed that all converts to the new movement should adhere to Torah pre-cepts, against the (notional) background of thousands of Jews having already rallied to Jesus' message during his lifetime.

This message would have included the proclamation that Jesus was the long-awaited messiah and King David's succes-sor (in the New Testament, of course, Jesus himself makes no such explicit claim[400]). In turn, this would have resulted in Jesus' execution, since the Romans were ruthless in eliminat-ing messianic contenders (his death was certainly "political", but not occasioned by Zealot-like activities).

Soon afterwards, word began to circulate about Jesus' res-urrection. What would have been the outcome had this be-lief been accompanied not by an emphasis on some kind of primitive atonement theory but an emphasis instead on the pre-eminence of the forgiveness of sin? On the assumption that such a development had occurred, along with the above-mentioned *rapprochement between Paul and James*, the result – far more likely than not – would have been the Jesus movement's continued status as a sect within Judaism, with outcomes very different from those familiar to us:

- ❖ What, by c. 80, had become known as "Christianity" (see Acts 11:26) would never have spread throughout the Roman Empire and, later, the wider world, and 'there would have been no Western civilization as we know it'.

- ❖ As a sect, Christianity would have disappeared in the fallout from the *First Great Jewish-Roman War*, similar to the fate that befell the Essenes and Sadducees (see Chapter 2).

Islam would probably have arisen, however, and Rabbinic Judaism, born in the aftermath of the trauma of the Second Temple's destruction (Israel's greatest catastrophe until the Holocaust), would have developed into the forms of Judaism known today.

These expressions of Judaism subscribe to belief in the general resurrection of the dead without any need to invoke Jesus as "proof" or "evidence" for that belief, contrary to St Paul's famous assertion:

> Christ has been raised from the dead, the first fruits of those who have died. For since death came through a human being, the resurrection of the dead has also come through a human being (1 Cor. 15:20-21).

Here, the context is important. Paul is not making a

throwaway comment; going on to draw a parallel between Adam and Christ, his point is that Jesus is the agent of life for everyone – in other words, "universalism" is the proper focus of the Gentile mission (see Gal. 3:28, where all are said to be 'one in Christ Jesus'.)

Rom. 8:29 complements this claim, referencing Jesus as 'the firstborn within a large family', the enabler of a new, re-deemed, humanity, to be realised by virtue of his role as *the* messiah.[401]

What Judaism, from the first century, disputes with Christianity is not the general circumstances of Jesus' death (though great care needs to be exercised here), but the question of his messiahship and it is mistaken to think that a majority of Jews rejected Jesus, for this simple reason: few of them knew anything about him.

Related to this fact are the considerations, previously indicated, that the messiah of expectation was not a divine figure, no more than it was expected he would come back from the dead. It is utterly mistaken, therefore, to accuse Jews then, now or at any time, of having failed to recognise their messiah. Owing to Christian claims that Jesus was the long-awaited messiah, overmuch attention has been paid to its role in first century Jewish thinking, 'giving it an exagger-ated importance'.[402]

This exaggeration is a consequence of Christians think-ing, again mistakenly, that belief in the resurrection of Jesus somehow clinches their arguments promoting his messianic status, which in time also served as "proof" that he is divine.

Allied to this observation is the further consideration that, because Paul links the notion of "resurrection" with "univer-salism", Christians tend to infer, understandably, that the latter concept was central to the Judaism of the late Second

Temple period. It is St Paul who, as with so much else, is responsible for the dominance of this idea in Christianity.

Or, to express this thought another way: Judaism has always emphasised the sanctification of the world; Christianity generally insists on saving the world, and its rationale for that imperative centres on the belief that Jesus is 'the first fruits of those who have died', in the context of Paul's further claim that if justification comes through the Law, then 'Christ has died in vain' (Gal. 2:21).

Returning to our 'thought experiment', is it possible that Paul (a genius, if a tortured one) has taken a story about Jesus' resurrection and transformed it, as "midrash", into a narrative about universal salvation that had little, if anything, to do with the historical Jesus and those who accompanied him during his ministry?

It is also necessary to remember that, following the researches of Vermes and other scholars, Christianity remains faced with the awkward dilemma that the historical Jesus seems not to have exhibited greet interest in resurrection belief.

Would Jesus, dying on a cross the victim of Roman hegemony, have identified explicitly or implicitly with what Paul claimed in his name?, for Jesus 'was sent only to the lost sheep of the house of Israel' (Mt. 15:24).

Vermes, the late doyen of Jesus scholarship, certainly thinks not, arguing that, within a generation of Paul's death, no Jew was able to find acceptable the incultured legacy of Jesus: 'In fact, I think he himself would have failed to acknowledge it as his own.'[403]

In other words, could the Apostle's purpose have been served by utilising any other idea current at the time (*forgiveness of sins*, for example)?

Were there to be an affirmative answer to this question, it would suggest that "resurrection" need not have become the litmus test of belief so identified with Christians' faith in Jesus as the messiah, and that had it not been for two "accidents of history", the "conversions" of Paul and Constantine, the *Jesus Sect* would have been little more than a footnote in the history of Judaism, since it is difficult, but not impossible, to imagine how *forgiveness* could have been the disciples' focal point of their mission subsequent to Jesus' ignominious death.

Not even someone of the genius of Saul of Tarsus could have made *forgiveness of sins* the raison d'être of the Gentile mission.

Should this hypothesis (or something comparable) have materialised, there would have been no *good* and *bad anti-Semitism*, no *Anguish of the Jews*, no *Holocaust* and no *Holocaust Deniers*, but there would still have been that *First Easter*, with this difference: No one, 2,000 years later, would be reading books about it, notwithstanding the probable certainty that the New Testament would have been completed by c. 125.

Like the *Dead Sea Scrolls* (discovered in 1947), only a small number of academic specialists would be studying the New Testament today, but "midrash" would have endured for centuries after Jesus' death as a way of making sense of the Jewish experience of God.

This genre, by the early centuries of the Christian era, was well established in the life of Jews; the *Mishnah* (a collection of oral legal traditions dating from c. 200) has many examples of it. Some experts limit their use of the term to 'rabbinic commentaries in which part of the history of Jewish interpretative activity is collected', but all examples of biblical interpretation from the late Second Temple period (c.

167 BCE to 70/73 CE), including the New Testament, 'are midrashic', though they could also be termed "midrsh-like", observes Peter Enns.[404]

Kunst's account of *The Road to Emmaus* in Chapter 9 of this book is illustrative of what Enns means, where we are told that the risen Jesus explained to Cleopas and his companion that the messiah had to suffer 'and then enter into his glory' (Lk. 24:26).

"Emmaus" is part-derived from Hos. 6:1-2 ('... on the third day he will raise us up, that we may live before him'), and its original context, in addition to the speaker being Israel, was to castigate believers for having compromised their commitment to Yahweh in favour of a Pagan fertility cult.

Luke uses it to provide support from the Hebrew Scriptures for his community's belief that a morally perfect Jesus, raised from the dead, has redeemed Israel's rebellion against Yahweh, but – for obvious reasons – this interpretation was by no means shared by everyone.

The overwhelming majority of Jews (about one million lived in Palestine and a further five million in the Diaspora, on one estimate) had no interest in this midrashic "take" on Hosea, understanding it to run counter to the text's plain meaning.

The phrase 'their eyes were opened' (Lk. 24:31) makes sense, in the judgement of some Jewish scholars, only if 'what Jesus meant to do was found a new religion'.[405]

Jesus, of course, never had any such intention, but by the time St Luke wrote his gospel the movement founded in Jesus' name had begun to move in a new direction. The main purposes of the *Emmaus Story* is to indicate that, like the rabbis, Jesus was authorised to interpret the scriptures: 'Beginning with Moses and all the prophets, he interpreted to them all the things about himself in all the scriptures' (24:27).

Moses was regarded as author of the Torah, which Jesus was now said to fulfil, and so it was important for Luke to establish that Jesus was passing on both his own authority and the mediating role exercised by Moses to the newly established movement. This claim, encapsulated in the phrase 'all the things about himself', was jaw-dropping in its implications.

It is no exaggeration to say, with the benefit of hindsight, that it constituted a major turning point in the history of the West, if not the entire world, particularly when read in conjunction with the verse below from the same author and attributed to James, leader of the church in Jerusalem. He is proposing a compromise for Gentiles who wish to embrace Christianity, thereby avoiding the *circumcision problem*[406] :

> We should write to them, merely to abstain
> from anything polluted by idols, from illicit
> marriages, from the meat of strangled animals
> and from blood (Acts 15:19).

These conditions can be summarised in two minimal requirements: the avoidance of non-kosher foods and immoral sexual practices. In time, only the latter prohibition survived into subsequent centuries, and the rest - as the saying goes - *is history.*

When, taken together with 1 Cor 57b ('Christ, our paschal lamb is sacrificed'), these passages provided a mandate for Paul's outreach to the Gentiles, a mission that succeeded in ways far beyond his expectations.

Indeed, it is not hyperbolic to suggest that, because the vast majority of Jews rejected Paul's teachings, 'there is such a thing as Christian civilization' (see endnote 413).

The New Testament, in various ways, makes claim to this mandated authority derived from Jesus, via Paul, with consequences that have been mostly calamitous for Judaism. We Christians understandably view passages such as "Emmaus", "Acts" and "1 Corinthians" through the filter of 2,000 years of doctrinal development, but Jews understand them very differently, and with good reason.

Christians interpret the *Emmaus Story*, for example, as validating *The First Easter*, forgetting that 'the resurrection works as a proof that Jesus was "the Christ" only if you have already accepted *his authority* to render interpretations of scripture contrary to the obvious meaning of the words'.[407]

In this regard, whilst the genre of midrash has shaped the New Testament, it should be remembered - contrary to the impression given by Kunst (and other Evangelical Christians) - that many Jews consider Christians' use of it an abuse, for the reason that it can imply abrogation of the Sinai Covenant, exemplified by *Emmaus Exegesis*.

And, in turn, this can amount - without people realising it - to giving Hitler a posthumous victory, as well as potentially offering a twisted rationale for the repulsive lies promoted by *Holocaust Deniers*.

"Abrogation" has a long history, extending back to the New Testament, but it was an infamous homily preached by Melito, Bishop of Sardis (*the poet of deicide*, d. 190), that set the pattern for the Jewish-Christian relationship up to virtually our own time.

The sermon was delivered on a year when Passover and Easter coincided, always a particularly volatile situation in the early centuries, and it provides us with the first known reference to deicide, a charge levelled by a pope as recently as the 1840s (see above):

> God has been murdered; the King of Israel has
> been slain by an Israelite hand.[408]

Jews, for centuries, have suffered the anguish of persecution consequent upon the promotion of this warped narrative. It marks a point by which time Christianity had truly emerged as a religion in its own right, having effectively perfected *exegetical acrobatics* in its interpretation of Old Testament passages, with particular – but certainly not exclusive – regard to explanations of Jesus' resurrection, described by one commentator as 'the greatest escape fantasy ever told'.[409]

This sceptical assessment of the data, contrary to the position adopted by Tom Wright and Sandra Schneiders, has the merit nonetheless of reminding us of the circularity in Christian thinking (indicated above) that is often a feature of this discussion – that, for example, Jesus' resurrection is "proof" of claims made about him (see 'Maccoby', below).

Matthew Tindal, referenced in the previous chapter, had his finger on the pulse of this difficulty when he pointed to the 'odd jumble' caused by trying to establish the truth of religious propositions on the basis of the concepts themselves.[410]

Applying Tindal's witty observation to the resurrection, the problem, too often, is that many Christians make their case largely on the basis of an appeal to the authority of the Bible, but this approach assumes what it sets out to establish.

And when Christians argue for the resurrection as the ultimate evidence that Jesus and his mission were vindicated by God, they don't have in mind only that *First Easter* (the story of the empty tomb etc.). Their point is that it was the resurrection by itself, on its own merits and entirely inde-pendent of other criteria, that elevated Jesus 'from the rank of mere prophet and wonderworker to that of Son of God'.[411]

The vast majority of Palestinian Jews at the time did not see matters that way, and it is a virtual certainty that Jews in the Diaspora knew nothing of Jesus during his lifetime, similar to how St Paul had very limited knowledge of the his-torical Jesus.

There are three summary reasons why Palestinian Jews in particular would not have shared the views of Jesus' followers:

- A standard criterion for the acceptance or rejection of religious claims was what Scripture taught about these matters, and no passages therein pointed to resurrec-tion as a touchstone for recognising the coming of the messiah, for this reason: the New Testament's authors devoted much effort to making such connections (see 1 Cor. 15:3-4, for instance), where in reality none existed. Such a hypothetical event, therefore, would not prove anything, regardless of who proclaimed it.

- Another feature of Jesus' resurrection is the paucity of witnesses to it (with the possible exception of what Paul relates in 1 Cor. 15:5[412]), whereas 'Jews were accus-tomed to far higher standards of reliability'. When God spoke at Sinai, for example, the entire nation is said to have been present: 'On the morning of the third day, ... there was thunder and the blast of a loud trumpet ..., and Moses brought the people out of the camp to meet God' (Ex. 19:16-17). The "third day" symbolism is clear-ly significant (see Chapter 5), and the point of these observations is that 'if it was God's habit to seek mass witness to his greatest deeds, then why not with Jesus' resurrection?'

✥ Even if, following Wright and Schneiders, the historical veracity of the resurrection is taken as a given, it's still not clear what, if anything, it would mean or prove. The implication has always been that it transcends, if the resurrection does not actually abrogate, the Sinai covenant, but Jesus thought no such thing. Generations of Jews to this day (*Messianic Jews* and *Jews for Jesus* are exceptions proving the rule) have never subscribed to the notion that *The First Easter replaces Sinai*. Paul, who certainly thought that Gentile Christians had no need of "Sinai", nonetheless recognised that God's promises to the Jews endures forever (see Rom. 9 and 11:1-2, previously referenced), which is the context for understanding problematical verses such as 'Christ is the end of the law, so that there may be righteousness for everyone who believes' (Rom. 10:4).[413]

If, as seems likely from the perspective of the overwhelming majority of Jesus' contemporaries, the resurrection did not elevate him 'from the rank of mere prophet', there is no doubting the fact that whilst the Jews' rejection of *Jesus the Jew* was one thing (and for good reason), their rejection of *the Christian Jesus*, that is, the Christ of the church once it had become established as an exclusively Gentile entity, was a very different matter altogether.

Christianity, of course, did not emerge as a separate religion until long after the outcome of the First Great JewishRoman War, but it is reasonable to suppose that its seeds were planted once the presumed messiah had been crucified, which necessitated a radical reinterpretation of everything Jesus' followers thought they knew about the anticipated messiah.[414]

The focus of this book, concluding a trilogy devoted to the furtherance of Jewish-Christian dialogue, has been how belief in Jesus' resurrection was the main response to the dissonance consequent upon the violent death of he whom Peter proclaimed to be 'the Christ, the Son of the living God' (Mt. 16:16), and by this appellation Jesus has been known for 2,000 years.

For much of that time, Christianity ignored the full significance of its *midrashic origins* in the religion of Jesus, *the resurrected Jew*, with disastrous consequences for his people.

The rabbis, observes David Klinghoffer, had taught that the messiah, son of David, would not die before the completion of his mission, and so Christians drew the inference that the rabbis must be wrong – that they were *Christ Deniers*.

And from this assumption it was a small step to the scapegoating of Jews as *Christ Killers*: 'a nation of deicides and blasphemers' (Pope Gregory XVI).

St Paul, our first witness to the story of Jesus' resurrection, has frequently in the course of Western history been identified with Pope Gregory's excoriating sentiment. The truth of the matter, however, is very different.

Once we realise, to echo Charles Freeman, that accounts of Jesus' resurrection have for too long been removed from 'the context of the times in which it is said to have happened' - making of it a unique historical experience - it becomes possible to see Paul and the writers of the gospels in a new light, as authors 'who were placing Jesus within Jewish tradition rather than alienating him from it' (*A New History of Early Christianity*, p. 39; for a somewhat contrary view, see endnotes 203 and 208).

When that tradition, from c. 90, became incultured in Gentile contexts far removed from its originating matrix availing of 'midrash', there developed an understanding of Jesus and Judaism that was alien to the first century reality of vibrant, if fragile, communities.

These were characterised by an appreciation of diversity as a medium for communicating the universality of God's love, a perspective soon lost by Christians who prioritised *orthodoxy* over *orthopraxis*; and, in the process, failed to do justice to history's most famous Jew, born in Nazareth, who proclaimed the good news of the Kingdom.

It was Paul, however, following a mystical experience of the crucified-risen Jesus, who transformed that message into a mission that has swept the world; and, to paraphrase Paula Fredrikensen's words in the Introduction, the world still awaits Jesus' return in glory: the Kingdom of good news is yet to come. For some commentators, that 'mystical experience' was the manifestation of 'a mere psychological seizure' (see endnote 208), and yet it has changed the world!

There is no doubt that belief in the resurrection of Jesus identified the movement after his death and to which he has given his (*sur*)name; without that belief, it – like other messianic movements – 'would simply have ceased to exist' (Hyam Maccoby).

It is wholly mistaken, however, to imagine that this conviction implied the abandonment of Judaism, 'as long as it did not involve a deification of Jesus or the abrogation of Torah as the means to salvation' (MPC, p. 125).

In this context, the Church, until fairly recently, effectively adopted a supersessionist view of Judaism, that its prophets were said to have prepared the way for Jesus and that the

Jewish people were blind to the presence of the messiah in their midst. This was the background to the notorious Good Friday prayer, revoked by Pope John XXIII:

> Let us pray for the perfidious Jews, that our
> God and Lord may remove the veil from their
> hearts ... Hear our prayers, which we offer for
> the blindness of that people ..., that they may be
> rescued from their darkness.

The Resurrection of Jesus the Jew and its two accompanying volumes are a small contribution to reanchoring Jesus and Paul in the flow of history, once again mindful of Geza Vermes' observation that, for Christians, 'the dilemma to be confronted and resolved is how to reconcile the extreme importance ascribed to the resurrection by Christianity with the very limited amount of discernible interest in the subject in the authentic teaching of Jesus' (see endnote 35).

When Christians place disproportionate emphasis on the miracles of Jesus (miracle-working was typical of the era, attributable to wholly human figures), in addition to failing to contextualise his resurrection appearances (which were experienced by people of faith alone), they risk wrongly separating Jesus from his Jewish milieu, argues James Carroll, in *Christ Actually* (pp. 133, 139).

The long history of the Jewish-Christian relationship is testimony to the appalling consequences of indulging this form of theological amnesia, to the extent that Harry J. Cargas poses this question: 'Will there be, can there be, a resurrection for Christianity?' (*Shadows of Auschwitz: A Christian Response to the Holocaust*, p. 1)

The question haunted Cargas (d. 1998) and it haunts me,

alive to these words from one of the lesser known documents of Vatican II: 'Truth cannot impose itself except by virtue of its own truth' (*Dignitatis Humanae*). Transformation, not improvement, is now an urgent imperative, for Christianity still has a long way to go if it is to be rescued from its blindness and darkness.

The story told of the old lady at the end of the Introduction to this book, '*I just glories to hear it again*', reminds us that whatever truth (however we understand it) is affirmed by Christians' proclamation of that *First Easter*, it must forever more be lived, 'as hope and obligation', with our faces turned to Auschwitz, in the spirit of this sentiment:

If ever it comes to a choice between Jesus and truth, we must always choose truth, because disloyalty to truth will always prove in the long run to have been disloyalty to Jesus the Jew. (Simone Weil, slightly adapted)

Timeline

Many of the dates in this *Timeline* are approximations, with some obvious exceptions – the destruction of Jerusalem's Second Temple in 70 CE, for example.

The *Table* has been compiled from a variety of sources, with particular regard to Paula Fredriksen's *When Christians Were Jews: The First Generation*, Edward Kessler's *An Introduction to Jewish-Christian Relations*, Simon Schama's *The Story of the Jews: 1000 BCE – 1492 CE* and Geza Vermes' *The Authentic Gospel of Jesus*.

BCE

1600 Abraham

1500 The first recorded historical reference to Israel, on a stone slab

990 David consolidates the cult in the Temple; Solomon, his son, builds the First Temple

928 Israel divides into Judah and Israel

722 Assyria conquers the North (Israel); deportation of the *Ten Tribes*

628 The probable year of Zoroaster's birth

551 Zoroaster's likely year of death

597 Nebuchadnezzar lays siege to Jerusalem and deports its elite

587 The final destruction of Solomon's Temple by the Babylonians, led By Nebuchadnezzar

538   Cyrus, King of Persia, after conquering Babylon, permits Jews to return from their *Babylonian Exile*

520 to 515   Building of the Second Temple

332   Alexander the Great (d. 323) conquers Judaea

200   The Bible, at Alexandria, is translated into Greek (*the Septuagint*, known also as the *the LXX*)

167 to 161   The Hasmonean Revolt against the Seleucids, led by the Maccabees, after Antiochus IV had forced Greek customs on the Jews

166   Approximate date for the emergence of the Pharisees (*Qumran Community*)

165   Antiochus IV "abolishes" Judaism

130   Possible date for the start of the Essene settlement at Qumran

74   Birth of Herod the Great

63   Pompey in Jerusalem; Judaea becomes a Roman province

37   Herod establishes the Herodian dynasty

27   Augustus becomes emperor (until 14 CE)

4   The probable year of Jesus' birth (but see 'Luke', below)

4   Death of Herod the Great and the kingdom is divided between his three surviving sons; Archelaus is appointed ethnarch of Judaea and Samaria (until 6 CE) and Antipas becomes tetrarch of Galilee (until 39 CE)

CE

6   Judaea governed by Roman prefects (until 41); Census for tax purposes; birth of Jesus, according to Luke's Gospel (2: 1-7)

10   Birth of Saul ('Paul') of Tarsus

14   Tiberius becomes emperor

18   Caiaphas appointed high priest (until 36)

26   Pontius Pilate appointed prefect of Judaea (until 36)

29   Ministry and execution of John the Baptist; ministry of Jesus, born in Nazareth, begins

30	Crucifixion of Jesus (7th April in our calendar); the *First Easter* (9th April)

30   Crucifixion of Jesus (7th April in our calendar); the *First Easter* (9th April)

35   The Jesus movement begins to spread in the Diaspora

37   Birth of Flavius Josephus (died c. 100); Caligula becomes emperor

49   Council of Jerusalem

50   1 Thessalonians, first known letter of Paul (Romans is the last known one, c. 57)

62   Death of James, brother of Jesus

64   Martyrdom of Peter, in Rome, related by Eusebius (see below)

64   Nero's persecution of Christians in Rome (until 67)

66   Outbreak of the (first) Great-Jewish War (until 73)

68   As the Roman armies move south from Damascus, they obliterate the Essene settlement at Qumran; Nero dies by suicide

70   Destruction of the Second Temple, by Titus (emperor from 79 to 81)

67   Martyrdom of Paul, in Rome, related by Eusebius

70   Gospel of Mark (2 Peter is the last 'book' of the New Testament, c. 125)

73   Fall of Masada

78   The probable year Josephus completed *Jewish War*

90   The Council of Jamnia

120   Gospel of Peter

120   Earliest known extant New Testament fragment [a copy of John 18:38 ("Pilate asked him, 'What is truth?'") and preserved in the *Rylands Library*, Manchester] is dated to this year

132   Second Great Jewish-Roman War (until 135), led by Bar Kochba

200   Codification of the Mishnah

500s   Talmuds: "Babylonian" and "Palestinian" – the "Heart of Judaism"

Endnotes

1   *Vicars of Christ: The Dark Side of the Papacy* (VoC, Bantam Press, 1988; the references to Gladstone and Lincoln in Chapter 12, and the "shepherds' quotation", are from pp. 135 and 246.)

2   Its full title is *The Pope at War: The Secret History of Pius XII, Mussolini, and Hitler* (PaW , Oxford University Press, 2022)

3   Ibid, p. 480

4   Ibid, p. 162

5   Ibid, pp. 195 and 528 – The 'man sent from God' is an obvious allusion to John the Baptist (see Mk. 1:1-11 and parallels). For this bishop, it would seem that Mussolini was "John the Baptist" to Hitler's "Jesus".

6   Ibid, p. 195

7   Ibid, p. 121

8   Ibid, p. 200

9   *DJJ* recognises that Pius XII's wartime record continues to have many defenders, one typical example of which is Rodney Stark in *Bearing False Witness: Debunking Centuries of Anti-Catholic History* (SPCK, 2017, pp. 29-35). Quoting the Jewish academic Pinchas Lapide, Stark (d. 2022) claims that Pius was instrumental in saving perhaps as many as 860,000 Jews from 'certain death' (p. 31), and he suggests further that the 'historical libel' perpetrated against Pius has come mainly from 'alienated Catholics'. In addition, Stark dismisses Kertzer's academic work as 'unscholarly' (p. 33), presumably a reference to some of Kertzer's thirteen other books – *The Popes Against the Jews: The Vatican's Role in the Rise of Modern anti-Semitism* (PAJ), for example. The claim is preposterous. Chapter 12 will be referring to some material in this book, which was written in response to Pope John Paul II's *We Remember: A Reflection on the Shoah* (1998). In addition, readers are referred to Michael Burleigh's writings, an English expert on Nazi Germany. He says that Kertzer's books are 'prejudiced',

failing to reference the fact that the Nazis were the quintessential party of many disgruntled Lutherans, and that liberal Protestantism often licensed unsupported racial views, and that 'many leading Protestant theologians were anti-Semitic in ways that had no Catholic equivalent'. Interested parties should also consult what Eugene Fisher, formerly chief adviser to the *Secretariat for Catholic-Jewish Relations of the United States Bishops' Conference*, observes about Kertzer's books. The essence of these criticisms of Kertzer (some better than others) is that he does not give sufficient attention to the 'multi-pronged strategies' adopted by Pius (William Doino, who says that the pope 'served both truth and love'). Mgr. Hugh O'Flaherty (d. 1963) was a senior Vatican figure, amongst others, who was not intimidated by the Nazis. From the Vatican, he organised and led a very successful resistance movement, and O'Flaherty's brave efforts have been immortalised in the film *The Scarlet and the Black*, starring Gregory Peck (1983). In Killarney, Co. Kerry, there is a powerful and moving street memorial honouring this brave man, and there is good reason for thinking that Pius XII applauded his efforts. This inference is supported by an article by Felicity O'Brien (at the time a lecturer in history at King's College London), in the 4th May 1996 issue of The Tablet, where she notes that criticisms of Pius XII have ignored 'the many Jewish tributes to his courageous stand on their behalf'.

10   Fischer, Klaus P. *Nazi Germany: A New History* (*NG*, Constable, 1995, p.363)

11   John T. Pawlikowski, referencing Nora Levin, in his essay *The Challenge of the Holocaust for Christian Theology*, in *Thinking The Unthinkable: Meanings of the Holocaust* (*TTU*, Paulist Press, 1990, editor Roger S. Gottlieb, p. 265)

12   Ibid, slightly adapted

13   This distinction is from Robert Funk's *Honest to Jesus* (*HTJ*, Harper 1996, p. 300).

14   *Guidelines for Catholic-Jewish Relations* (Catholic Truth Society, 1994, n. 23)

15   Kelly, Peter. *Searching for Truth: A Personal View of Roman Catholicism* (*SfT*, Collins, 1978 , p. 124) – the 'three characteristics' are sourced from p. 123

16   Quoted in David Mishkin's *Jewish Scholarship on the Resurrection of Jesus* (*JSJ*, Pickwick Publications, 2017, p. 74)

17   Ibid, p. 76

18   Crossan, John Dominic. *Who Killed Jesus? – Exposing the Roots of anti-Semitism in the Gospel Story of the Death of Jesus* (WKJ?, Harper, 1995, p. 38)

19   *Dominus Iesus: On the Unicity and Salvific Universality of Jesus Christ and the Church* [DI, Congregation For The Doctrine Of The Faith (CDF), Catholic Truth Society, n.22, August 2000]

20   This verse is part of *The Great Commission* (28: 16-20). It is a likely midrash on Dt. 32:48, where Moses gives final instructions from a mountain. The reference to 'Father, Son and Holy Spirit' is clearly Trinitarian and could not have been spoken by Jesus. Mt. 15:24, 'I was sent only to the lost sheep of the house of Israel', is considered by the vast majority of reputable scholars to represent Jesus' own position, whose activities were focused 'solely on Palestinian Jews' (Geza Vermes).

21   Quoted by Hubert Richards in *The First Christmas – What Really Happened?* (TFC, Collins, 1973, pp. 118-9)

22   1,300 years ago, Muslims forced its adherents to migrate there, from Iran.

23   This paragraph, the preceding endnote and most of the other information about the Parsees and Zoroaster are sourced from Richard Holloway's *A Little History of Religion* (LHR, Yale University Press, 2016, pp. 71-7).

24   Ibid, pp. 74-5, much adapted – the above dating with regard to Zoroastrianism's origins reflects best known historical findings, but it is very likely that Zoroastrian beliefs have a long prehistory.

25   *TFC*, p. 18

26   *LHR*, p. 75

27   Siedentop, Larry. *Inventing the Individual: The Origins of Western Liberalism* (ItI, Penguin Books, 2015, p. 11, which is also the source of the preceding paragraph).

28   Ibid, p. 13, adapted (Siedentop does not make the urban planning connection)

29   Harari, Yuval, N *Sapiens: A Brief History of Humankind* (Penguin Books, 2011, p. 23)

30   O Murchu, Diarmuid, *The God Who Becomes Redundant* (Mercier Press, 1986, pp. 15 and 7) – fire was 'controlled' about 600,000 years ago (p. 16)

31   Scholars are divided regarding the extent to which Zoroastrianism has

influenced Jewish resurrection belief. One argument questioning this supposed influence is that there are no known Zoroastrian texts prior to the emergence of the belief in Judaism, meaning that – in the words of Bart D. Ehrman – 'it is not clear who influenced whom'. An additional consideration is that Judah emerged from Persian rule in the fourth century BCE, thanks to Alexander the Great (d. 323) sweeping through the eastern Mediterranean, but the idea of bodily resurrection does not appear in Jewish texts for well over a century later.' (Ehrman, in *Heaven and Hell: A History of the Afterlife* (H&H, One World, 2021, pp. 104-5)

32   *Is Religion Dangerous?* (Lion Hudson, 2006, p. 104)

33   *H&H*, p. 105 – an additional consideration is that when Alexander the Great (d. 323 BCE) swept through the eastern Mediterranean, and defeated the Persian Empire, 'the idea of bodily resurrection does not appear in Jewish texts for well after a century after that'

34   Ibid

35   *Nativity * Passion * Resurrection* (NPR, Penguin Books, 2010, pp. 364 and 370); the quotation from Vermes at this work's conclusion is from p. 294. The reference to Maurice Casey in the Introduction is sourced from Hilde Brekke-Moller's *The Vermes Quest: The Significance of Geza Vermes for Jesus Research* (Bloomsbury, p. 6), where she also provides two extensive footnotes on Casey's view of Vermes, inclusive of this statement: 'Casey also has critical remarks about Vermes. Most importantly, he points out that Vermes never has been able to provide a "convincing explanation" about why Jesus was crucified.' In addition, Casey suggests that Vermes' religious beliefs 'block him from seeing that Jewish opposition against Jesus led to his death'. [For more on this, see endnote 208.]. Brekke-Moller notes (p. 31) that, ever since the 1910 English translation of Schweitzer's *Quest of the Historical Jesus*, it has become standard to delineate four phases in 'Jesus Research': 1) 1174-1902; 2) 1953-1980; 3) from 1980. The 'no quest period' is dated from 1906 to 1953, making up the *four epochs/phases classification*, and 'each period is typically defined by features that are perceived as characteristic and common to research from the time' (p. 31). The reference to James Dunn, also in the Introduction to *RJJ*, comes from Brekke-Moller's p. 5, and the quotation from Meier comes from p. 9, and his "cliché point" is adapted from quotations provided by Brekke-Moller (p. 123).

36   Reza Aslan, *Zealot: The Life and Times of Jesus of Nazareth* (Z, Westbourne Pres, 2014, p. 7, slightly adapted) – some of the succeeding paragraph is

sourced from p. 8

37 *Catechism of the Catholic Church* (CCC, n. 404)

38 Shelby Spong, John. *Resurrection: Myth or Reality?* (*RMR?*, Harper Collins, 1994 , p. 113)

39 Ibid, p. 114, much adapted, and the preceding paragraph is based on page 113 and the succeeding one is loosely derived from p. 114; the "bride threshold" quotation is Larry Siedentop's (see endnote 27)

40 Lohfink, Gerhardt. *Is This All There Is? – On Resurrection and Eternal Life* (*ITA*, Liturgical Press Academic, 2018 edition, pp. 87-8 (the 'translation information' is also derived from these pages). In Chapter 11, Lohfink's account of the resurrection is summarised under the rubric of his book's subtitle.

41 This paragraph is sourced from Stuart E. Rosenberg's *The Christian Problem – A Jewish View* (*TCP*, Hippocrene Books, 1988, p. 93). The succeeding paragraph's points also derive from this page. See endnote 203 for an important criticism of John Gager's position outlined in endnote 50.

42 *The Gospel According to Judas, by Benjamin Iscariot* (Macmillan, 2007, pp 89-90) – 'Benjamin' is supposed to be Judas' son, narrator of this fictional tale. Its authors and this writer agree that there is probably a historical basis of sorts to Judas, but Archer and Moloney give too much credence to the 'Betrayal Narratives' in the Gospels – they are a product of Midrashim. 'Judas' effectively represents 'Judah', the Jewish people.

43 Vermes, Geza. *The Changing Faces of Jesus* (*CFJ*, Penguin Books, 2001, pp. 123-4)

44 Ibid, p. 124

45 Ibid, and this association of ideas, once Christianity became the state religion of the Empire in the fourth century, had tragic if unintended consequences for the Jewish people.

46 *The Story of the Jews: Finding the Words, 1000BCE to 1492CE* (*SoJ*, Vintage Books, 2013, p. 150; this and the preceding page provide different versions of the tradition)

47 *TCP*, p. 142

48 Ibid

49 *TCP*, Chapter 8, pp. 131-152, provides a fascinating explanation of these claims – it is the Pharisees, not the Greeks, for example, who originated

the notion of universal education for all male children, now extended to all children by the *Universal Declaration of Human Rights*.

50   Interested readers are referred to John Gager's chapter, Paul the Apostle of Judaism, in *Jesus, Judaism & Christian anti-Judaism: Reading the New Testament after the Holocaust* (*JCC*, editors Paula Fredriksen and Adele Reinhartz, Westminster John Knox Press, 2002 edition). Gager writes that it is difficult to imagine how St. Paul 'could have been converted to Christianity while at the same time serving as its founder' (p. 56). In context, he does not mean Christianity as we understand it, but the Jesus movement, using 'Christianity' as convenient shorthand. The Birth of Jesus the Jew, *The Death of Jesus the Jew* and *The Resurrection of Jesus the Jew* subscribe to the belief that St Paul is Christianity's 'true founder', in the sense that he provided it with its distinctive theology of atonement, reflected in the account of the Institution of the Eucharist (1 Cor. 11:23-24), part of which almost certainly derives from Hellenistic mourning rites, with particular regard to the words, 'Do this is memory of me.' Jesus was and always remained a faithful Jew. The religion about him, whose foundation he inspired, is Christianity (see endnote203).

51   For a detailed treatment of this matter, see Étienne Trocmé's *The Childhood of Christianity* (SCM Press, 1997, with particular regard to its Preface). Scholars, for good reason, dispute the historicity of the 'Jamnia Council', as they do the 'Council of Jerusalem' (Acts 15), but there can be little doubt that, by the end of the first century, the 'two daughters' were already set on a course that would lead eventually to disastrous consequences for the two emerging faith traditions, Rabbinic Judaism in particular.

52   Quoted from Marc Saperstein's *Moments of Crisis in Jewish-Christian Relations* (*MoC*, SCM Press, 1989, p. 6)

53   Ibid, p. 7

54   *Christ in the Light of the Christian-Jewish Dialogue* (*CLJ*, Paulist Press, 1982 , p. 87)

55   Scholarly writings on this matter are extensive, with regard to the provenance of Hebrews 4:14-5:10, for example, where Jesus is described as 'the great High Priest'. *RJJ, DJJ* and *BJJ* adopt the position that the historical Jesus never ascribed such a status to himself, and that 1 Cor. 11:23-24, *the Institution of the Eucharist* and paralleled in three of the Gospels, should not be interpreted as a real time event. It is best understood as a midrash, developed from the fellowship meals that Jesus shared with his disciples

and friends, and probably narrated at least partly against the background of Hellenistic funerary and other rituals (It is significant that St Paul, a Jew of the Diaspora, had no knowledge of the historical Jesus, apart from the bare fact of the crucifixion – the narratives about it, both canonical and apocryphal, are chiefly midrashic interpretations). In addition, to paraphrase Dr Kieran O'Mahony (OSA), Jesus never ordained anyone, for the simple reason that the 'Last Supper' was not an ordination service – he never envisaged a body separate from his own faith. In the light of these considerations, there is irony in the fact that Christianity went on to develop its own hierarchy of priesthood, focused on the notion of 'sacrifice', a concept central also to those churches, Evangelical communities, for example, that eschew formal hierarchical structures.

56 *CLJ*, p. 88

57 *CFJ*, p. 200

58 *The Mythmaker: Paul and the Invention of Christianity* (*MPC*, Weidenfeld & Nicholson, 1986, p. 29)

59 Ibid

60 Ibid

61 This paragraph is partly sourced from John Dominic Crossan's *How to Read the Bible and Still be a Christian* (*HRB*, Harper Collins, 2015, p. 5), with particular regard to the 'acclamations' and 'condemnations' observation. *RJJ*, towards the end of Chapter 12, refers to the Church's pre-Vatican II *Good Friday Liturgy*.

62 See *CLJ*, Chapter 4, for a detailed study of the arguments.

63 Ibid, p. 93 – Of course, common sense suggests that Jesus, like all of his contemporaries, would have been exposed to the variety of Jewish schools of thought at the time; in addition, the New Testament is hardly a dispassionate account of historical events: it presents Jesus within its own multiple contexts of interpretation.

64 *MPC* devotes an entire chapter ('6') to this matter (see also endnote 208), and Klinghoffer's book (see endnote 399) also addresses it (pp. 93-99).

65 Vermes, Geza. *The True Herod* (*TTH*, Bloomsbury, 2014, p. 19).

66 Fredriksen, Paula. When Christians *Were Jews: The First Generation* (*WCJ*, Yale University Press, 2018, p. 10)

67 Ibid

68   Ibid

69   Ibid, p. 11

70   It is mistaken to attribute real time status to the 'words of institution'.

71   Segal, Alan, *Life After Death: A History of the Afterlife in Western Religion* (*LAD*, Doubleday, 2004, p. 351) The above statement does not mean that St. Paul was unaware of, and not influenced by, Hellenism. Indeed, the previous endnote implies otherwise (a number of scholars argue that the Eucharist is his sole creation). But the Apostle seems to have understood eternal life chiefly in terms of bodily resurrection, though care needs to be taken when interpreting that term. And Jesus, if Vermes is right, may have drawn little distinction between bodily resurrection and some kind of spiritual survival.

72   Ehrman, Bart D. *How Jesus Became God: The Exaltation of a Jewish Preacher from Galilee* (*HJBG*, HarperOne, 2014, p. 258)

73   Ibid

74   This is the real meaning of 'I will never again drink of the fruit of the vine until that day when I drink it new in the Kingdom of God' (Mk. 14:25).

75   *The Universal Christ* (*TUC*, SPCK, 2019 edition, p. 143)

76   From *Re-Imagining Paradise*, a lecture by Rita N. Brock 19th. June 2006 (reference: *Voices of Sophia Breakfast*, Presbyterian General Assembly and rita@faithvoices.org)

77   Perrin, Norman. *The Resurrection According to Matthew, Mark and Luke* (*MML*, Fortress Press, 1977, pp. 81-2 – Perrin makes the additional point that we cannot treat as historical the three accounts in Acts of St Paul's conversion experience (p. 81)

78   It is best understood as a *literary Semitism* – that is, 'burial' is a synonym for 'death', the point being to emphasise the reality of Jesus' death by crucifixion. Carl E. Olson (see the following endnote) disagrees, maintaining that burial is much more than a generic reference to the fact of Jesus' death: 'It describes what happened to his body after death' (p. 157).

79   Carl E. Olson, in *Did Jesus Really Rise from the Dead?* (*DJRD?*, Ignatius Press, 2016), with particular regard to Chapters 2 and 8, provides counter arguments.

80   This paragraph and the succeeding three are derived and much adapted from *MML*, pp. 9-13. Interested readers are referred also to Karen F. McCarthy's *The Other Irish: The Scots-Irish Radicals Who Made America*

(*TOI*, Fall River Press, 2011 edition) for a comprehensive, entertaining and moving account of how 'The Other Irish' have contributed in so many ways to the contemporary identity of the United States.

81   *HMG*, SCM Press, 1973 edition, p. 191

82   *The Story of the Jews: Finding The Words* – 1000 BCE to 1492 CE (*SoJ*, Vintage, 201, p. 65)

83   Ibid, p. 66

84   St John's Gospel makes no reference to 'Simon', maybe because by the time it was written stories had begun to circulate that 'Simon' had died as a substitution for Jesus (see 19:17, with its reference to 'by himself').

85   Much adapted from pp. 83, 85 and 86 of *CFJ*.

86   *Maranatha: Women's Funerary Rituals and Christian Origins* (WFR, Fortress Press, 2010, p. 118,)

87   *RMR?*, Chapter 17, addresses this matter in detail, briefly summarised in this chapter.

88   Ibid, p. 212, and it is noteworthy that Mithraism's 'first day of the week' was known as 'the Day of the Conquering Sun', from which our 'Sunday' derives (from TCP, p. 44)

89   *RMR?*, p. 212

90   Of related interest, Reginald Fuller has argued convincingly that the celebration of the Lord's Day 'on the first day of the week' was instituted by Hellenistic Christians, one that would have been familiar to St Paul, who – for obvious reasons – moved in Gentile circles. It was unknown to Jewish Christians in Jerusalem, a consideration supporting the claim of the previous Chapter that Jesus had no knowledge of the Eucharist as we have come to know it: 'Christianity's great cultic edifice'.

91   Ibid, p. 215; *Rabbinic Writings* record this interpretation, which must have had an oral prehistory, as far back as the first century, and possibly earlier

92   Ibid, p. 217

93   Ibid, p. 219

94   *HMG*, p. 194 and *DJJ* treat extensively of the role of Joseph of Arimathea in the Passion Narratives.

95   Ibid

96   Ibid

97 Ibid, p. 196

98 Ibid, p. 197

99 Ibid, p. 199

100 Ibid, p. 196

101 *MML* p. 80

102 Docetism in its mature version maintained that Jesus' suffering on the cross was apparent, not real (that is, he only *seemed* to have the body of a human being). Other representations of the belief held that Judas Iscariot or Simon of Cyrene exchanged places with Jesus immediately prior to the crucifixion.

103 *TOI*, pp. 61-5

104 Ibid, p. 63

105 *The Dignity of Difference* (*DoD*, Continuum, 2002, Chapter 3)

106 No reputable biblical scholar or historical theologian regards these to be the words of the historical Jesus, but that is not to say that they are without significance, once their context is understood.

107 *DJJ* examines this matter in some detail, but suffice to say that whilst the passion narratives are largely an exercise in midrash and religious propaganda/theatre, there nonetheless remains a nucleus of historical truth behind them, contrary to the opinion of some academics that the passion narratives are 100% 'fictional'.

108 *CFJ*, p. 173

109 *HJBG*, p. 166

110 Ibid

111 'Junia' is 'Junias' (a man's name) in some translations of this verse.

112 *HJBG*, p. 166

113 *WFR*, from the *Foreword* by John Dominic Crossan, p. XII)

114 *WFR*, pp. 48, 49, 52 and 53

115 Ibid, pp. 111, 112

116 Ibid, pp. 115, 40

117 Ibid, p. 115

118 Ibid

119 Ibid, p. 116

120 Ibid, pp. 127-8

121 Ibid, p. 129

122 Crossan, John Dominic. *Jesus – A Revolutionary Biography* (*JRB*, HarperOne, p. 158)

123 *Was Jesus God?* (*WJG?*, Oxford University Press, 2008 edition, p. 119)

124 *JRB*, p. 158

125 Shelby Spong, John, in *Biblical Literalism: A Gentile Heresy* (*BLH*, HarperOne, 2016) explains this hypothesis in great detail, with particular regard to *Part IX: Passover and Passion – The Climax*

126 The story was related to the author during the course of a meal in January 2023.

127 *WFR*, page XII and p. 121

128 *TFCK* (Random House, 1986 edition, p. 173); the 'K' distinguishes it from Hubert Richards' book (see endnote 21)

129 Later in the narrative, it is clear that the soldiers are Roman, but the point of the above observation is that it seems very unlikely that the Jewish leaders would have had protection of this kind, thereby underlining the central point that the entire section is not historical.

130 2014 edition, Viking, quoted in O'Murchu, *When The Disciple Comes of Age: Christianity in the 2st. Century* (Orbis Books, 2019, pp. 156-7

131 *The Jewish Annotated New Testament* (*JANT* Oxford University Press, p. 62)

132 This is a clear allusion to *The Transfiguration of Christ* (Mt. 17:1-13, redacted from Mk. 9:2-8).

133 *NJBC*, p. 673

134 *An Introduction to the New Testament* (*INT*, Doubleday 1997 edition, pp., 202, 203 and 176)

135 In a fascinating book, *The Jewish Gospels: The Story of the Jewish Christ* (*TJC*, The New Press, 2012) Daniel Boyarin, an expert on the Talmud (a comprehensive, 'definitive', account of Jewish oral traditions) argues that 'Jews, it seems, had no difficulty whatsoever with understanding a messiah who would suffer vicariously to redeem the world' (p. 133), and he maintains also that, contrary to the view of most biblical scholars, Is. 53 can be interpreted to refer to 'a suffering Messiah', to be understood in a literal sense and not merely as a metaphor for Israel's sufferings, (p. 131). Boyarin devotes much of his book to an analysis of 'Daniel', addressed in Chapter 8 of this book, claiming that 'many Jews came to

believe that Jesus was divine because they were already expecting that the Messiah/Christ would be a god-man' (p. 56). Even if Boyarin is right, this does not suggest that there was Jewish uniformity about such views. Christians, owing to the long and strong tradition of orthodox beliefs, often fail to appreciate how diverse was "Jewish theology" of the first century.

136   Quoted in *WKJ?*, p. 36

137   Condensed and adapted from pp. 7 and 386, derived from the summary in *WKJ?*, p. 36 (the words in italics are mine, but faithfully representing Brown's meaning)

138   *NPR*, p. 22

139   These points are much edited versions of conversations and e-mail exchanges between O'Murchu and this writer.

140   The book's full title includes the 'header' *Is God Violent? – An Exploration from Genesis to Revelation* (*HRBC*, Harper One, 2015, p. 67)

141   Ibid, p. 137

142   Vermes, in *CB* Chapter 4, deals extensively with this matter: 'Paul's Christ truly became the Lord of the Universe, standing somewhat below the Father' (p. 114), and he also provides a convincing interpretation of the famous *Hymn to Christ* (Phil. 2: 6-11, claiming that *Jesus was in the form of God*), to the effect that it does not reflect the theology of St. Paul's seven genuine letters (p. 109).

143   The book's subtitle is *The Jewish Christ* (The New Press, 2012, p. 56)

144   Ibid, pp. 72-73

145   Ibid

146   Ibid, pp. 133, 131

147   *HJBG*, p. 49 – Ehrman devotes the whole of Chapter 2 (pp. 48-84) to an analysis of *Divine Humans in Ancient Judaism*

148   *MPC*, p. 77

149   *NJBC*, p. 406

150   Ibid, p. 1058

151   *Z*, p. 139, abridged

152   *RMR?*, p. 68

153   Ibid

154   Ibid, p. 71

155 *NJBC*, p. 673

156 *RMR?*, p. 71

157 The source of this information is in Josephus' *Jewish War and Jewish Antiquities*, and 1 Maccabees 4 tells of 'The Battle at Emmaus'. This book, originally in Hebrew, was written c. 90 BCE and it deals with the Maccebees' struggle against the Seleucid Empire

158 Paraclete Press, 2006 edition, p. 128

159 Ibid, p. 126

160 Dan. 9:26, which may have influenced Boyarin's thesis (see Chapter 8) refers to the death of 'an anointed one', an exclusively human, political figure, notes Paula Fredriksen.

161 The Ebionites subscribed to the position that Jesus was the messiah, but that he was not conceived virginally and that St Paul was a 'false prophet' (for a full, if contested, treatment of this matter see *MPC* pp.174-183 and endnote 352).

162 The idea that God, beginning with creation, progressively brings humankind to completion (at the Second Coming) , by virtue of Christ's atoning death and resurrection.

163 *Jesus of Nazareth, King of the Jews* (*JoN*, Random House, 1999, p. 247). I consider Fredriksen's interpretation of the data involving this issue to be persuasive, but the matter is very complex and Hyam Maccoby, for example, maintains that 'Jesus regarded himself as the messiah in the normal Jewish sense of the term' (*MPC*, p.15).

164 This observation derives from the hypothesis that the practice of 'the breaking of bread' (see Acts 2: 42-46, for example) is not a synonym for the Eucharist as represented by 1 Cor. 11:23-26 and its parallels in the synoptic gospels. *MPC*, pp. 116-118, explores the issue.

165 *The Eucharist: Origins and Contemporary Understandings* (*EOU*, Bloomsbury, 2015, p. 87, and see endnote 391)

166 Ibid, p. 86

167 *JRB*, pp. 170, 178, 180 – readers are directed to Chapter 7 for a full account of this hypothesis. In summary, Crossan's argument is that the 'nature miracles' (Jn. 6:1-15, *Feeding the Five Thousand*, and Jn. 21:1-14, *Jesus Appears to Seven Disciples and eats Breakfast with Them*, for example) are patterned, as with the words of the Last Supper, 'using the four key verbs describing Jesus' action: *took, blessed (or gave thanks), broke and gave*' (p. 180).

168   *JANT*, p. 218

169   *CB*, p. 92

170   See Bradshaw and Johnson, *The Eucharistic Liturgies* (TEL, SPCK, 2012, Chapter 1, especially pp. 13-14)

171   Chapter 2 of *The Death of Jesus the Jew*

172   *JRB*, p. 180

173   *The Didache* (*Training of the Twelve Apostles*) is the earliest document providing instruction about 'Church order', prepared for Gentile converts to one branch of the Jesus movement. Originally in oral form, the written text was for centuries dated to after 80 (it was believed to have cited a combination of Matthean and Lucan traditions), but the majority of scholars now date it much earlier. Interested readers are referred to Aaron Milavec's 2003 translation (Liturgical Press) for a detailed account of its origin and purpose.

174   *JRB*, p. 130

175   Ibid and *The Tablet*, 29th. February 2020

176   *EOU*, p. 146, in which he criticises the understanding of the Eucharist portrayed in the Catholic document *One Bread One Body* (1998), which O'Loughlin characterises as an inability to move beyond understanding it other than 'as some kind of capstone on a systematic theological edifice'.

177   Ibid, pp. 70 and 196 – O'Loughlin, it must be emphasised, is criticising a particular theological position (see above endnote), not the practices of believers, most of whom will not be cognizant of what he says and, should they be, O'Loughlin has no problem with their decision to interpret the tradition in a manner at variance with his 'take' on it.

178   Ibid, pp. 70, 196 and 23

179   Ibid, p. 23

180   *JRB* elucidates this matter, particularly in chapter 3

181   *EOU*, p. 196

182   *JRB*, p. 130

183   According to the three synoptic gospels, Jesus celebrated a Passover meal on the day of his death. St John, however, has Jesus celebrate a non-Passover meal with his disciples on the Preparation Day for Passover, and he dies on the same date (the Jewish day runs from sunset to sunset). One or the other is mistaken and it is probable that, whilst Jesus was

certainly executed by the Romans (probably in 30), these four narratives largely reflect theological, not historical, considerations. In my opinion, the four passion narratives provide us with little credible historical data, being largely the product of pre-midrashim, inspired in all likelihood by two key passages in St Paul's First Letter to the Corinthians: 'Christ, our paschal lamb, is sacrificed' (5:7b) and the account of *The Institution of the Eucharist* (11: 23-24). The reference in the latter to 'on the night of his betrayal' is not, I believe, a genuine historical memory (St. Paul does not name Judas). It is far more likely to be his brief midrash on 2 Sam. 15:12 – 17:23 (Absalom's failed conspiracy to murder King David), in the context of an emerging atonement theology (c. 52 or earlier), which by c. 70 had been 'fleshed out' in *The Passion of the Christ*, as represented in the canonical gospels. One reason for advancing this hypothesis (examined in great detail in *DJJ*) is that the gospels' accounts of Judas' betrayal of Jesus, no more than the stories about his "trials", make no sense when examined by the best methods available to modern scholarship. These considerations, according to one interpretation, should not matter (on a particular faith understanding of *Jesus as the Christ*), but in reality they matter very much. Christianity, unlike most approaches to Buddhism, for example, makes claims of an historical, not just a metaphysical, nature and it cannot be allowed to shelter under the umbrella of 'special pleading'. Christianity, at the level of common sense, is accountable to the responsible court of public (and scholarly) opinion: and if mainstream Christianity in the twenty-first century is not up to this muscular challenge, it will fall prey to the guiles and deceits of fundamentalism(s). Truth matters; it matters very much indeed.

184   *JANT*, p. 166

185   *The Tablet*, 19 May 2017, reproduced in Stanford's engaging book *What We Talk About When We Talk About Faith* (Hodder & Stoughton, 2019, pp. 217-221)

186   Ibid. McGovern does not use the words 'heart' and 'spirit', but I believe them to represent his meaning.

187   *RMR?*, p. 204

188   *JANT*, p. 166

189   *TFCK*, p.106

190   Ibid, p. 101

191   Ibid, p. 254, referencing Aquinas' *Summa Theologiae* III (55,2,c)

192 Ibid

193 Versions of it have Jesus, amongst other ludicrous scenarios, migrating to India.

194 This idea derives from Mt. 28:11-15, which is best understood in terms of the anti-Jewish polemic characteristic of Matthew's Gospel. *JANT* (p. 66) further observes that v. 15b, 'And this story is told among the Jews to this day', echoes a 'biblical formula', to be found twice more in this gospel (11:26, 27:8) and in the 'Old Testament' (Gen. 35:20, Dt. 11:4).

195 *WCJ?*, p. 75

196 Z, p. 182, slightly adapted

197 *Paul: The Pagans' Apostle* (*PPA*, Yale University Press, 2017)

198 David Mishkin provides this information in his *Jewish Scholarship on the Resurrection of Jesus* (*JSR*, Pickwick Publications, 2017, p. 29. Lapide's book was published in 1983 (SPCK) and the 'second Jew' is Geza Vermes (see footnote 35; his 'Resurrection' was first published as a single volume, in 2008)

199 Z, p. 186

200 *JJC*, p 69 and see endnotes 50 and 203

201 Ibid, adapted; the biblical references are Rom. 11:26 and Gal. 3:10 respectively

202 Ibid, p. 8, adapted from some observations by Paula Fredriksen

203 Ibid, pp. 69-70, JJC The substance of Gager's thesis is that neither Paul's enemies nor his audience in general were from outside of the Jesus movement, and that in the Letter to the Galatians, for example, where he talks of the Law as 'a curse' (3:10-11), the context is his criticism of Gentile believers, not Jews; he is describing a situation pertaining to the former, not to the latter. Another central theme of Gager's article is that 'we surely read back into Paul's own time the opinions, debates and circumstances that emerged only later on, long after Paul's period, when Christianity really did emerge as something distinct from, and even opposed to, Judaism' (JJC, p. 59; see endnote 50). Stuart Rosenberg (see endnote 41) is very critical of Gager: 'Despite Gager's valiant and appealing efforts to save Paul from the charge of anti-Judaism, relying on earlier efforts in this direction of people like E.P. Sanders ..., the fact remains that even if Gager is right, he is wrong. It is one thing for a modern ecumenist, seeking rapprochement between Jews and Christians to "reinvent" the historical Paul, in order to help Christians change their

attitudes to Jews. It is quite another to obliterate from history the manner in which traditional Church leaders used what they believed Paul had (negatively) taught about Jews and Judaism, and then proceeded to translate into official Church policy. ... We cannot change the historical and *phenomenological* dynamics of Paul, to "reinvent" him by means of novel exegetical twists and turns' (*TCP*, p. 96). Rosenberg continues by criticising other academics in this field (Paul van Buren, for example): 'Some of these scholars miss the more important point, namely that irrespective either of the sources of his theology or of a new exegesis of his teachings, it is the politics of Paul, the pragmatic ways in which he redirected the idea of the Jewish mission that is crucial. In this process, he virtually behaves as an anti-Semite, using Jewish ideas while denying the Jewish nation any significant right to continue its covenantal group existence (*TCP*, pp. 96-7). Rosenberg also notes the view of Michael Grant, writing in 1976, that 'had it not been for Paul, Judaism might eventually have conquered the Roman Empire instead of Christianity' (p. 97). I disagree. Bart D. Ehrman's treatment of this hypothesis is far more convincing, in *The Triumph of Christianity: How A Forbidden Religion Swept the World* (ToC), where he argues that 'Judaism was looked upon with real suspicion in the empire' (p. 112), noting that, amongst other factors, the practice of circumcision in particular was 'what made Christianity more acceptable than Judaism to the wider populace' (p. 112; see also Chapter 2 – *The Conversion and Mission of Paul*; see endnote 240). In addition, David Klinghoffer's book (Doubleday, 2005, Chapter 4), referenced in the *Introduction*, is also critical of attempts to "rehabilitate Paul ", doubting that he was a Jew, making this comment: 'Jews who observed the commandments, even if they also believed in Jesus, found something suspect about Paul's Jewishness' (p. 115). In Chapter 10, the Martin Goodman reference to St Paul is from his *Mission and Conversion: Proselytizing in the Religious History of the Roman Empire* (p.105), quoted in *ToC*, p. 118.

204 *Unitarian Church, Cork*

205 *JSR*, p. 116, quoting Rabbi Michael Cook and see endnote 203

206 Ibid, p. 193

207 This verse claims that Paul supported the stoning of Stephen (Acts 7:1-8:3, with particular regard to7:54-8:1), but scholars have long recognised that the account of Stephen's death is riddled with problems and contradictions. '8:1' may well be an embellishment.

208 *MPC*, p. 101; Maccoby also notes that 'the dying and resurrected deity was always the same under all his names and guises, whether Adonis, Osiris or Attis' (p. 101). Of Attis, Maccoby writes that 'Saul would have become aware of Jesus as a figure that seemed strangely familiar to him, answering a need in his soul. .. In particular, his strong imagination would have been captured by the picture of Jesus dying on the cross, which would have reminded him of the icons he had seen in Cilicia of the god Atis in his various guises – the hanged god, whose dripping, flayed body fertilized the fields and whose mysteries renewed the souls of his frenzied devotees' (p. 102 and see "Dt. 21:7", below). For Maccoby, St Paul's vision of the resurrected Jesus ('a mere psychological seizure', he terms it), 'made sense out of the meaningless into which his life had degenerated. For instead of being merely a hireling of the quisling high priest, he now saw himself as a historically significant person – he who had persecuted the dying and rising god and who, by his very guilt, could switch to the antithetical role of the god's chief acolyte' (p. 103, slightly adapted). Paul is the focus of *MPC*: 'Paul made the crucifixion of Jesus into the centre of his thinking. Paul's view of Jesus has coloured the story told in the Gospel and has thus influenced the imagination of Western civilization. To search for the historical facts of Jesus' death is thus to uncover the real world in which Paul's thinking had its origin and to explain the motivation of Paul in transforming a historical event into a cosmic myth. Blaming the Pharisees or Jewish religion generally for Jesus' death was one of the by-products of this transformation of a man into a myth' (p. 46 and see endnote 35). Maccoby also maintains that the famous passage in Galatians 3, which speaks of Christ redeeming us from the curse of the law and referencing Dt. 21:7 – 'Cursed is everyone who hangs on a tree' – reflects how Paul's troubled imagination came to associate Jesus' ignominious death with the cult of Attis, thereby effectively 'founding Christianity' . In a recent book, *Ignorance and Bliss: On Wanting Not to Know* (Hurst & Co, 2024), Mark Lilla writes scathingly of that development, accusing Paul of having transformed the message of Jesus into an anti-intellectual ideology that has much influenced modern secularism, according to a review by John Banville in *The Observer* (24th November 2024).

209 *JSR*, p. 209, quoting Mishkin's paraphrase of Segal (page not specified)

210 Penguin Books, p. 59

211 Since c. 1970, scholars have paid a great deal of attention to the contribution of sociology to the study of conversion experiences; indeed, this

discipline has now overtaken psychology as a medium for researching the phenomenon. For obvious reasons, *RJJ* cannot address this matter, which is covered in *PtC*. Such considerations throw doubt on the traditional interpretation of the "sudden nature" of Paul's conversion.

212   The conviction that God was about to inaugurate a universal reign of justice and peace by vanquishing evil forever.

213   Lev. 16:1-34 and 23:26-32, in addition to Num. 29:7-11, are often used as "evidence" of 'Old Testament' atonement teaching supporting Christianity's 'midrash' on the concept.

214   Mk. 10:45 – 'The Son of Man came not to be served but to serve, and to give his life as a ransom for many' – is interpreted to mean that Jesus' death brought about a new relationship between God and his people, thereby *atoning* for their sins. In *JANT* (p. 90), Lawrence M. Wills explains that this verse is 'the climax of the middle section of Mark's Gospel, and it expresses a great irony.' James and John expect the Son of Man to come in great power, but this is not to be the case. The reference to "ransom" is most likely from the *Suffering Servant* of Is. 52-53, and its meaning remains the focus of much scholarly debate.

215   Spong, John Shelby. *Why Christianity Must Change Or Die* (WCC, HarperOne, p. 98)

216   This paragraph is adapted from Diarmuid O'Murchu's *Incarnation: A New Evolutionary Threshold* (Orbis Books, 2017, p. 158)

217   Ibid, p. 98

218   *The Concise Oxford Dictionary of The Christian Church* (COD, Oxford University Press, editor; Elizabeth Livingstone, 1977, pp. 162-3)

219   *JSR*, p. 105 (slightly adapted) – the *Mishnah*, a compilation of oral law, ethical principles and rules concerning worship, is the foundation document of Rabbinic Judaism, dating from the third century CE.

220   Cohen, Jeremy. *Christ Killers* (CK, Oxford University Press, 2007, p. 181, quoting Rabbi Michael Cook)

221   *JSR*, p. 41, from *The Resurrection of Jesus: A Jewish Perspective* (SPCK, 1983, p. 93)

222   From a paper delivered to the Oxford Socratic Club, 1945

223   *JSR*, p. 41

224   Ibid.

225   Ibid, p. 207

226   *NPR*, p. 422

227   Ibid, p. 421, which states that only Heb. 11:17-19, three verses in a deu-
teron-Pauline letter, provides support for the idea this interpretation of
Abraham's willingness to sacrifice Isaac, thereby providing a basis for
Paul's approach to 'atonement'. In *CB*, Vermes writes: 'The post-biblical
Jewish notion of the 'Binding of Isaac', combining the biblical idea of the
epic subservience of Abraham with positive cooperation by Isaac, the
victim in the sacrifice, seems to have provided the inspiration for Paul's
discovery of the redeeming character of the death and resurrection of
Christ' (p. 101). On the same page, he says that, for fifty years' (that is,
since 1962), he has been arguing this point (see Rom. 8:31-32). Vermes
also notes the significance of the fact that the Church Fathers saw in
Isaac 'the prototype of Jesus the Redeemer' (pp. 101-2).

228   Ibid.

229   *JSR*, p. 212

230   *INT*, p. 534 – Brown observes on the next page that much has been made
of Paul's silence about the empty tomb, arguing that 'there is no a-prio-
ri reason why he had to mention the tomb, and the burial/resurrection
sequence (*of the 1 Corinthians passage*) virtually presumes that the risen
body is no longer where it was buried'. The words in italics are mine, and
I remain unconvinced of Brown's "presumption" – such explanations
are used far too extensively throughout his two major works: *The Birth of
the Messiah* and *The Death of the Messiah*.

231   This paragraph is sourced from Peter Cole's *Religious Experience: Access
to Religious Studies* (*RES*, Hodder Murray, 2005, Chapter 9)

232   *INT*, p. 535, slightly redacted

233   *Beyond the Quest for the Historical Jesus: Memoir of a Discovery* (*BQHJ*,
Sheffield Phoenix Press, 2012, p. 35) – Brodie's magnum opus is *The
Birthing of the New Testament: The Intertextual Development of the New
Testament Writings* (Sheffield Phoenix Press, 2004/6). It was only in the
later *BQHJ*, however, that he fully articulated the view, long held, that
Jesus never really existed (see p. 41). I have used the term 'midrash'
loosely as a description of Brodie's approach, but he eschews the con-
cept, believing that it is not adequate to explain the extent to which the
New Testament is almost solely dependent upon the 'Old Testament' for
its portrait(s) of Jesus.

234   Few scholars believe this passage to be historical (its *Trinitarian formula*,

for obvious reasons, cannot go back to Jesus, and it probably has been influenced by 'Numbers' and other material from the 'Old Testament'), but they do not deduce from this consideration that Jesus himself was not a historical figure, a position argued for in Bart Ehrman's *Did Jesus Exist? – The Historical Argument for Jesus of Nazareth* (2012). Brodie correctly identifies flaws in Ehrman's book (its uncritical treatment of 'Josephus' and 'Tacitus', for example; see pp. 226-231 of *BQHJ*), but in my estimation it remains sound in its essential methodology.

235 *BOP*, Atlantic Books, 201, pp. 152-3 (edited)

236 Ibid, p. 157

237 It is noteworthy that it is the Father who designates Jesus "Son of God" in consequence of the resurrection effected by Him. There is no indication in this verse of Jesus being in any sense God's "equal", that is, of an incarnational theology as it later developed.

238 This paragraph and the previous one are adapted from John S. Spong's *Eternal Life* (EL, HarperOne, 2009, p. 181)

239 Ibid.

240 Gibbon advanced primary (spiritual) and secondary ('doctrinal') reasons for Christianity's success, predicated upon the premise that it was religiously and ethically superior to all forms of Paganism. Ehrman's *ToC* (see endnote 203), Chapter 4, provides an excellent summary account of the pertinent issues (including Nock's position), upon which I have drawn.

241 Z, p. 215

242 *HJBG*, p. 184

243 *The Resurrection of Jesus: The Crossan-Wright Dialogue* (RCW, Fortress Press, Robert B. Stewart, editor, 2006, pp. 17-18)

244 Wright, NT. *Paul: A Biography* (PAB, SPCK, 2018, p. 9)

245 Ibid, p. 42

246 Established by Robert Funk and John Dominic Crossan (1985), it is a controversial group of scholars ostensibly dedicated to communicating the work of the academy to as wide an audience as possible. Whilst having merits, it has also been much criticised by other scholars, both "conservative" and "liberal".

247 Sourced from an online review of the book

248 NPR, page 396, quoting from *Der alte und der neue Glaube* (1872, p. 72)

249 *HMG*, p. 194

250 Ibid, pp. 195 and 204

251 Ibid, p. 203

252 Ibid.

253 Ibid.

254 Bultmann's interpretation of the *virginal conception* in Matthew (1: 18-25) illustrates this point, by arguing that the original Aramaic version of this gospel said nothing about the *virgin birth*: 'It was a motif unheard of in the Jewish environment of the age,, and it was first added to the gospel account in the course of its transformation in Hellenism' (NPR, p. 22; Vermes is paraphrasing Bultmann in *The History of the Synoptic Tradition*, 1963, p. 291).

255 Armstrong, Karen. *The Bible: The Biography* (Atlantic Books, 2015, p. 238)

256 *New Testament Interpretation: Essays on Principles and Methods* (NTI, editor, l.H Marshall, The Paternoster Press, 1979, p. 298)

257 Ibid, p. 300

258 In *Jesus Before the Gospels: How the Earliest Christians Remembered, Changed and Invented their Stories of the Saviour* (JBG, Harper One, 2016, pp. 173-6), Bart Ehrman provides a comprehensive analysis of this verse, part of Chapter 4 – *Distorted memories and the Death of Jesus*. It is the basis for the information provided above. On p. 174, Ehrman notes that Mt. 27: 51-52 is absent from the Fourth Gospel, and the synoptic gospels have discrepancies in their accounts of the event: 'One of them appears to be irreconcilable. In our earliest account, Mark, the curtain rips the moment after Jesus dies (15:38); in Luke's version, it rips while he is still living (23:45). They both obviously can't be right.' Ehrman's account of distorted memories will be further examined later in this chapter. They are 'recollections – often quite vivid – of things that did not happen' (p. 139).

259 Ibid, p. 175

260 *JANT*, p. 65; it also gives four references from the Book of Revelation: 6:12, 8:5, 11:13, 19, and the remaining 'Old Testament' ones are Judg. 5:4, Is. 24: 19-22 and Ps. 18: 6-8.

261 *NJBC*, p. 983

262 *Who Do Men Say I Am?* (WDI, Orbis Books, 1994, p. 90)

263 *JSR*, pages 4 and 183

264 HMG, Chapter 2: *The Symbol of Light in the Hebrew Tradition*, addresses the issue.

265 Ibid, p. 75, much adapted, and the 'Steiner quotation' is sourced from *DJJ*, p. 47, in the chapter arguing for Judas' disputing Judas' alleged betrayal of Jesus (pp. 47- 62)

266 HMG, p. 80

267 Hodder, 2019, p. 243

268 HJBG, p. 185

269 *The Resurrection: Did it Really Happen and Why Does That Matter?* (RHM, Marymount Institute Press, 2014, p. 43)

270 HJBG, p. 186

271 Ibid, p. 187

272 Ibid, p. 188, quoting from *The Resurrection of Christ: a Historical Inquiry*, Prometheus, 2004, p. 19 (also p. 378 of *HJBG*)

273 Ibid, pp. 188-189, abridged and redacted

274 ITA, p. 114 (see endnote 40)

275 RMR?, p. 79, referring to Gen. 18:1-9, 19:1-3; and Heb. 13:2 has a similar reference: 'Do not neglect to show hospitality to strangers ..., some have entertained angels without knowing it.'

276 ITA, p. 114

277 Ibid, and p. 115

278 Ward Keith. *God: A Guide for the Perplexed* (GGP, Oneworld Publications, 2002 edition, p. 183, in a chapter exploring the differences between 'the facts of science and the beliefs of religion' (p. 179)

279 RHM, p. 20, much adapted

280 Chesterton, GK, *Orthodoxy* [(O, Bodley Head, 1909, p. 258, quoted by Alister McGrath in *Lord and Saviour: Jesus of Nazareth* (LS, SPCK, 2014, p. 20)]

281 LS, pp. 20-1

282 These points are adapted from Mark L. Strauss' *Four Portraits, One Jesus: A Survey of Jesus and the Gospels* (FPOJ, Zondervan, 2007, p. 457

283 RHM, p. 38 and see endnote 269

284 Ibid, p. 40

285 Ibid, pp. 41-2

286 In *The Resurrection of God Incarnate* (*RGI*, Oxford University Press, 2003), Richard Swinburne argues that 'God must put a certain "epistemic distance" between himself and human beings. He must not make his presence and his intentions for us too obvious. The point of his intervention in human history was to help us to make the right choices, by making available atonement and teaching; to encourage us, but not to overwhelm us so that we have no options left. Otherwise, he would have abandoned his method for dealing with humanity in the pre-Christian era' (p. 172). The matter is addressed in some detail in the book's Chapter 2 - *God's Reasons for Incarnation* - and Swinburne continues by suggesting that, had God made his intervention 'equally evident to all', then it would not be possible 'to help others to learn about it' (p. 173). Swinburne's approach derives substantially from St Anselm's theory of the Atonement. His argument for Jesus' resurrection is based on "probability", concluding the book (aside from *Appendix: Formalizing the Argument*, to do with applying numerical values to probabilities) with this statement: 'If the background evidence leaves it not too improbable that there is a God likely to act in the way discussed, then the total evidence makes it very probable that Jesus was God Incarnate who rose from the dead' (p. 202). Swinburne's sophisticated thesis is problematic, but two observations will suffice by way of illustration: 1) Based as it is chiefly on Anselm's *Ontological Argument for God's Existence*, many philosophers (Kant, in particular) have shown how the *Argument* is flawed, not least because, to paraphrase Gary Cox (in *The God Confusion*, p. 80), it relies on logical hypotheses that are themselves illogical. 2) Swinburne's use of biblical texts, with particular regard to his interpretation of *Atonement teaching* attributed to Jesus, fails to take proper account of the findings of *historical-critical scholarship*. For these (and other) reasons, I do not judge his comments about "resurrection appearances" to be a valuable contribution to this discussion.

287 *RHM*, p. 42, redacted

288 Ibid, p. 29

289 Pp. 25-32 of *RHM* explains this approach, using the events of 9/11 to illustrate her thesis, which can be summarised by noting that what happened on 9/11 is still happening, in the sense that it 'infinitely overflows the boundaries of that one day in September', and its meaning 'we will be unpacking, sifting, arguing over, narrating, and ordering our lives in terms of, probably as long as there is a United States' (page 28). Schneiders has adapted the philosophy of Hans G. Gadamer to her study of the *Easter*

Experience. It will continue to generate an "effective history", that is, 'a progressive deepening of the event itself by what flows from it and back over it' (p. 29). Her analysis applies also to how, in Ireland, the 1916 Rising continues to be perceived (see Chapter 4).

290   *NPR*, p. 434 – the context is Vermes' claim that evidence provided by female witnesses had no standing in a male-dominated society, but it fails to address the likelihood that the *tomb tradition* is a midrash on the story of *Daniel in the Lions' Den* and, secondly, that the "women argument", according to Ehrman, does not carry the force popularly attributed to it.

291   *HJBG*, pp. 189-190

292   Ibid, p. 191

293   Ibid, p. 192

294   Ibid

295   *JBG*, p. 91 – this book provides an excellent account of the role played by "memory" in the narratives about Jesus (see endnote 258)

296   Ibid

297   *JBG*, pages 92 and 307 – Clancy, it should be noted, does not believe that aliens exist, that there is no veridical basis to people's belief that they have been abducted.

298   Ibid

299   Ibid, p. 93

300   Ibid, pp. 94, 95 and 307 provide background information on the experiment, conducted by three psychologists at Wesleyan University (involving forty students over some weeks), and pages 95 to 100 offer a detailed evaluation (based on a series of stories) of memories about Israel ben Eliezer (d. 1760). He was a charismatic Jewish teacher, adored by his followers, who performed wondrous actions similar to those attributed to Jesus, including miracle-working powers (their messages, however, were not particularly similar), and the followers of this 'Baal Shem Tov' (the Hebrew name bestowed upon him, meaning 'Master of that Good Name', or –as an acronym – *the Behst*) told of eyewitness reports about *the Behst's* 'wondrous actions' that were regarded as historical, yet 'virtually everyone realises that these allegedly eyewitness reports are anything but historical' (p. 100).

301   Ibid, p. 101; the subtitle of Bauckham's book (JE) is *The Gospels as Eyewitness Testimony* (Erdmans, 2006). It has come in for much criticism, addressed in (the) *Journal for the Study of the Historical Jesus* (JHJ,

7, 2008), for example, and by Judith Redman who has critiqued the book from a psychological perspective. In *JHJ*, Bauckham has answered his critics (see *JBG*, p. 307).

302 *JBG*, pp. 101-2 gives a comprehensive account of these difficulties, emphasising how Bauckham's treatment of Jesus' sayings in John's Gospel is counter to the findings of most scholars.

303 Ibid, pp. 102-3, and Ehrman provides a useful *eleven points summary* (pp. 103 to 104) of what Paul tells us about Jesus. He notes that *Item 9* (from 1 Tim. 6:13, regarding the appearance before Pilate) almost certainly could not have come from Paul himself. Ehrman's list includes what Jesus supposedly said at the Last Supper (see 1 Cor. 11:23-26; *The Death of Jesus the Jew*, Chapter 2, argues that these words are not Jesus' ipsissima verba) and two other teachings attributed to Jesus: about *divorce* and *pay the preacher* (1 Cor. 7:10, 9:14). His final point, concerning responsibility for Jesus' death (see 1 Th. 2:14-15), will be addressed in Chapter 12; it is one of the New Testament's most controversial passages: *a text of terror*, similar to Mt. 27:25. Gal. 4:4, 'born of a woman', is often dismissed as "blindingly obvious", but this is to miss the point. It is a theological statement, reflecting Paul's belief that, in some way, Jesus was a *pre-existent divine being* (see Phil. 2:6-8).

304 Lk. 1:1-3, addressed to 'most excellent Theophilus', with its reference to 'delivered over to us by eyewitness and ministers of the word', is frequently misunderstood. Luke, notes Ehrman, 'does not say that he himself interviewed eye witnesses or bases his account on what he learned from eyewitnesses' (*JBG*, p. 107). This is not to deny, of course, that stories about Jesus were first told by people who knew him, and transmitted (adapted and embellished) to others in the years before the gospels were written ("invention" also played a role in this process).

305 Erhman, Bart D. *Forged: Writing in the Name of God – Why the Bible's Authors Are Not Who We Think They Are* (*F*, HarperOne, 2011 edition, p. 243)

306 *CFJ*, p. 171

307 Ibid – Vermes, unlike the premises, following Crossan, of *The Death of Jesus the Jew* and of this book, is willing to accord some historical basis to the (formal) burial tradition recounted in the gospels. This does not mean, however, that he believes Jesus' body to have survived post-mortem, in the manner championed by Schneiders, for example.

308 Ibid, adapted; Mk. 8:31, 9:9, 31 and 14:28 are four other references

309 In the liturgical calendar, this is celebrated on *Palm Sunday*, the Sunday preceding Easter Day, and it commemorates Jesus' entry into Jerusalem. According to Mark, Jesus entered the city on a colt, with people spreading their cloaks on the road, 'and leafy branches that had been cut in the fields' (11:8). The story is an obvious midrash on Zech. 9:9 and other 'Old Testament' passages: Zech. 14:4, Ps. 118: 25-26 and Gen. 49:11, for instance. It is probable, however, that there may be a historical basis to the story, especially if Ehrman and others are right that Jesus claimed some kind of messianic status for himself. It is of interest that Josephus recounts the story of a contemporary messianic figure, the so-called *Egyptian Prophet*, who announced that God would appear on the Mount of Olives, which was designated the place of the coming eschatological battle, and this is alluded to by 11:1, 'When the were approaching Jerusalem ... near the Mount of Olives' (*JANT*, p. 93).

310 *CFJ*, p. 171 adapted, providing dates, for example; we do not know the year of Jesus' death, except that, on the presumption it was during Pilate's time as procurator, it was between 26 and 36 CE. "30" is the year favoured by most scholars, using the dating of the Gregorian calendar and "Good Friday" that year would have been 7th. April, assuming, of course, that Jesus died at Passover – a contested claim, as referenced already in this book. The author of Luke's Gospel was aware of the problem that he disciples did not have knowledge of the "prophecy", and at 24:7-8 he rather clumsily addresses it by having the women at the empty tomb reminded of the prediction, which reinforces Vermes' point.

311 Ibid, p. 172

312 *NPR*, p. 408; the 'non-Jewish world' is a reference to Syria, Asia Minor, Greece and Italy

313 The full verse reads: 'The Lord says to my lord, "Sit at my right hand until I make your enemies your footstool.."' Vermes (*NPR*, p. 408) explains that 'lord' is here a synonym for 'messiah'.

314 Ibid, p. 409, much abridged and adapted

315 Ibid, p. 324

316 Another example of this *Moses-Jesus Parallelism is the Forty Days Symbolism*. Moses spends forty days and nights fasting on Mount Sinai, where he writes down the *Ten Commandments* (Ex. 34:28) and Jesus goes into the wilderness for the same period of time (Mk. 1:12-13; cf. Mt. 4:1-11).

317 *JANT*, p. 88, commenting on *The Transfiguration of Jesus* (Mk. 9: 2-13; cf. Mt. 17:1-13, Lk. 9:28-36)

318 John D. Crossan and Sarah Sexton-Crossan. *Resurrecting Easter: How The West Lost And The East Kept The Original Easter Vision* (RE, HarperOne, 2018, p. 171). Their book, with its beautiful images of Eastern iconography, argues that the Eastern Church, with its emphasis on *Jesus' universalistic Resurrection*, has a better understanding than the Western Church, with its *individualistic focus*, of the *Easter Experience*. Interested readers may wish to access their arguments, with particular regard to the importance of this distinction: 'Ascension and Resurrection refer to divergent theological visions within at least pre-Pharisaic Judaism, because "ascension" is for an individual – like Enoch or Moses or Elijah – but "resurrection" is for all of humanity. Put bluntly, Jewish tradition never imagines an individual "resurrection" for one, but only a universal "resurrection" for all '(p. 173).

319 See *The Birth of Jesus the Jew*, especially Chapter 2 (Herod, of course, was a historical figure, who died in 4 BCE, a likely date for Jesus' birth, who was born almost certainly in Nazareth.)

320 Aristotle (d. 322 BCE), in *Poetics*, set the tone for centuries to come of the way in which history was reported, and it did not 'place the same high value on the accurate recording of historical events that we generally do today' (Jeremy Cohen, *Christ Killers: The Jews And The Passion From The Bible To The Big Screen* (CK, Oxford University Press, pp. 16-17). Cohen's point is that Josephus and other first century Jews, including the evangelists, were not concerned primarily with preserving a record of the past. His focus is the passion narratives, but Cohen's observations apply also to the resurrection narratives.

321 This is according to the Venerable Bede (d. 735), and *Easter Eggs* seem to have originated in "Christian Mesopotamia", then adopted by the Eastern Church and later spread to the West.

322 *CFJ*, p. 174

323 Ibid, and p. 175; a paraphrase from Paul Winter's book, *On the Trial of Jesus* (1974, p. 208)

324 At the time, Jewish apocalaypticisits (*apocalypse* means 'revealing') were dualists, meaning that there were two aspects to reality: 'the forces of good and the forces of evil. God, of course, was in charge of all that was good; but for these Jews, God had a personal opponent, the devil, who was in charge of all that was evil. ... The powers of good and evil, for

these apocalypticists, were engaged in a cosmic battle; everyone had to take a side, there was no neutral territory' (*HJBG*, pp. 99-100). And *eschatology* (the "last things") refers to the consummation of God's purpose for the creation, which many Jews of the first century believed to be at hand. *Apocalyptic-Eschatology* was a key tenet of Paul's thinking, one that he shared with Jesus and his disciples, though their emphases were somewhat different.

325   *RCW*, p. 18

326   *Doing Christianity: How Religion Is About What You Do, Not What You Believe* is published by *Columba Books* (2023)

327   *H&H*, p. 160

328   *NJBC*, p. 985

329   *TFCK*, p. 226

330   *RHM*, p. 12

331   Ibid, p. 39

332   Holloway, Richard. *Doubts and Loves: What is Left of Christianity* (D&L, Canongate, 2001, p. 139)

333   Ibid

334   Ibid, p. 140

335   *INCARNATION: A New Evolutionary Threshold* (IET, ORBIS BOOKS, 2017, p. 164)

336   *RHM*, p. 20

337   *IET*, pp. 169-70; p. 82: 'Whether we attribute the flawed perception of the human to Aristotle's philosophy or to the later theory of Original Sin, perpetuated by St Augustine (and others), our view of the human person, up to the mid-twentieth century was largely devoid of incanational value. There then ensued a momentous shift, which many theologians have not yet come to terms with. ... Many know little about the study of human origins, known as palaeontology, going back to an estimated *seven million years*. And regarding *Original Sin*, O'Murchu writes: 'It is not a foundational truth, but a dangerous and deceptive heresy that morphed into a dominant myth, developed from a Judaeo-Christian ideology of humans being inherently evil and aggressive' (p. 89, redacted slightly).

338   This paragraph is sourced from O'Murchu's *Doing Theology In An Evolutionary Way* (*DTEW*, Orbis Books, 2021). It provides a comprehensive account of his thoughts on the need for Christian theology to

reconfigure itself in the light of the findings of modern science, and with regard to O'Murchu's treatment of the 'Great Spirit' in the lives of indigenous peoples (see p. 46, for example; the book's Index should also be consulted under these headings, and '*Quantum*').

338   The term *Companionship of Empowerment* (CE), borrowed from Dom Crossan, is preferred by O'Murchu to 'Kingdom', on the grounds that the latter's 'imperial tenor' is a barrier to assessing the true meaning of Jesus' ministry and resurrection. CE, whilst clumsy, better represents the idea of *collaborative mutual engagement* (DTEW, pp. 178-9, and see Index).

339   *TFCK*, p. 224

341   *DTEW*, p. 41

342   Ibid

343   Ibid

344   O'Murchu, Diarmuid. *Paschal Paradox: Reflections on a Life of Spiritual Evolution* (PP, Franciscan Media, 2022, p. 71)

345   Ibid, pp. 71-2

346   *Panentheism* has been very influential in *Process Theology*, associated with A.N. Whitehead and Charles Hartshorne. Pantheism is usually a feature of *Polytheism*: Hinduism, for example, has many gods. And many great mystics have been "pantheists", if it is understood to mean that the world is divine. *Pantheism* can also be understood to be atheistic, in the sense many academics interpret Spinoza (d. 1677) and Hegel (d. 1831). C.F. Crause, in 1828, coined the term 'Panentheism', and 'Pantheism' first appears in a work by John Toland, *Socinianism Truly Stated* (1705). Most of this information is edited from *The Penguin Dictionary of Philosophy* (edited by Thomas Mautner, 1997, p. 407). Orthodox Christian belief holds that God pre-existed the (*creation of*) the world, that He is *wholly other* yet also *present* in the world. The ultimate exemplification of that presence is the doctrine of the Incarnation, the belief that, in Jesus, God became true man. Panentheists, notes Keith Ward, see 'the whole universe in which human beings live as a tiny part of the infinite reality of God', and this means that 'God will be constantly developing and changing as the universes develops and changes, so he will be a partly imperfect and limited sort of God'. Ward continues with this observation: 'If everything is part of God, we ought to worship everything – including murderers, thieves, frogs and tadpoles, as well as stars and beautiful

sunsets. Just to drive the point home, I certainly do not feel that I am God, and I hope you do not either. So I might want to make quite a distinction between you and me and God, and hope that God is much wiser and better than either of us' (*God: A Guide for the Perplexed*, Oneworld Publications, 2002, p. 162). Ward continues, however, by noting that 'God changes and develops in knowledge without getting any more perfect ..., and since time is not really spread out all at once, but things really do happen one after the other, the classical God cannot really see things as they are – or so it seems to people who take time more seriously than Plato did' (p. 164). This latter observation goes some way towards accommodating O'Murchu's vision of God as *Great Spirit*, and 'we come to know the Great Spirit through our convivial relationship with nature at large', in such manner that 'indigenous peoples do not worship the *Great Spirit*', but strive to work collaboratively with it, in ways mediated through rituals focused on 'the fertility of soil and land' (*DTEW*, p.19). Referencing Philip Clayton's understanding of (the Christian) *Holy Spirit* 'as an emergent life force of cosmic significance', and adopting the notion of *Panentheism* to describe the immanent presence of the Spirit throughout the evolving process of creation, O'Murchu endorses the view that 'in so far as this emergent theology remains panentheistic, it holds that the physical world was already permeated by, and contained within, the Spirit of God, long before cosmic evolution gave rise to life and mind'. This endorsement implicitly rejects the largely neo-Platonist approach adopted by Ward, recommending that such dualism, the basis of much Christian theology (inclusive of the doctrine of the Trinity), needs to be reinterpreted in categories better suited to contemporary scientific and related findings (*DTEW*, pp.107-108). On p. 19, O'Murchu writes that such perspectives should 'not be confused with either pantheism or panentheism', but his thesis seems to embrace some form of the latter, which is hardly surprising given the nature of the paradigm shift required if Christianity is to be a coherent, prophetic voice as the twenty-first century progresses, having to face this question: 'Do we need the postulate of an *original divine Creator*?' (p.119, slightly redacted and see next endnote).

347   *Intelligent Design* proposes that 'biological accounts of the adaptations of living things are incomplete unless they allow room for theistic explanation' (Peter Harrison in *The Cambridge Companion To Science And Religion*, Cambridge University Press, 2010, p. 2). In the comment about "O'Murchu and *intelligent design*", I use the term in the way understood by

Harrison (O'Murchu is well-aware of problems inherent in the concept "theism"), in the context of the above endnote. In reality, O'Murchu's "philosophy" resembles aspects of *Process Theology*, developed in a creative and life-embracing manner.

348 1Williams, Harry. *True Resurrection* (TR, Mitchell Beazley, 1972, pp. 174 and 178, adapted)

349 *HJBG*, p. 197 and the preceding paragraph also derives from this page

350 *RHM*, p. 40

351 Quoted in *The Good Book: How To Read The Bible*, by Richard Holloway (GRANTA, 2014, p. 1, from Tindal's *Christianity as Old as the Creation*, published 1733, and see endnote 451).

352 In *MPC*, Hyam Maccoby deals extensively with the known history of the Ebionites. There are serious weaknesses in this book, but his treatment of the Ebionites is very plausible, noting that, after 70, they were increasingly cut off from mainstream Rabbinic Judaism and, c. 135, they were finally declared "Jewish heretics". It is of interest that 'Gentile Christianity, unlike Ebionite Christianity, was never declared heretical, since it was too far removed from Judaism to be regarded as a heretical form of it' (p. 179 and see endnote 161).

353 Hick, John. *Death And Eternal Life* (DEL, Macmillan, 198, p. 371)

354 Ibid, p. 179 - Hick proposes an interesting idea concerning 'the resurrection of the body', known as *Replica Theory* (Chapter 15): 'We can think of it as the divine creation in another space of an exact psycho-physical 'replica' of the deceased person' (p. 279). His proposal is an attempt to elucidate St Paul's understanding of 'the resurrection of the body' related to 'how, if at all, we can intelligibly think of it today' (p. 279). The theory is expounded by reference to three cases, which Hick claims to be 'logically possible of fulfilment' (pp.280-288), concluding with the claim that his theory preserves the notion of continuity of identity between the resurrected person and the pre-resurrected person (page 294). It is effectively a sophisticated version of the Schneiders and Wright proposals.

355 Bethany, where the Ascension takes place (see Lk. 24:36-53; cf. Acts 1:6-11) comes under this heading, and it is significant that Matthew has the eleven disciples meet with the resurrected Jesus in Galilee (28:16-20; cf. 28:7,10).

356 Found in Egypt by a monk (1886), it is a fragment (60 verses dealing with

the passion and resurrection) of what was most likely a complete narrative of Jesus' ministry. It relates closely to Matthew's account of Jesus'
death and resurrection, but with a far more pronounced anti-Jewish bias.
Scholars debate, however, the extent to which it is dependent upon the
canonical gospels, and Dom Crossan, in *WKJ?*, argues a contrary view:
'I maintain the opposite, that the canonical versions are dependent on
a section of Peter' (p. 24). 'Peter' has a strong docetic emphasis, that is,
it denied the reality of Jesus' suffering and death. We have knowledge
of sixteen *apocryphal gospels*. See Bart D. Ehrman's *Lost Christianities:
The Battles for Scripture and the Faiths We Never Knew* (Oxford University
Press, 2003) for a comprehensive account of *Major Christian Apocrypha*.

357 *NJBC*, p. 672, explains that the "washing of the hands" has been sourced
from Dt. 21; 6-9, Ps. 26:6 and Ps. 73:13, and that the practice had no place
in a Roman trial. Similarly, the notorious *Blood Cry* (v. 25) comes from 2
Sam. 1:16, Jer. 26:15, 51:53 and 1 Kgs. 2:33

358 WKJ?, p. 210

359 Holloway, Richard. *Stories We Tell Ourselves: Making Meaning in a
Meaningless Universe* (SWO, Canongate Books, , pp. xx- xxi)

360 See David Kertzer's *The Popes Against the Jews* (*PAJ*, Vintage Books, 2002,
Chapter 6 (*The Catholic Press*), for a comprehensive account of how
Catholic newspapers (Italy alone had 500 publications, thirty of which
were "dailies") had assisted, by 1900, 'the transition to a modern form
of anti-Semitism', by making use of older means of demonizing Jews,
and none of these was more dramatic than the charge of ritual murder
(p. 151). The 'Dreyfuss reference' is sourced from pp. 182- 185; he was
not finally exonerated until 1930, though released from confinement (on
Devil's Island) in 1899. Dreyfuss died in 1935.

361 Ibid, p. 147

362 Ibid - Russia and Poland (and other states in the region) had a long history of pogroms. At the beginning of the twentieth century, for example, the *Kishniev Pogrom* (1903) received much attention in the West; it
lasted three days and led to many fatalities, orchestrated by anti-Semites, after a Russian (Czarist) official had promised to drown revolu-
tionaries (those opposing Czarist rule) 'in Jewish blood'. Poland, in the
wake of World War I, also witnessed pogroms, most notably that at Lvov
(November 1918).

363 Mt. 16:13-20 (a redaction of Mk. 8:27-30), where the resurrected Jesus
gives authority to Peter (the famous *rock and keys* passage) is chiefly a

midrash on Old Testament sources, and Jesus could never have founded a "Church", for the simple reason that he never envisaged a religion separate from Judaism.

364 *PAJ*, p. 225; in the decree *Lamentabili* (3rd. July 1907), Pius X condemned Modernism (it sought to bring Catholic beliefs into closer alignment with contemporary philosophical, historical and scientific developments) and sixty-five propositions associated with it.

365 Ibid, p. 220; the biography's preface (1933) was written by Eugenio Pacelli, the future Pope Pius XII (elected 2 March 1939)

366 See Jeremy Cohen's *Christ Killers: The Jews And the Passion From the Bible to the Big Screen* (*CK*, Oxford University Press, 2007) for a comprehensive history and analysis of this appalling phenomenon. Part II, consisting of five chapters and concluding with Vatican II, merits close study, where Cohen explains how what were originally two discrete accusations (*ritual murder and blood libel*) had morphed into a single entity by the time of Simon of Trent (see main text, above, and endnote 368, below). The first known documented medieval blood libel charge appeared at Christmas 1235 in the German town of Fulda (p. 110).

367 *PAJ*, p. 14

368 In an 1890 article, Fr Raffaele Ballerini SJ, wrote that, long ago, the Jews had stopped following Mosaic law, and 'now followed only the execrable Talmud', having rejected and murdered the Messiah, they now believed they were divinely ordained to rule the world: 'brotherhood and peace were and are merely pretexts to enable them to prepare – with the destruction of Christianity, if possible – the messianic reign that they believe the Talmud promises them' (*PAJ*, p. 143). The same year, Leo XIII blessed the Jesuits' efforts, commenting that 'they have pursued the study of truth combined with the law of justice, and, having employed great intelligence in their works, have acquired great fame' (*PAJ*, p. 312).

369 For a detailed account of this incredible story, see *PAJ*, pp. 213-222. On p. 221, Kertzer relates that an extraordinary note accompanying the decision was found in the archives of the Inquisition, stating that although nothing had been found either in the Holy Office or at the Secretariat of State bearing on the *ritual murder charge*, it is nonetheless 'a historical certainty, citing cases in Austria and Bohemia as "proof" of the allegation, and referring to the English protesters (that is, chiefly Cardinals Manning and Vaughan, Lord Russell and the Duke of Norfolk) as 'a few dupes in England'.

370 Ibid, p. 234; pp. 152-6,, 159 and 161 provide a full description of the

appalling story centred on Simon of Trent, as does CK, pp. 110-112. In modern times, the two most notorious *ritual murder charges* were the 1840 *Damascus Case* of a Capuchin friar, Fr Tomasso, and the of *Mendel Beilis Case*, Kiev 1913, both of which receive extensive treatment in *PAJ*. Between 1887 and 1891 alone, the press reported at least twenty-two *ritual murder accusations*.

371 Flannery, Edward. *The Anguish of the Jews: Twenty-Three centuries of Anti-Semitism* (AoJ, Paulist Press, 198, p. 188; originally published 1965)

372 Pope Francis, with Antonia Spadaro. *My Door Is Always Open: A Conversation on Faith, Hope and the Church in a Time of Change* (Bloomsbury, 2013, p. 167; the pope gave this address on 14th. June 2013)

373 As late as 1914, *Civilitá Cattolica* was publishing articles, copies of which were sent in advance to the papal secretary of state, defending the authenticity of *ritual murder claims*, with one article maintaining that 'Jews consider blood to be a drink like milk', continuing with the monstrous libel that, when Jews murder young Christian children, 'the child dies in the most painful manner possible' (*PAJ*, pp. 232-236).

374 This dangerous hoax, which endures in various guises to this day (see later in this chapter), originated as a political satire in 1864, written by Maurice Joly attacking the ambitions of Napoleon III (d. 1873; abdicated 1870 after the disastrous Franco-Prussian War of that year). It featured a secret meeting in hell and was then plagiarized by a German anti-Semite; his version fantasized a secret gathering of rabbis, held every one hundred years, at which nefarious plans for the next century were hatched. By the 1890s, agents of the Russian secret police had transformed this version into a text labelled "Protocols of the Elders of Zion" ..., first printed at the turn of the century, 'and used in an effort to discredit the Russian reform movement, which backers of the czar identified with the Jews' (*PAJ*, p. 265). By 1919, translations had appeared in eastern and Western Europe, including London. '*The Protocols* purported to be the newly-found minutes of a meeting held by a secret international directorate of Jews plotting world conquest. Of course, no such directorate ever existed, nor had such meeting ever taken place' (*PAJ*, p. 266).

375 The Jn. 11:39 reference by Martha to 'four days' is, of course, to emphasise that Lazarus was really dead. There are two Talmuds, one from Palestine, completed c. 450, and the Babylonian Talmud, completed c. 550. The word 'Talmud' literally means 'teaching'.

376   *PAJ*, p. 82

377   Sourced in part, and adapted, from *PAJ*

378   Rotschild, Mike. *The Storm Is Upon Us: How Qanon Became A Movement, Cult, And Conspiracy Theory Of Everything* (*SUU*, Melville House, 202, p. xiv)

379   Ibid, and referencing *The Protocols* and related matters (pp. 51-55); also Fintan O'Toole, writing in *The Irish Times* (9th January 2024) about The Irish Light (TIL). This publication attacks the findings of reputable climate scientists and medical experts; a recent edition included an article with the heading *The Jewish Cycle of Hate*. It claims that 'the Jews deserve to be destroyed because they rejected Christ', and other recent editions have had articles saying that Jews are responsible for 'every single aspect of the "Covid agenda"'. *TIL* had an image of the globe with a gigantic snake bearing the *Star of David*, the suggestion being that Jews are controlling the "dangerous vaccine programme". O'Toole observes rightly that this repulsive publication is 'a mishmash of Medieval hate-mongering, the fake Elders of Zion and revived ul-tra-reactionary Catholicism' (page 14), continuing by remarking that anti-Semitism is the default mechanism (template) of *TIL*'s conspir-acy mania. With regard to the Israel-Hamas Conflict, O'Toole writes that the upsurge in anti-Semitism everywhere, including Ireland, should not be understood as a response to 'the horrors of Israel's bom-bardment of Gaza, but that the mass killing of Palestinian civilians has created a space in which anti-Semitism can be manifest 'in all its naked savagery'. Many Jews, he notes, are appalled by Israel's response, and it is deplorable, a trivialization of the Holocaust, to accuse those who protest the response as 'anti-Semitic'. O'Toole points, correctly, to the deep roots of anti-Semitism in Christian Europe: 'anti-Semitism is hard-core racism', and that 'fighting anti-Semitism must always be an entry-level requirement for progressive politics: any society in which Jewish people do not feel safe is one in which no one who can be de-fined as "other" can be safe either' (p.14). *TIL* also promotes Holocaust Denial. Issue 14 (November 2022), for example, has three pages devot-ed to a notorious, long discredited Holocaust-denier – (Prof) Robert Faurisson - who "proved" that 'it was technically and physically impos-sible for the gas chambers at Auschwitz to have functioned as extermi-nation facilities' (Deborah Lipstadt).

380   *SUU*, p. 52: 'The term has never appeared in a Q *drop*, but andrenochrome

is referenced constantly in the discourse of Q promoters, to the point where a number of major news outlets wrote about it in the struggle to understand why so many people were getting sucked into Q. Androenochrome and Q fit together easily'.

381   Ibid, pp. 53-54

382   *Apostolic Letter* (27th August 1989) marking the fiftieth anniversary of the outbreak of World War II (1st September 1939)

383   Adapted from a *Catholic Holocaust Memorial Service* of the 1990s

384   Seidel, Gill. *The Holocaust Denial: Anti-Semitism, Racism & the New Right* (HD, Beyond The Pale Collective, 1986, page xxiv)

385   *NJBC*, p. 972

386   Amy-Jill, Levine. *The Misunderstood Jew: The Church and the Scandal of the Jewish Jesus* (TMJ, 2006, p. 99). This quotation should be understood in the context of another explanation: that the word "Jews" should be translated "Judaeans", referencing a geographic reason, but people reading the passage typically understand it to refer to 'all who identify with the Jewish way of life' (page 96). Levine observes, rightly, that the "interpolation arguments" may not be sustainable – Paul, after all, may, in this context, have meant what the text says. Interested readers are referred to Levine's full account of the possibilities (pp. 95-99), with particular regard to what she has to say about 1 Cor. 14:33b-36 ("women in church") and Jn. 7:53-8:11 ("the woman taken in adultery"). Her analysis of the material is important for an adequate understanding of the Jewish-Christian relationship.

387   Ibid, paraphrase of p. 97

388   JANT (p. 692) notes that 'the first Jewish text to depict in detail an afterlife as a venue for righting earthly wrongs is the *Book of the watchers*, as scholars call the work preserved as *1 Enoch 1-36*.' This work had reached its final form by the end of the third century BCE. It was very influential towards the end of the Second temple period.

389   This paragraph is sourced from *JANT*, page 421 and *NJBC*, p. 775.

390   *TMJ*, page 200 addresses this issue, from which the above paragraph derives.

391   EOU (see endnote 165), Chapter 6 (*Distinctive Memories*, pp. 145-90), comprehensively addresses this matter, and on p. 23 O'Loughlin writes that the *Last Supper* is 'not immune to all the problems, long recognized, about the historicity of events in the life of the historical Jesus',

where on the same page he is very critical of a pronounced tendency in Catholic teaching which 'sees history as an apologetic arm of its catechesis', whereby its understanding of the *development of doctrine* 'is defined in such a way as to make it the opposite of real historical change'. In other words, he objects to the Church's present teaching – defined in councils, laws and catechisms – as 'that which is the mind of Christ', resulting in the logical fallacy which confuses "history" with "apologetics".

392 *TMJ*, p. 200

393 The first part of Acts 18:6 has Paul, in protest, shaking dust from his clothing, which is a biblical expression for symbolising separation, and the verse clearly reflects a general condemnation of "the Jews" for their unwillingness to recognise Jesus as the messiah, most infamously represented by Mt. 27:25.

394 Raphael, Frederic. *Anti-Semitism* (*AS*, Biteback Publishing, 2015). The quotation, on the back cover, is preceded by this anecdote: "There is an old story about Adolf Hitler, in post-war hiding, telling someone that, 'next time', he will finish off the Jews and also two ballet dancers. 'Why two ballet dancers?' says the other man. 'See what I mean?' says Adolf. 'Who cares what happens to Jews?'

395 From an article, *Facing the Jews: Christian Theology After Auschwitz*, *Concilium* (1984, its special edition, *The Holocaust As Interruption*, pp. 29 and 31)

396 These observations, and some related comments, are sourced from a letter to the author.

397 Crane, Tim. *The Meaning of Belief: Religion From an Atheist's Point of View* (*MOB*, Harvard University Press, 201, p. 79)

398 Ibid, pp. 78-9

399 The scenario is based upon David Klinghoffer's suggestion in *Why The Jews Rejected Jesus* (*WJRJ*, Doubleday, 2005, pp. 6-8). His treatment of *Oral Torah* is covered in pp. 54-60: *Jesus the Rabbi*.

400 This statement is predicated upon what I believe to be the correct assumption that passages such as Mt. 16:13-20 [where Jesus acknowledges Peter's profession of him as "the Christ", redacted from Mk. 8:27-30] and Mk. 14:53-64 [where, at the so-called *Trial Before the Sanhedrin*, Jesus says he is "the Christ" (v. 62)] do not reflect historical events, though it is possible, as referenced earlier in this volume, that the historical Jesus may have accorded some inchoate messianic status to himself, but not

in the manner interpreted by the nascent church.

401   This verse includes a reference to "predestination", to be understood not as a statement about free will, but in the sense of 'God's sovereignty over the future' (*NJBC*, p. 855).

402   Braybrooke, Marcus. *Time To Meet: Towards a Deeper Relationship Between Jews and Christians* (TtM, SCM Press, 1990 edition, p. 62)

403   *CFJ*, p. 265

404   Enns, Peter. *Inspiration And Incarnation: Evangelicals and the Problem of the Old Testament* (IAI, 2015 second edition, p. 189). Scholars date this period in slightly different ways; this form coincides with the rise of the Maccabes culminating with the destruction of the Temple (70 CE), followed by the fall of Masada (73). Others give an end date of 135, when the Second Jewish-Roman War (beginning 132) came to an end. The entire Second Temple period extends from 520 BCE (when construction began on the Temple) to 135 CE.

405   *WJRJ*, p. 87

406   'Had the "circumcision party" won the day, Christianity would have remained a Jewish sect whose members obeyed Jewish law, at least of the written Torah' (*WJRJ*, p. 99)

407   Ibid

408   There is an extensive body of scholarly work about Melito, of which the most famous is Eric Werner's *Melito of Sardes: The First Poet of Deicide* (1966). Jacques Dupuis SJ, in *Who Do You Say I AM?: Introduction to Christology* (Orbis Books, 1994, p. 91), provides this account of the "proper understanding" of how Jesus is said to be God and man: 'Jesus is the Son of God as man. This does not mean that he is Son of God because of his humanity, which is created, but because of the Incarnation, his humanity is that of the Son of God. ..., the human story of the man Jesus is that of the Son of God, and Jesus' human death is God's own'.

409   Rev Mike O'Sullivan, Unitarian minister, in a conversation with the author

410   *Christianity as Old as the Creation* (1733), quoted in Richard Holloway, *The Good Book: How to Read the Bible* (TGB, Granta Books, 2014, p. 1). Tindal's book argued that all creedal systems are about 'a religion of nature', and see endnote 351

411   This paragraph is sourced from *WJRJ*, page 87

412   Brodie argues that it is a midrash on he Book of Numbers

413   These points are sourced and adapted from *WJRJ*, pp. 87-9

414   Ibid, p. 89; Klinghoffer's remarks about the 'Davidic Messiah' have much
      influenced the closing paragraphs of *The Resurrection of Jesus the Jew:
      Midrash and the First Easter*, as have the observations about Acts 15:19
      and St Paul (*WJRJ*, pp. 98-100).

Bibliography

Borg, Marcus; Crossan, John D. The Last Week, SPCK, 2008

Boyarin, Daniel. The Jewish Gospels: The Story of the Jewish Christ. The New Press, 2012

Brekke-Moller. *The Vermes Quest: The Significance of Geza Vermes for Jesus Research.* Bloomsbury (T&T), 2017

Brodie, Thomas. *Beyond the quest for the Historical Jesus: Memoir of a Discovery.* Sheffield Press, 2012

Brown, Raymond. *The Virginal Conception & Bodily Resurrection of Jesus.* Paulist Press, 1973

    The Death of the Messiah: From Gethsemane to the Grave. Doubleday, 1994

    An Introduction to the New Testament. Doubleday, 1996

Cargas, Harry James. *Shadows of Auschwitz: A Christian Response to the Holocaust.* The Crossroad Publishing Company, 1990

Carroll, James. *Constantine's Sword: The Church and the Jews.* Mariner Books, 2002

    Chris Actually: The Son of God for the Secular Age. HarperCollins, 2014

Cohen, Jeremy. *Christ Killers: The Jews and the Passion from the Bible to the Big Screen.* Oxford University Press, 2007

Cohn-Sherbok, Dan. *The Crucified Jew: Twenty Centuries of Christian.* Anti-Semitism HarperCollins, 1992

Crane, Tim. *The Meaning of Belief: Religion from an Atheist's Point Of View.* Harvard University Press, 2017

Crossan, John D. *Who Killed Jesus? – Roots of Anti-Semitism in the Gospel Story of the Death of Jesus.* Harper, 1995

    How to Read the Bible and Still be a Christian: Is God Violent? Harper One, 2016

    Resurrecting Easter (with Sarah S. Crossan). Harper One, 2018 de-Rosa Peter. *Vicars of Christ: The Dark Side of the Papacy*. Bantam Press, 1988

Dupuis, Jacques, SJ. *Who Do You Say I Am?* Orbis Books, 1994

Ehrman, Bart. *Misquoting Jesus: The Story Behind Who Changed the Bible and Why*. Harper One, 2005

> *How Jesus Became God: The Exaltation of a Jewish Preacher from Galilee*. Harper One, 2015

> *Forged: Writing in the Name of God – Why the Bible's Authors Are Not Who We Think They Are*. HarperCollins, 2012

> *Jesus Before The Gospels*. HarperOne, 2016

> *The Triumph of Christianity: How a Forbidden Religion Swept the World*. Oneworld, 2019

Evans, Richard J. *Lying About History: Holocaust and the David Irving Trial*. Basic Books, 2002

> Fawcett, Thomas. *Hebrew Myth and Christian Gospel*. SCM Press, 1973

Fischer, Klaus, P. *A New History of Nazi Germany*. Constable, 1995

Flannery, Edward. *The Anguish of the Jews: Twenty-Three Centuries of Antisemitism*. Paulist Press, 1985

Fredriksen, Paula (ed.). *Jesus, Judaism and Anti-Semitism: Reading the New Testament After the Holocaust*. Westminster John Knox Press, 2002

> *Paul: The Pagans' Apostle*. Yale University Press, 2017

> *When Christians Were Jews: The First Generation*. Yale University Press, 2018

Freeman, Charles. *A New History of Early Christianity*. Yale University Press, 2011

Funk, Robert. *Honest to Jesus: Jesus for a New Millennium*. Harper Collins, 1996

Goodman, Martin. *A History of Judaism*. Penguin Books, 2019

Halik, Tomás. *The Afternoon of Christianity: The Courage to Change*. University of Notre Dame Press, 2024

Hilberg, Raul. *The Destruction of the European Jews*. Holmes and Meier, 1973

Higginson, Paul. *Doing Christianity: How religion is about what you do, not what you believe*. Columba Books, 2023

Holloway, Richard. *A Little History of Religion*. Yale University Press, 2016
Stories We Tell Ourselves: Making Meaning in a Meaningless World. Canongate, 2020

Horvilleur, Delphine. *Anti-Semitism Revisited*. MacLehose Press, 2019

Keenan, Peter. *The Birth of Jesus the Jew: Midrash and the Infancy Gospels*. Columba Books, 2021

> *The Death of Jesus the Jew: Midrash in the Shadow of the Holocaust*. Columba Books, 2023

Kelly, Peter. *Searching for Truth*. Collins, 1978

Kertzer, David I. *The Popes Against the Jews*. First Vintage, Books, 2002

> *The Pope at War: The Secret History of Pius XII, Mussolini & Hitler*. Oxford University Press, 2022

Klein, Charlotte. *Anti-Judaism in Christian Theology*. Longman, 1978

Klinghoffer, David. *Why The Jews Rejected Jesus: The Turning Point In Western History*. Doubleday, 2005

Levine, Amy-Jill. *The Misunderstood Jew: The Church and the Scandal of the Jewish Jesus*. Harper One, 2006

> Lilla, Mark. *Ignorance and Bliss: On Wanting Not to Know*. Hurst & Co, 2024

Lippstadt, Deborah. *Denying The Holocaust: The Growing Assault on Truth and Memory*. A Plume Book (Penguin), 1993

Lohfink, Gerhard. *Is This All There Is? On Resurrection and Eternal Life*. Liturgical Press, 2020

Maccoby, Hyam. *The Mythmaker: Paul and the Invention of Christianity*. Weidenfeld and Nicolson, 1986

Mackey, James P. *Jesus of Nazareth: The Life, the Faith and the Future of the Prophet*. The Columba Press, 2008

Marshall, Howard (ed.). *New Testament Interpretation: Essays on Principles and Methods*. The Paternoster Press, 1979

Mishkin, David. *Jewish Scholarship on the Resurrection of Jesus*. Pickwick Publications, 2017

Maté, Gabor. *In the Realm of Hungry Ghosts: Close Encounters with Addiction*. Penguin, 2018

O'Loughlin, Thomas. *The Eucharist: Origins and Contemporary Understandings*. Bloomsbury, 2015

O'Murchu, Diarmuid. *Incarnation: A New Evolutionary Threshold*. Orbis Books, 2017

When The Disciple Comes of Age: Christian Identity in the 21st Century. Orbis Books, 2019

Doing Theology in an Evolutionary Way. Orbis Books, 2021

Paschal Paradox: Reflections on a Life of Spiritual Evolution. Orbis Books

Pawlikowski, John, OSM. *Christ In The Light Of Christian-Jewish Dialogue.* Paulist Press, 1982

Perrin, Norman. *The Resurrection According to Matthew, Mark and Luke.* Fortress Press, 1976

Rohr, Richard. *The Universal Christ.* SPCK, 2019

Rosenberg, Stuart. *The Christian Problem: A Jewish View.* Hippocrene Books, 1986

Rotschild, Mike. *The Storm Is Upon Us: How QAnon Became A Movement, Cult and Conspiracy Theory of Everything.* Monoray, 2021

Saperstein, Marc. *Moments of Crisis in Jewish-Christian Relations.* SCM Press, 1989

Schama, Simon. *The Story of the Jews: Finding the Words 1000BCE – 1492 CE.* Vintage Books, 2014

Schneiders, Sandra, IHM. *The Resurrection: Did It Really Happen And Why Does That Matter?* Marymount Institute, 2014

Segal, Alan F. *Paul the Convert.* Yale University Press, 1990 *After Death: A History of the Afterlife in the Religions of the West.* Doubleday, 2004

Seidel, Gill. *Anti-Semitism and the New Right.* Beyond the Pale Collective, 1986

Sheehan, Thomas. *The First Coming: How the Kingdom of God Became Christianity.* Random House, 1986

Siedentop, Larry. *Inventing the Individual: The Origins of Western Liberalism.* Penguin Books, 2015

Spencer, Nicholas. *Magisteria: The Entangled Histories of Science and Religion.* Oneworld, 2024

Spong, John S. *Biblical Literalism: A Gentile Heresy.* Harper One, 2016

Resurrection: Myth or Reality? Harper SanFrancisco, 1994

Stanford, Peter. *What We Talk About When We Talk About Faith.* Hodder & Stoughton, 2018

Stark, Rodney. *Bearing False Witness: Debunking Centuries of anti-Catholic History.* SPCK, 2017

Stewart, Robert B (ed). *The Resurrection of Jesus: The Crossan-Wright Dialogue.* Fortress Press, 2006

Strauss, Mark L. *Four Portraits, One Jesus.* Zondervan, 2007

Swinburne, Richard. *The Resurrection of God Incarnate.* Oxford University Press, 2003

Trocmé, Étienne. *The Childhood of Christianity.* SCM Press, 1997

Vermes, Geza. *Jesus the Jew.* Collins, 1973

  The Changing Faces of Jesus. Pengiun, 2000

  The Authentic Gospel of Jesus. Penguin, 2003

  Jesus: Nativity – Passion – Resurrection. Penguin, 2010

  Christian Beginnings: From Nazareth to Nicaea, AD 30-325. Allen Lane, 2012

  The True Herod. Bloomsbury, 2014

Ward, Keith. *God: A Guide for the Perplexed.* Oneworld, 2002

  Is Religion Dangerous? Lion Hudson, 2006

  Re-Thinking Christianity. Oneworld, 2007

Wilson, Barrie. *How Jesus Became Christian.* Weidenfeld & Nicolson, 2008

Works of Reference

Holy Bible – New Revised Standard Version. Cambridge University Press, 2007

Catechism of the Catholic Church. Geoffrey Chapman, 1992

Documents of Vatican II (Abbott and Gallagher translation). Geoffrey Chapman, 1967

Guidelines for Catholic-Jewish Relations. Bishops' Conference of England And Wales (published by Catholic Truth Society), 1994

The Jewish Annotated New Testament. Oxford University Press, 2016

An Introduction to the New Testament. Raymond E. Brown. Doubleday, 1997

The New Jerome Biblical Commentary. Geoffrey Chapman, 1992